WARD'S HISTORY
Of
COFFEE COUNTY

BY
WARREN P. WARD

Southern Historical Press, Inc.
Greenville, South Carolina

This volume was reproduced from
An 1985 edition located in the
Publisher's private Library,

All rights reserved. No part of this publication may be reproduced, stored in a retrieval system, transmitted in any form, posted on to the web in any form or by any means without the prior written permission of the publisher.

Please direct all correspondence and orders to:

www.southernhistoricalpress.com
or
SOUTHERN HISTORICAL PRESS, Inc.
PO BOX 1267
375 West Broad Street
Greenville, SC   29601
southernhistoricalpress@gmail.com

Originally published: Atlanta, GA 1930
Reprinted with New Material by:
Southern Historical Press, Inc.
Greenville, SC
New Material Copyright 2018 by
Southern Historical Press, Inc.
Greenville, SC
ISBN #0-89308-976-1
All rights Reserved.
Printed in the United States of America

WARREN P. WARD

Ward's History
of Coffee County

A story dealing with the past and present of Coffee County. Beginning with the early settlers about the year 1800,—discussing the Creek Indians and the Pioneers. Leading up to the creation of Coffee County in 1854 —Old families, old schools and churches, showing the conditions during the Civil War and ending up with the spirit of progress, which is evident in better schools, and a more intelligent civilization. Showing that Coffee County, in South Georgia, is God's Country and a good place to live in the year 1930.

Dedication

This book is dedicated to the memory of:

The Creek Indians: who occupied this territory and preserved it till the coming of the early settlers;

To the Pioneers: who cut the first logs and built the first houses, who split the first rails and fenced the first fields;

To the Old School Teachers: who wore cotton breeches and taught our children how to read and write in log huts;

To the Old Preachers: who preached the old time Gospel and sang the old time songs;

And to everyone, who has in any way helped to make Coffee County a good place in which to live.

The Author.

Contents

	Page
Dedication	III
Preface	XIII
An Ideal Wedding	144
Atkinson County Creation	13
Automobiles	244
Banking Business	233
Big Court, October Term	118
Big Four	230
Billy Bow-Legs	34
Boll Weevil	248
Boy Scout Movement	239
Bright Leaf Tobacco	241
Camp Meetings	201
Carding Machine	185
Catching Fish	190
Coffee County, 1930	293
Coffee County In War	135
Coffee County Officers, 1854	343
Confederate Soldiers Who Went to War from Coffee County	331
Constitution and the Flag	147
Cotton Picking Time In Georgia	246
Creek Indians	24
Doctors	245
Doctors and Medicine	93
Douglas Cemetery	277
Douglas, Dunk	90
Douglas, the Capital City of Coffee County	297
Early History of Coffee County	20
Early Steamboat Navigation on the Ocmulgee	255
Education	320

v

Contents

	Page
English Gold	137
Fifty Uses of Turpentine	314
Fraternal Orders	233
Gaskin, William	324
Georgia Colonel	164
Georgia Laws Creating Coffee County	5
Georgia Militia Districts	18
Georgia Normal Business College	291
Grady's Tribute to Negro Slaves	223
History of Newspapers of Coffee County	326
Hour of Prayer in a Saw Mill	162
Indians Rob Dr. Parker's Home	100
Inferior Courts and Courts of Ordinary	322
Jeff Davis County, Creation of	11
Killing Deer	195
Ku Klux Klan	276
Ladies' Clubs	235
Land Districts of Coffee County	15
Language of the Birds	206
Lawyers	245
Liquor Laws	252
List of Some Old People of Coffee County Married More Than Fifty Years Ago	78
Log Rolling, Quilting and a Frolic	159
Map of Coffee County	329
Member of Confederate Cabinet	219
Meningitis Epidemic	228
Negro Race	221
Negro Funeral	225
Newspapers	155
Ocmulgee River Section	260

Contents

	Page
Old Churches In Coffee County	102
Arnie	104
Bethel	115
Carver	109
Catholic	115
Elam Primitive Baptist	112
Elizabeth	110
Gravel Hill	110
Hebron	102
Lone Hill Methodist	108
Lott Memorial	107
Midway Methodist	110, 115
Mormon	105
Mount Pleasant	114
Mount Zion Baptist	114
Mount Zion Methodist	111
New Hope	114
Oak Grove	115
Pleasant Grove Baptist	111
Rehoboth Primitive Baptist	111
Roberts Methodist	113
Royals' Methodist	113
Sand Hill Baptist	106
Old Families In Coffee County	38
Burkett	68
Carver	70
Davis	40
Gaskin	52
Kirkland	63
Lott	47
Meeks	59

Contents

	Page
Old Families in Coffee County—Cont'd.	
Newbern	41
Paulk	52
Sapp	71
Tanner	66
Vickers	43
Ward and Hargraves	55
Wilcox	53
Old Graveyards	125
Lone Hill	125
Mount Zion	126
New Hope	126
Sand Hill	125
Old School Houses	116
Kirkland School	117
Old Time Singers	121
Ordinary	166
Pioneers of Coffee County	84
Public Health Work	237
Public Schools	280
Railroads in Coffee County	148
Brisbane Railroad	148
Douglas and McDonald Railroad	150
Georgia and Florida Railroad	150
Railsplitters	181
Regulators	141
Resolution of General Assembly	1
Resolution of Grand Jury	3
Sand Hill Church	153
Saw Mills and Lumber	171
Scab Timber	316

Contents

	Page
Snakes in Coffee County	186
South Georgia State College	288
Spivey, Erwin	87
Stills and Mills	179
Storms	250
Stormy Night on Seventeen-Mile Creek	197
Strange Phenomenon	254
Study in Human Hands	318
Teachers in Coffee County Public Schools	284
Teachers in Douglas Public Schools	287
The Pine Tree	174
Towns in Coffee County	302
Ambrose	302
Broxton	303
Nicholls	306
West Green	308
Tribute to Monroe Wilcox	98
Tribute to the Women of the South	133
Trees	208
Turpentine Industry	311
Two Boys from Clinch	168
Ward, Old Man Billy	95
Ward, Priscilla (Jones) and Her Ward Boys	72
War Times and Hard Times	127
Wheat and Flour Mill	184
Where Uncle Jim Lives	157
Wilcox, Capt. Jefferson	88
Wild Turkeys	192
Women of the South	134
World War Veterans	333

Illustrations

	Page
Warren P. Ward	Frontispiece
J. H. Peterson, M. D. Dickerson, Warren P. Ward	3
Senators	6
Riley Wright	12
Judges Superior Court	16
Senators	22
Jim Boy, a Creek Indian	24
Daddy Ward's Mill	27
Billy Bow-Legs	34
Representatives	46
Representatives	58
Solicitors Superior Court	86
Erwin Spivey	87
Jeff Wilcox	88
Dunk Douglas	90
Dr. Staff Davis	93
Billy Ward	95
Dr. Calvin Parker	100
Superior Court Clerks	124
Spinning Wheel	129
James K. Hilliard	136
Abraham Hargraves and Wife	140
Parker, William	155
J. M. Freeman	157
M. D. Dickerson-W. C. Lankford	168
The Pine Tree	174
Ordinaries	182
Stormy Night on Seventeen-Mile Creek	197
Rev. Green Taylor	201
Sheriffs	214

Illustrations

	Page
Big Four—Dan Gaskin, R. S. Smith, Dan Newbern, Elias Lott	230
J. M. Ashley	233
Archie Bagwell	239
Tanner, Melvin	280
Douglas Public Schools	287
South Georgia State College	288
Georgia Normal Business College	291
Courthouse, Douglas, Georgia	297
Broxton High School	303
Nicholls Public School	306
William Gaskin	324
Map of Coffee County, Georgia	329
Arthur Lott	259
Major John M. Spence	259

Preface

I have been selected by the grand jury of Coffee County, to prepare a complete history of the county and its people, covering the formation, development and progress of the county from its creation in 1854 to the present date, 1930. The result of my labor is now before you.

No country is greater than its people. I have tried to give a history of many of the old families who have helped to make Coffee County what it is. No book could contain the names of all the worthy people of Coffee County; consequently I have been compelled to omit the names of many families. I regret this, but have done the best that I could with the space at my disposal.

Inasmuch as the Creek Indians occupied this territory before the Pioneers came, I have given much space to the story of the Indians. I note with pleasure that the Indians destroyed nothing while they lived here, and when we came we found plenty of game, birds, and fish. The country was in a primitive condition when the Indians left it, and they gave us but little trouble while they were here.

I am giving you a special write-up of Billy Bow-Legs, celebrated Indian chief, who was the most talked-about Indian in South Georgia. I am proud to be able to give you his picture. It is the first time his history has been printed.

I am giving you biographies, stories and incidents tending to illustrate the social and economical life of our people.

I have spent much time and have done a lot of work in giving you the early history of Coffee County, covering old schools, old churches and old methods of life. To those of you who read this history, you will now be able to see what wonderful progress has been made in Coffee County within recent years.

WARREN P. WARD,
Historian for Coffee County.

A Resolution of General Assembly

WHEREAS, the founding of the colony of Georgia by General James Oglethorpe occurred in 1733 and the two hundredth anniversary of that venturesome, political and philanthropic event will occur in 1933 and should be marked in some way proper to its historic character, so as to perpetuate for our posterity and the records of the State and Nation the facts of the evolution and progress of the commonwealth that became a constituent State of the Federated republic of the United States; and

WHEREAS, no provision has been made by the State Government to celebrate and memorialize the momentous establishment of the colony and subsequent sovereign State, and

WHEREAS, there is not in existence today a comprehensive and contemporaneous history of the State, therefore, be it

RESOLVED, by the General Assembly of Georgia, both houses thereof concurring herein, that the Judges of the Superior Courts of the State are hereby earnestly requested to give in charge to the grand jury of each county in their several circuits, at the next term of the court herein, the urgent consent of some competent person in their county to prepare between now and February 12th, 1933, being Georgia Day, as nearly a complete history of the formation, development and progress of said county from its creation up to that date, together with accounts of such persons, families and public events as have given character and fame to the County, the State, and the Nation. And that said county histories be deposited on Georgia Day in

1933 in the State's Department of Archives and History, there to be preserved for the information of future citizens of the State and prospective biographers and historians. And this action is recommended to the judges, grand juries, and the people of all the counties of the State, for early procedure because delay will leave action in this behalf too short a time for the necessary research and accumulation of data to make the county histories as full and accurate as they should be for full historic value.

RESOLVED, FURTHER, that the Governor of the State is respectfully requested to transmit an officially certified copy of these resolutions to each of the judges of the Superior Courts of the State.

W. CECIL NEILL, RICHARD B. RUSSELL, JR.,
  President of Senate.   Speaker of House.
D. F. McCLATCHEY, E. B. MOORE,
  Secretary of Senate.   Clerk of House.

Approved: L. G. HARDMAN, Governor.
This 23rd day of August, 1929.

Resolution of Grand Jury of Coffee County

The grand jury, as a whole, following up the fine sentiment developed by the last General Assembly of this State in designating the year 1933 for celebrating the 200th anniversary of the establishment of the Colony, now the Commonwealth of Georgia, and the same being transmitted to this body in the able charge of its esteemed Judge M. D. Dickerson, does hereby

1. J. H. PETERSON, Chairman County Commissioners
2. M. D. DICKERSON, Judge Superior Court
3. WARREN P. WARD, Ordinary Coffee County

designate and recommend that His Honor, Judge M. D. Dickerson, Ordinary W. P. Ward and Chairman of County Commissioners J. H. Peterson be authorized to appoint and fix compensation of a competent person, to gather, compile and write a complete history of Coffee County and its establishment in 1854 up to the present date, and that such complete history be delivered to the keeper of Archives and History for the State of Georgia as a permanent record constituting our County's part in the glowing history of the Empire State.

Having completed our investigation,

>Respectfully submitted,
>
>>W. T. Cottingham, Foreman.
>>T. A. Mitchell, Clerk.

Georgia Laws Creating Coffee County
Coffee County Boundaries Defined

SECTION I. Be it enacted by the Senate and House of Representatives of the State of Georgia in General Assembly met, and it is hereby enacted by the authority of the same, That from and immediately after the passage of this act, a new county shall be made out from the counties of Clinch, Ware, Telfair and Irwin, to be included within the following bounds, viz: Beginning at the corners of lots numbers One Hundred and Fifty-six and One Hundred and Sixty-seven in the Tenth District of formerly Irwin, now Clinch County, running from thence due east, along the original line, to the district line dividing the Tenth District of formerly Irwin, now Clinch, and the Seventh District of formerly Appling, now Clinch County, to the corner of lots number One Hundred and Sixty-one and One Hundred and Sixty-two in the Seventh District, thence due east along the original line, to the line dividing Clinch and Ware, thence up said line to Red Bluff Creek, thence along said creek to the Satilla River, thence down said river to the dividing line of the Seventh and Eighth districts of formerly Appling, now Ware County, thence due north along the district line dividing said districts, and the districts number five and six in originally Appling, now Ware County, thence along the line dividing the counties of Appling and Telfair to the Ocmulgee River, thence up said river to Coffee's Road, thence taking the road to the Lowndes County line, thence due east to the Alapaha River to the place of beginning.

Districts, Etc.

SEC. II. And be it further enacted by the authority aforesaid, That the new county described by the first section of this act shall be known by the name of Coffee County, and be attached to the Southern Judi-

SENATORS FROM COFFEE COUNTY.
1. E. L. GRANTHAM, 1923-1929.
2. J. M. WILCOX, 1882-1883-1884-1885.
3. S. F. MEMORY, 1925-1926.
4. WILLIAM A. McDONALD, 1882-1883.
5. GEORGE W. DEEN, 1907-1908.
6. CAPT. J. W. BOYD, 1890-1891.

cial District, to the first Congressional District, and to the Second Brigade of the Sixth Division, Georgia Militia.

County Officers, How and Where Elected, Militia Districts

SEC. III. And be it further enacted by the authority aforesaid, That the persons included within the said new county, entitled to vote for representatives of the General Assembly, shall, on the first Monday in April next, proceed to elect five Justices of the Inferior Court, a clerk of the Superior Court, a clerk of the Inferior Court, a sheriff, coroner, a tax collector, a receiver of tax returns, a county surveyor, and an ordinary for said county; the election for said officers shall be held at the house of Daniel Lott, and shall be conducted in manner as is now prescribed by law, and the Governor, on the same being certified to him, shall commission such persons as returned to him as elected at such elections, to hold their respective offices for and during the terms prescribed by law, and that the Justices of the Inferior Court, after they shall have received their commissions, shall proceed to lay out and divide said new county into Militia Districts, and advertise for the election of the requisite number of Justices of the Peace, said Governor, on being duly certified of the election of such Justices of the Peace, shall commission them according to law.

County Site and Buildings

SEC. IV. And be it further enacted by the authority aforesaid, That the Justices of the Inferior

Court of said county shall have full power and authority to select and locate a site for the public buildings in said county, and the said Justices, or a majority of them, are hereby authorized to purchase a tract or lot of land for the location of the county site, lay off the same into lots, and sell the same at public sale for the benefit of said county, or make such other arrangements or contracts in relation to the location of the county site and public buildings as they may deem most advantageous to the public good.

Precincts

SEC. V. And be it further enacted by the authority aforesaid, That the elections of the county generally, and by the precincts, for all elections, shall be established at the place of holding Justices' Courts in the several districts in said county, and votes received at them accordingly.

Justices and Bailiffs

SEC. VI. And be it further enacted by the authority aforesaid, That all Justices of the Peace and bailiffs, within the limits of said new county, shall hold their commissions and exercise the duties of their several offices within the said limits of the aforesaid county, until their successors shall have been elected and commissioned.

Processes and How Executed, Publication

SEC. VII. And be it further enacted by the authority aforesaid, That all mesne process, executions, and other final process in the hands of the Sheriffs, Coroners, and Constables, of the counties of which the new county may be formed, and which properly belong to said new county, and which have been levied, or in part executed, and such proceedings therein not finally disposed of at the time of passing this act, shall be delivered over to the corresponding officers of said new county, and such officers are hereby authorized and required to proceed with the same, and in the same manner as if such process had been originally in their hands: Provided, That in all cases publication of the time and places of sale, and proceedings of the like character, in the new county, shall be made for the time now prescribed by law, and all such process which properly belongs to the counties out of which said county may be formed, which may be in the hands of the officers of said new county, shall in like manner be delivered over to the officers of said county, to be executed by them in the manner herein prescribed.

Courts

SEC. VIII. And be it further enacted by the authority aforesaid, That the Superior Court for said county shall be held on Friday after the time of holding Appling County courts.

Extra Tax

SEC. IX. And be it further enacted by the authority aforesaid, That the Justices of the Inferior Court of Coffee County be authorized to levy an extra tax, not exceeding fifty per cent upon the general tax, for the purpose of erecting public buildings in said county.

SEC. X. And be it further enacted by the authority aforesaid, That all laws and parts of laws militating against the provisions of this act, be and the same are hereby repealed.

Approved, February 9, 1854.

Creation of Jeff Davis County

New County from Appling and Coffee named "Jeff Davis" and Attached to Brunswick Circuit and Eleventh Congressional District

An Act to lay off and organize a new county out of portions of Appling and Coffee Counties, and for other purposes in connection therewith.

SECTION I. Be it enacted by the General Assembly of the State of Georgia, and it is hereby enacted by authority of the same, That from and after the first day of January, 1906, a new county shall be, and the same is, hereby laid off and organized from portions of the counties of Appling and Coffee.

SEC. II. Be it further enacted, That said new county shall be named and called "Jeff Davis," and it shall be attached to the Brunswick Judicial Circuit, to the Eleventh Congressional District.

Territory

SEC. III. Be it further enacted, That the said County of "Jeff Davis" shall be included within the following boundaries: Beginning at a point on the Altamaha River which bounds the present counties of Appling and Tattnall, being at the northeast corner of land lot No. 695; thence running the land line south to the southeast corner of land lot No. 443; thence due west the land line to the southwest corner of land lot No. 448; thence again due south the land line to the southeast corner of land lot No. 272; thence again due west the land line to the southwest corner of land lot No. 271; thence due south the land line to the northeast corner land lot No. 222; thence due east the land line to the northeast corner of land lot No. 224; thence again due south the land line to the southeast corner of land lot No. 122; thence again due west the land line to Coffee County line dividing Appling and Coffee counties at the southwest corner of land lot No. 116; thence beginning at the southeast corner of land lot No. 116 in Coffee County and running west the land line to the southwest corner of land lot No. 129; thence running north the land line to the Ocmulgee River, which now forms the present boundary line between the counties of Coffee and Telfair, all being in the first district of Coffee County; thence along the Ocmulgee and the Altamaha Rivers to the point of beginning.

RILEY WRIGHT
Clerk Superior Court
1873-1875-1877

Creation of Atkinson County

Boundaries of New County. Name of County and Site Districts and Circuits.

An act to propose to the qualified electors of this State an amendment to Paragraph 2, Section I, Article II, of the Constitution of the State of Georgia, as amended by the ratification by the qualified electors of this State of the acts approved July 19, 1904, July 31, 1906, July 30, and August 14, 1912, July 7, 17, 27 and August 11, 1914, and for other purposes.

SECTION I. Be it enacted by the General Assembly of the State of Georgia, and it is hereby enacted by the authority of the same, That the following amendment is hereby proposed to paragraph 2, section I, article II, of the Constitution of the State of Georgia, as amended by the ratification by the electors of said State of the acts approved July 19, 1904, July 31, 1906, July 30 and August 14, 1912, July 7, 17, 27 and August 11, 1914, to-wit: By adding to said paragraph the following language: "Provided, however, That, in addition to the counties not provided for by this Constitution, there shall be a new county laid out and created from territory embraced in Coffee and Clinch Counties within the following boundary lines: Beginning at the point where the southern boundary line of lot of land No. 334, in the Fifth Land District of Coffee County, intersects the middle of the run of Willacoochee Creek, then to follow said land line directly east to the southeast corner of lot of land No. 15, in the Sixth Land District of Coffee County to the southwest corner of said lot of land; thence along the land line directly east to where it intersects the middle of the run of the Satilla River; thence, in a southeasterly direction along the run of the said Satilla River to where the same intersects the northern boundary of lot of land No. 250, in the Sixth (6) Land District, thence directly east along said line to where it intersects the Ware County line; thence in a southerly direction along the Ware County line to the southeast corner of lot of land No. 234, in the Seventh Land District of Clinch County; thence directly westward along the land line of said lot of land No. 234 on the south, to where it intersects the middle of the run of Alapaha River; thence in a northerly direction along the middle of the run of the Alapaha River to the mouth of Willacoochee Creek; thence along the middle of the run of Willacoochee Creek to point of beginning. That said new county shall be known as "Atkinson County," and the "City of Pearson" shall be the county seat thereof. That said "Atkinson County" shall be attached to the Eleventh Congressional District, the Waycross Judicial Circuit and the Fifth Senatorial District.

Land Districts of Coffee County

These land districts were surveyed, platted and mapped by various surveyors under the authority of the State of Georgia. It is worthy of note that the Sixth Land District of Coffee County, Georgia, is the largest land district in the county. It was surveyed by Reuben Neel. It was begun the 23rd day of July, 1819. The chain bearers were Riley King and Enoch Johns.

The boundary of the Fourth Land District of Coffee County is as follows: Beginning at the southwest corner of the lot of land number 30 in the Fourth District: South along the land lot line to the southwest corner of lot of land 20. West across 41. South to lots 41-42. West to lot of land 46 and south along south side 72 to the land district line and lot 72. East along the land district line to the southeast corner of lot 15. North along the land district line to the Ocmulgee River. West of said river to the beginning.

First land district of Coffee County is as follows: Beginning at the northwest corner of 322 of the First District and on the Ocmulgee River. South along said land district line to the southwest corner of lot of land Number 1. Thence in an easterly direction to the southeast of lot of land 23. North along the original land line beginning at the county line of Appling to the northeast corner of lot of land 115 and being the corner of Jeff Davis County, then following Jeff Davis west and north back to the river.

Fifth District of Coffee County, Georgia, being as follows: To the northeast corner of lot of land Number 23. South along the land lot line to the southeast corner of 345. The same being the boundary of

Coffee County, thence west along the boundary line of Coffee and Atkinson Counties, to the Irwin County line. Northeast direction to lot of land 18. Easterly direction to the northeast lot of land 23 to the point of beginning.

Sixth Land District of Coffee County, Georgia, is as

JUDGES SUPERIOR COURT

1. R. G. DICKERSON, first Judge of Alapaha Circuit.
2. J. I. SUMMERALL, 1915-1924.
3. J. W. QUINCEY, 1914-1915.
4. FRANCIS WILLIS DART (the youngest judge in Georgia at the time of his service.)
5. CALVIN A. WARD, Judge Inferior Court.

follows: The northwest of land lot Number 1 and running south along the land lot line to the southwest corner of Number 15. East along the south line of 15 to the southeast corner of said lot. South along the west line of 31 to the southwest corner of 31. East along the land lot line to the Satilla River, being about or between 200-201, down the Satilla River in a southeasterly direction to the south line of 249. East along the Coffee County and Atkinson land line to the southeast corner of lot of land 525, same being the corner of Ware County. North along the land lot line 507. West along the land lot to the point of beginning.

Beginning at the northwest of lot of land 510 of the Fifth District of Coffee County, Georgia, thence east across 510. South on the east side of 510. East to line 502. South along the east line of 502 and south down to the southeast corner of 496. South line 496 going west 496-517 to the land district line of the Sixth District down north along the land district line to the northwest corner of 510.

The land districts of Coffee County were surveyed by the state in 1819. A land district in the original survey contains 529 lots of land. The land districts remaining just as they were originally surveyed, but the changing of county lines has cut off land districts lying in one county and added to the new county that was cut off from the old county. There are part of two Fifth Land Districts in Coffee County. A portion of the Fifth Land District of Irwin and Appling County was cut off into Coffee County.

NOTE: This information is furnished to the History of Coffee County by D. H. Peterson, County Surveyor, and is therefore correct and authentic.

Georgia Militia Districts of Coffee County

BROXTON 1127 G. M. is bounded as follows: Beginning on the east side of lot of land 103 in Land District Number 1; thence south along east side to lot of land Number 231; thence west along the south side to lot of land 46; thence north to lot of land 95; thence west to lot 20, the boundary line; thence north along boundary line to Ocmulgee River; thence running south back to the point of beginning.

AMBROSE 1556 G. M. is bounded as follows: Beginning on the west side of lot of land 170; thence running southeasterly to lot of land Number 46; thence east to lot of land 250, thence southeasterly to lot of land 254; thence south to boundary line; thence east to lot of land 33, then north to lot of land 95; thence west to boundary line, then south to point of beginning.

DOUGLAS 748 G. M. is bounded as follows: Beginning on the northwest side of lot of land 48, thence running south to lot of land 60, then west to lot 33, then south again to boundary line; thence east to lot of land 169; thence southeasterly to boundary line; thence west to lot of land 341; thence north to lot of land 326; thence east to land lot 232; thence west again to lot 48, the point of beginning.

NICHOLLS G. M. is bounded as follows: Beginning on the northwest side of lot of land 365; thence south to lot 350, the boundary line, thence east to lot 525; thence north to lot of land 517; thence east to lot 496;

thence north again to 502; east to 511; thence north to 509, thence east to lot 365, the point of beginning.

WEST GREEN 427 G. M. is bounded as follows: Northwest by lot of land 104; in the Fifth Land District of Coffee County; thence south to lot of land 274; thence east to lot of land 509; thence north to lot 115; thence west to lot 104, the point of beginning.

BRIDGETOWN 1804 G. M. is bounded as follows: Beginning at the southeast corner of lots of land numbers 15 and 14 in the Sixth District of Coffee County, Georgia; running along east lines of said lots 15 and 14 to the Satilla River, thence in a westerly direction along said river to Hebron Bridge; thence along the Douglas and Willacoochee road northwest to the bridge across the Satilla River on said road; thence in a westerly direction along the Satilla River to the Irwin County line, said district being bounded as follows: on the south by Atkinson County Line; east by the east original line of lots 15 and 14 in the Sixth District of Coffee County, Georgia, and the Douglas and Willacoochee public roads; north by the Satilla and the Douglas and Lax road and west by Douglas and Lax road and the Irwin County and Berrien County lines.

Early History of Coffee County

First County Officers—The List of Juries—Population in 1860

Since the removal of the Indians and the building of the Columbus and Blackshear roads, immigration came more rapidly to this section of Georgia. The class of people who came in were sturdy men and women from Virginia and the Carolinas. They had large families. Conditions of all kinds were improving; churches and schoolhouses were being built; roads were being opened; farm land being fenced and cultivated, and there was an era of progress and prosperity on every side. And so, in 1854 Coffee County was created, being carved out of Appling, Telfair and Irwin Counties. The county was named for General John Coffee. Hon. James Pearson gave the county fifty acres of land, on which the courthouse was built in 1858. The county site was named Douglas, after Hon. Stephen A. Douglas, who had been the South's candidate for President.

All the citizens of Telfair County on the south side of the Ocmulgee River and all the citizens who formerly lived in Appling County, later included in Coffee County, and also citizens of Irwin County, then included in Coffee County, all became citizens of the new county of Coffee. The county was duly organized on the 17th day of April, 1854, by the Justices of the Inferior Court of the County of Coffee, whose names were as follows: Alex Mobley, Joel Lott, Mark Lott, Hardy Hall, and Elijah Pickren.

The first officers of Coffee County, which are as follows: B. H. Tanner, Sheriff; Whitington S. Moore,

Clerk Superior Court; Whitington S. Moore, Clerk Inferior Court; Thomas Mobley, Ordinary; John W. Matchet, Tax Receiver; John R. Smith, Tax Collector; Carver, Surveyor; Sim Parker, Coroner.

Grand Jurors

In order to give you an idea of the leading citizens of Coffee County, at that time, I give you a list of the grand and petit jurors drawn for the June term of court of Coffee County, 1854. The list of the grand jury was as follows: Daniel Newbern, Nathan Byrd, Joseph Asbell, William C. Smith, Nathaniel Ashley, Abram Hargraves, Ivey Kirkland, William W. Creech, Seth Durham, Sherrod Roberts, Maddock H. McRae, Robert Roberts, Thomas Mobley, Archibald Miller, David Hutchinson, John J. Pickren, Arthur Turner, Elias Moore, Lewis Harper, Calvin Quinn, Roan Pafford, Daniel Lott, David Dyal, Daniel Morrison, Bartilery Burkett, William Hinson, Thomas Paulk, James Sermons, Bryant Wooten, Archibald McLean, Joel Ricks, Jackson Ward, Elijah Graham, Daniel Lott, Sr., Hiram Sears, Stafford Davis, Jacob J. Hill, William Dent, Allen Summerlin, Hiram Ellis, Joel Lott, Aaron G. Fryer, George Wilcox, William R. Manning, Calvin A. Ward.

Petit Jurors

The following is a list of the names of the petit jurors: Jackson Mills, Seaborn Bowen, James R. Smith, Alexander Chancey, Solomon Carver, Benjamin Thomas, Needham Purvis, John Middleton, John Passmore, John Douglas, James H. Wilcox, Elijah Tanner, James Gaskin, Johns Brooks, Alfred Merritt, Harris

Johnson, Mark Mobley, William Carver, P. Merritt, N. B. Sislar, Hiram Ellis, Jr., Mathew Benfield, Simon L. Wooten, E. S. Meeks, Angus Gillis, John Adams, Washington Nelson, Parrish Lankford, Jesse Bennett, John Ricketson, M. J. Kirkland, John Cothern, John P.

SENATORS.

1. Joe C. Brewer, 1929——.
2. W. T. Dickerson, 1911-12.
3. Lem Johnson, 1900-1901.
4. Leon A. Wilson, 1894-1895.
5. Mack Kirkland, 1871-72.
6. George W. Newbern, 1875-1876-1877.

Ricketson, Lovett Harrell, William Herrin, Thomas Minix, James Carver, Jr., William Everitt, Harris Kirkland, Benjamin Ricketson, Daniel Johnson, John Durham, John M. Lott, Willoby Adams, Demps Everett, Joseph Roberts, Henry Hutto and William Hutto.

Population

The population of Coffee County in 1860 was: whites, 2206; colored, 673. In 1870, ten years later, which covered the Civil War period, the population was white, 2514; colored, 678.

The Creek Indians

JIM BOY

A Typical Creek Indian Whose Indian Name Was Tustennuggee Emathla. He was born in 1793.

For several hundred years before Oglethorpe settled Georgia this territory was inhabited by thousands of Indians. The Wiregrass Country was occupied by the Muscogee, or Creek Indians. The Indian name for creek is Muscogee. The Creek Indian nation occupied the territory embraced in the area beginning at the Savannah River in Georgia, running to the St. Augustine in Florida, thence running west to the Flint River in Georgia and back to the beginning. The Indians known as the Cherokees lived in the middle part and northern part of the state; the Seminole Indians, which means wild men, lived in the east or southern part of Georgia and in Florida.

In my study of the Indians, in the Wiregrass Country, I have been surprised at the meager information to be found about their history, their manner and habits of life.

When the whites settled in the Wiregrass Country about the year 1800, it is estimated that there were twenty thousand Creek Indians in Georgia and eastern Alabama. They had thirty-seven towns; several of the towns were located on the Oconee River. Some twenty or thirty towns were located on the Chattahoochee and Flint Rivers; and so far as I have been able to ascertain, there were no towns in this part of Georgia.

The three tribes of Indians, which I have just named, were somewhat similar in their personal appearance, their habits of life, and also their language. One of the Indian commissioners of the United States government describes the Creek Indians as follows:

"The men are tall, erect and robust; their limbs are well shaped so as to form a perfect human figure; their features are such as to give them a dignified appearance; the eye is rather small and very black; their complexion is a reddish brown, or copper color; their hair long, coarse and brown. The Creek women are of short stature, well-formed round faces, the eye large and black."

The Cherokee men are very much like the Muscogee men, but the Cherokee women appear to be of a very different type from that of the Creek woman. The Cherokee women are tall, slender, erect, and of a delicate frame; their features formed with perfect symmetry, their countenance cheerful, friendly; they move with grace and dignity.

The Seminole Indians are of a copper color, over six feet tall. One of the best specimens of the Seminole race is that of Osceola, who died in prison in 1838. He was born and reared in Wiregrass Georgia. When he reached the age of twelve years, he moved to Florida.

In the study of the Indians of Georgia, and from such information as I could get from books, and from tradition, and from old citizens, I have been surprised at the intelligence and their high regards for justice and truth. If you have heard that the Indians who then lived in Georgia were something like the wild animals, you are very much mistaken. They had plenty of sense, had their own ideals of life, and as a rule they were no better and no worse than other nations of people. I wish to say to the credit of the Creek Indians that so far as I have been able to ascertain they gave the pioneer settlers of South Georgia little trouble. The white settlers lived among them for twenty years, and more, without having trouble of any sort. They often came to our home, ground their corn on our mill and swapped their guns with our boys. One of the first words the Indians learn is "swap." The reason for that is because of trade with the white people. We are accustomed to think that the Indians lived in the woods, had no houses and no clothes, and no means of warfare except with their tomahawks, and their bows and arrows, but in this we are very much mistaken.

The Creek Indians were religious in a way. They believed in the Great Spirit. They could not understand how you could get religion out of a book. They believed in a future state of rewards and punishments. They had some sort of religious ceremonies, but had no organization which in any way corresponds with our churches.

When Mr. Oglethorpe came to Savannah, he got in touch with that noble chief, Tommiechichi, made friends with him and entered into trade relations with him and all the Creek Indians. The following is a schedule of prices agreed upon by Mr. Oglethorpe and the Creek Indians; five skins for one white blanket; ten buckskins for a gun; five buckskins for a pistol; four buckskins for a gun; one buckskin for a couple of measures of powder; one buckskin for sixty bullets; two buckskins for one white shirt; one doe hide for a knife; two buckskins for a hoe; two buckskins for an axe; three doe skins for a large hatchet; one buckskin for a pound of brass; this being the 18th day of May, 1734. It will be seen by the above that the Indians buy all the guns and all the powder and all the bullets from the white people that they were able to pay for; it will also be seen that they bought blankets, shirts and cloth, consequently they wore clothes of some sort; generally, however, the clothes of the Creek Indians consisted of hunting shirt of some sort with buckskin breeches.

Old "Daddy" Ward's mill where the Creek Indians ground their corn —1810-1820.

I have said that so far as I could ascertain, the Creek Indians had no towns in this section of Wiregrass Georgia, but they often came to this section on hunting trips; they would select some camping ground and stay there for several weeks.

As it has been seen, the buckskins were very valuable for trading purposes and the flesh could be used for eating.

When the weather was good the Indians opened up the deer, cut out the bones and left the meat on the skin. When they traveled, the skin was rolled up with the meat inside, and when they stopped for camp the meat could be hung up in the sun to cure, and when thus cured could be kept for weeks.

The Indians, in passing from the Oconee River to Chattahoochee and Flint Rivers, and also from the Ocmulgee River down to the Okefenokee Swamp and into Florida, would pass through this section of Georgia. They had Indian trails, with regular crossing places at the rivers and creeks, and Indian Ford and Indian Spring on the Seventeen-Mile Creek, about five miles east of Douglas, was one of their crossing places; they had a regular camping place near the J. M. Lott old place, about fifteen miles northeast of Douglas. Many of the early settlers of this section used to go to the camp and trade with them. One of the Indian trails led from the Ocmulgee River down to Florida, and is known as the "trail ridge." Indian mounds are to be seen along the east banks of the Seventeen-Mile Creek. There is one near the Indian ford; one near Gaskin Springs and others in the hammocks along the creek. There is much speculation as to what use the Indians made of these mounds; they seem to be graveyards, places where they buried their dead. By digging in these mounds, you will find such implements as the Indians used, such as flints, pottery and sometimes human bones.

The Indian villages on the Chattahoochee, Flint and Oconee Rivers were built of logs and boards. In the center of the village some sapling poles were put up in a rough manner and covered. In cold weather a fire was built in the center of it, to this everybody was welcome, and there was plenty of room, as the structure covered about twenty by thirty foot space. The Indians had their little huts for their families, circled around this centrally located building in the same manner as many houses are today found around a mill quarter, but the buildings looked more like dog houses and goat houses.

Dr. Jefferson Wilcox, who has a wonderful memory, says that he heard a tradition of an Indian chief, by the name of Ocilla, who lived in Wiregrass Georgia, died in what is now Irwin County and was buried there. It may be that the name of Ocilla, now the county site of Irwin County, was named for him.

The Indians deserve our thanks for leaving this section of Georgia unharmed. The timber, the game and the fish were left here in good condition. They did not burn the woods, nor poison the fish, nor destroy the timber.

One of the strangest things about the Indians who lived in Wiregrass Georgia is that, although it has been only about one hundred years since they left this part of the country, no trace of them is left behind, except a few Indian mounds. No one has written their history in detail, and scarcely a name of the most prominent chiefs among the Creek nation can be found in any history. No one has undertaken to tell about the economic life of the Indians as they lived in the Wiregrass Country one hundred years ago. We hear Tommiechichi, who made friends with Oglethorpe, and Osceola, who grew up in South Georgia and became famous as an Indian chief among the Seminoles. We also hear something about Billy Bow-Legs, a great warrior among the Seminoles of Florida.

When General Oglethorpe made his treaty with the Creek Indians, in 1734, it also included the Seminoles, who at that time lived in South Georgia and Florida, but in 1750, the Creek and Seminole Indians had trouble among themselves, and, by mutual agreement, the Seminoles went to Florida and the Creeks remained in South Georgia.

By the study of the Indian language, we find that many of the principal streams in South Georgia were named by the Indians. The Indians named the Chattahoochee, Ocmulgee, Oconee, and Ohoope Rivers; they also named the Coochee Creek, and the Willacoochee Creek. The Indian names usually ended with "ee," however, it sometimes happened, owing to the meaning of the word, that the name of the creek or river ended with "a," such as Altamaha, Allapaha, and so forth. St. Illa and the St. Marys Rivers appear to be Spanish names.

When the whites would go into Florida after their slaves, the Indians would retaliate, coming into Georgia, stealing cows, hogs, and other property, and in some instances they killed and robbed the citizens of Wiregrass Georgia. To protect themselves against the attacks of the Indians, the white people built forts in South Georgia. There was one fort near what is now Homerville, Georgia, in Clinch County, Georgia; there was another fort about five miles northeast of Douglas, near the home of Mr. John Peterson, at Huffer, Ga. These forts were built with pine poles stood upon the ends around two- or three-acre tracts of land; they were braced inside with poles and made as strong as possible.

Inside the fort grounds, small houses or rooms were constructed for living purposes for women and children who went there for protection from time to time. About the year 1837, a band of robber Indians passed through this country. All the families in reach of the fort near the Peterson home were commanded to come to the fort, which they did. About three miles north of Douglas, on a high hill overlooking the Seventeen-Mile Creek, lived a man by the name of Metts. As it happened, his family had taken refuge in the fort. Mrs. Metts told a negro woman to slip back home and get some clothes for herself and the children; when she failed to return on time, investigation showed that the Indians had robbed the place and killed the negro woman.

About the same time, a whole family by the name of Granthams were robbed and killed by the Indians. Granthams lived near what is now Pridgen, Georgia. As soon as information of the murder reached the people, they hastily got up a small company of citizens to pursue the Indians. Among those in the company whose names I have secured were: Redding Metts, John Passmore, Dot Hill, David Collins, John G. Taylor, Fred Merritt, Mr. Maddox, and others. The Indians were pursued and overtaken at the Flint River, near Albany, Georgia. Many of the Indians were killed, some swam the river and made their escape. John G. Taylor, who since that time was a well known Baptist minister in South Georgia, dived down to the bottom of the river and brought many of the Indians to land.

I will tell you one more incident, because it puts the ingenuity of white men to test against the cunningness of the Indians. It is only through tradition that I have been able to get this story, which runs thus: Way back in the early days people living in South Georgia had no markets near and so the people would gather their little plunder together, go in carts to Centerville, Georgia. The Indians robbed and killed a good many of these people going to market at a point near the Okefenokee swamp. A company of brave pioneers decided to put a stop to this nefarious business, and, if possible, make it safe for people to go to market. And so with guns and such other necessaries as they would need, they went to the point near the Okefenokee swamp and pitched their camp. They cut small logs into pieces five or six feet long, about the length of a man. They laid the logs around the campfire and covered them over with quilts and blankets. On the ends of the logs they placed hats and fixed it up in such a manner as to make it look very much like a bunch of travelers lying around the campfire. The men, with their guns, went a short distance from the campfire and concealed themselves in the woods. Away in the midnight hour, as the fire burned low, the pioneers saw the heads of Indians beginning to peep out from behind trees and stumps and from over logs. In a minute there was a volley of shots fired and the Indians sprang to their feet and with the war whoop charged upon the campfire. As they pulled off the hats at the ends of the logs, instead of finding the heads of white men they saw the joke. For a moment they stood still in bewilderment; at that moment every Indian was shot dead, not one of them made his escape. Every hat had a bullet hole in it. That was the last of the robberies committed at Centerville by the Indians.

The Seminole Indians left Georgia and went to Florida in 1750. In 1837 the Cherokee Indians left the State of Georgia. In 1827 the last treaty was made with the Indians. By the year 1841 there was not an Indian in Georgia, who had a right to be here. The people in Georgia, and especially South Georgia, were happy indeed to be rid of the Indians and to have the Wiregrass land without fear of molestation. Some one wrote a song, about this time, which reads as follows:

"No more shall the sound of the war whoop be heard,
The ambush and slaughter no longer be feared,
The tommy hawk buried shall rest in the ground,
And peace and good will to the nation round."

Billy Bow-Legs

BILLY BOW-LEGS

The picture shown here is that of Billy Bow-Legs, the celebrated Seminole chief of Florida. His Indian name is Olac-to-mico. Billy Bow-Legs is supposed to have been born in Wiregrass Georgia about 1804. When he was about twelve years of age he moved to Florida and joined the Seminole nation of that state. Little or nothing is heard of him until about 1830 or '35 when he and his soldiers or braves would come to South Georgia and murder and kill the people and steal their horses and cattle. Billy Bow-Legs it seems was drawn into this sort of life as a matter of retaliation against the whites of South Georgia. During slavery times the negro slaves would sometimes run away and go to Florida and make their homes with the Indians. The Indians were glad to give them a warm welcome for they used them as slaves and as soldiers in the army. At this time Florida belonged to the Spanish Government and it required too much time and too much expense to take the matter up with the Spanish Government and get requisition papers for their slaves and so the South

Georgia slave owner would generally get up a bunch of his friends and go to Florida and take their slaves away from the Indians by force and sometimes, perhaps, they might bring back a few good horses for their trouble. Things went on like this for many years and so about 1841 the United States Government had ordered all the Indians to go west of the Mississippi and locate there. But Billy Bow-Legs and his band of Seminoles did not choose to go, and continued to remain in the neighborhood of the "Big Cyprus" in the State of Florida. At last the Government called for a show-down for Billy Bow-Legs, the Seminole chief, but instead of going west of the Mississippi river Billy Bow-Legs got on the steamboat and went to Washington City via New York. Billy was successful in his trip to the Government at Washington City. They advised Billy if he would be good and let the white people alone he might remain at the "Big Cyprus" for an indefinite period of time. This was about 1852 and so Billy went back to the "Big Cyprus" in Florida and opened up a big farm. He was also a big stock raiser. He had plenty of slaves to carry on a big business. He lived like a king and was lord of everything in sight but it so happened that the United States Government decided to make a survey of South Florida, including the "Big Cyprus" country. A crew of surveyors sent out by the Government ran into old Billy and his possessions one day and they said to themselves this is Billy Bow-Legs' plantation. We will go inside and destroy some of his orange trees and banana trees and other things and so they did. Next day old Billy Bow-Legs was walking over his plantation and discovered that somebody had been in his field and destroyed his crop. He made an examination of the tracks and decided it was the surveyors who had molested his farm. And so he went to the camps and made inquiry about what had happened. They said "yes, we are the boys who did it; they told us this farm belonged to Billy Bow-Legs and that they had entered the farm and destroyed the trees and fruit, etc., just to see old Billy 'cut up'," and so the old Indian straightened himself up, about six feet and four inches high, and said, "Young men, I am Billy Bow-Legs, and if you are not off these premises by sunrise tomorrow morning old Billy Bow-Legs will 'cut up'." And so Billy went home that night and called about a hundred of his braves together and the next morning at daylight he made an attack upon the surveyors who were soldiers and had commissions from the United States Government. And thus began the war with the Seminole Indians in 1858, when many people of South Georgia were called into service. Old Dr. Parker, M. L. Corbitt, C. A. Ward, Sr., and many others from Coffee County enlisted in this fight against the Seminole Indians. Billy Bow-Legs was a sly old fellow. He was hard to catch. He hid himself in the Okefenokee Swamp on an island which to this day is known as Billy's island.

The Government was very gracious toward Billy and his band of Indians. An order was passed giving a reward for every Indian that was captured and delivered at Ft. Brook, Fla., alive. The order was special that no Indian was to be killed. Under this proclamation a great many Indians went to Ft. Brook and surrendered themselves to the Government and in cases like that, the Indian who surrendered received the reward himself.

Billy Bow-Legs was the last Indian to go to Ft. Brook and surrender. Being the big chief of all the tribes he received a large sum of money and took his journey across the Mississippi into the sunset land and thus ended the Indian War under Billy Bow-Legs.

There are several hundred Seminole Indians living in Florida now. They give the whites no trouble and are fairly good citizens. Mrs. Minie Moore Wilson of Kissimmee, Fla., has written several books on the Seminole Indians of Florida. She knows hundreds of these Indians and has learned a great deal about them first hand. I am indebted to her books for some of the facts stated above.

Old Families of Coffee County
The Peterson Family

From the best information we can get the Petersons came to Coffee County from Bulloch County about 1810. Old man John Peterson had three sisters: Eliza Peterson, Lucy Peterson and Elizabeth Peterson. Lucy Peterson married old man Dan Lott, Sr. Eliza Peterson married Mathie McGovern and Elizabeth Peterson married Jim Davis. Fannie Peterson married Youngie Vickers and they had the following children: Tishie Burthnot, Lila Paulk, Little George Paulk, Beedie Carver and Hump Back Wiley Vickers. Lucy Peterson and Dan Lott had the following children: John Lott, Arthur Lott, Elisha Lott, Joe Lott, Mark Lott, Mrs. Jack Vickers, Mrs. Billie Meeks, Mrs. Benajah Pearson, Mrs. Elias Moore and Mrs. John Paulk, who lives in Irwin County. Eliza Peterson married Mathie McGovern and they have the following children: Tom Boy McGovern, John McGovern and Fannie McGovern, Tom McGovern. Thomas McGovern married a Ricketson. Tom Boy McGovern is deaf and dumb and has never married. Fannie McGovern who married Joe Day had several children.

John McGovern married a Neugent and had several children.

John Peterson married Betty Lott. He had two brothers. Hal Peterson, and Alfred Peterson. Hal Peterson married a Gaskin the first time and had the following children: Henry Peterson, Dan Peterson, Dave Peterson, Fannie Peterson and Betty Peterson. Fannie Peterson married Brooks Paulk, Betty Peterson married Jack Lott and had one girl, Sarah, who married R. G. Kirkland. Henry Peterson married a Miss Walker and they had the following children: Mary Peterson who married John Gaskins, and Emmitt Peterson who married a Miss Summerlin. Fannie Peterson who married Brooks Paulk had the following children: John Paulk, Elisha Paulk, Roy Paulk and Bessie Paulk, Dennis Paulk. Belle Peterson married a Mr. Corbitt. Dan Peterson married Elizabeth Lott and they had the following children: John Peterson, Lem Peterson, Tom Peterson and two girls: Mary Jane and one other.

John Peterson married Maggie Smith and they had the following children: Mary Peterson, Rexford Peterson, Gladys Peterson, Dan Peterson, Iris Peterson and J. H. Peterson, Jr.

Lem Peterson married Bertie Herrington and they have the following children: Rosa Mary Peterson, Robinetta Peterson and L. S. Peterson, Jr. Tom Peterson married Stella Stevens and they have the following children:

Alfred Peterson, son of old man John Peterson, married Betty Cato and they had the following children: Betty Peterson who married Henry Minix, Joe Peterson who married Lizzie Ward, Richard Peterson who married Lila Lott and William Peterson who married a Wooten.

Betty Peterson who married Henry Minix had the following children: Cyrus Minix, Lucy Minix, Lydia Minix, Joe Minix and Monroe Minix. Joe Peterson married Lizzie Ward and had the following children: Simon and Ruby Peterson. Richard Peterson married Lila Lott and have several children.

William Peterson married a Wooten and they have two children: Dave and Elizabeth.

Dr. John Peterson and Dr. Nicholls Peterson are sons of Mrs. Elizabeth Peterson.

Sheriff Manning Peterson was the son of Polly Peterson.

We are indebted to old man Essex Peterson for much of this information. He was a slave of old man Hal Peterson and is 88 years old.

The Davis Family

One of the first families who settled in Coffee County was Dr. Stafford Davis, a well known cancer doctor. He came to Coffee County from Montgomery County about 1820 and married Penny Lott who was a sister to the old members of the Lott family of this county. He lived to be 106 years old and died in the year 1900. He had the following children: Dan Davis, Joe Davis, Simon Davis, Mark Davis, Arthur Davis; the last named three sons died in the Confederate war. Mary married Travis Thigpen. Bettie married Perry Nettles, Patsy married Hymrick Meeks, Sr., Janie married William Bagley, Delilah married Hardy Hall, Sallie married Jackson Ward, Penny married Thad Douglas and Rhoda married B. W. Teston.

Following are the names of the children of Joe Davis, son of Staff Davis: Joe Davis married Roxie Kirkland, America married Dr. Frier, Penny married Tom Trowell, Margaret married Fred Tanner, Ella married High Davis, Emma married John Hersey, Martha married Josh Carter, Betty married Warren Smith, Mose married a Meeks, John married Mary Jane Little,

Travis married Miss Durhan and Rhoda married Jim Carter.

The following are the children of Janie Davis and William Bagley. Sarah Bagley married Jim Spell, Mary Bagley married Enoch Hersey, Rachell Bagley married Lem Courson, Penny Bagley married William Gilliard, John Davis married Liza Bennett, Lottie Bagley married Ben Teston, Mina married John Carter.

The following is the list of children of Delilah Davis and Dr. Hardy Hall: John Hall married Nettie Maulden, Mark Hall married Rachell Jorden, Dan Hall married a Miss Lee, Lee married Winnie Newbern, Delphia Ann Hall married Love Harrell, Pollie Hall married Newton Lee, Mattie Hall married Rev. H. M. Meeks, and Bettie Hall married Monroe Courson.

Sallie Davis, daughter of old Staff Davis, Sr., married Jackson Ward and they have the following children: "Big John Ward," Staff Ward married Mary Shuman, Tom Ward married Missouri Newbern, Joe Ward married Angeline Burkett, Penny Ward married Gaines Ellis, Janie Ward married William Courson, Bettie Ward married H. C. Ellis.

Mary Davis, daughter of old Dr. Davis, married Travis Thigpen and have the following children: Manning Thigpen, Joe Thigpen, who married a Mullis, Bartow Thigpen who married a Tanner, Susan Thigpen married Rev. A. B. Finely, Lila Thigpen married a Mr. Sweat.

The Newbern Family

Old man Jackson Newbern married Polly Lott and had the following children: Daniel Newbern, Jack

Newbern, Mark Newbern, Bill Newbern, and Joe Newbern. All but Dan Newbern went to Alabama about 1855.

Daniel Newbern, long before the Civil War, married Winnie Wilcox and settled in Coffee County about ten miles north of Douglas. He reared a large family, had a water mill and was a successful farmer. His children are as follows: Daniel Newbern, Sr., who married a Fussell, Lawrence Newbern who married Lizzie Douglas, and Willis Newbern who married Margaret Kirkland. She died early in life and he married Miss Polly Carver. The girls were Eliza, who married a Hinson who died soon after they were married. Later in life she married Robert "Dunk" Douglas. Mary married John Smith and died early in life. Winnie married Leon Hall and died young, Delilah married Mr. Davis and died soon.

About the year 1870 Dan Newbern, Sr., and his wife and four grown sons died with menengitis. The country was very much excited over this disease when so many in one family died within a week. Dan Newbern, Jr., had the following children: Jesse Newbern, Dan Newbern, Jr., married Miss Jackson, Winnie Newbern married Micajah Vickers and Eula Newbern married W. T. Cottingham. Emma Jane Newbern married Warren G. Meeks.

Rev. George W. Newbern was our senator from Coffee County in 1877 and also a Baptist minister. He organized Sand Hill Church about the year 1870. He was born in 1825 and died in 1892 at Homerville, Georgia.

The Vickers Family

Rebecca Paulk was born in 1815 and was married twice. Her first husband was Jesse Vickers who died in 1831. There was only one child by this marriage, which was Beedy Vickers and she married Joel Lott in 1826. Rebecca Paulk Vickers was married the second time to Ely Vickers, who was a brother to Jesse, her first husband. They had the following children: Rev. John Vickers, (Jack) born May 28th, 1836, died June 7th, 1900. Wiley Vickers, born May 8th, 1839. Henry Vickers, born Dec. 26th, 1837. Elijah Vickers was born Jan. 11th, 1842 and lived in Berrien County for many years. William Vickers, born Aug. 7th, 1843. Rebecca Vickers, born Jan. 6th, 1845. Mary (Polly) Vickers, born Nov. 3rd, 1845. She married Hamilton Sears. Micajah Vickers, born Oct. 8th, 1848. Ely Vickers, born Aug. 24th, 1850. He married Lucy Lott. Matilda Vickers, born Oct. 20th, 1852, and married D. P. Lott.

Beedy Vickers married Joel Lott and had the following children: Jesse Lott, Arthur Lott, Dan Lott, J. B. Lott (Babe), Elisha Lott, Wiley Lott, William Lott, Johnnie Lott, Rebecca Lott, Lucy Lott, Narcissus Lott, Beedy Lott, Martha Lott and Mary Lott.

Rev. John (Jack) Vickers married Martha Lott the first time and had the following children: Rebecca Vickers, Elizabeth Vickers, who married Lucius Paulk, J. J. Vickers married Eunnie Whiddon. Martha Vickers married G. G. Henderson. Beedy Vickers married Elmore Maine. Avie Vickers married Dempsey Whiddon, Daniel Vickers married Belle Bailey. Ely Vickers married Lilar Paulk.

Rev. John Vickers married Sarah Jane Graves, a second wife, and they had the following children: Joseph Vickers, married Elizabeth Daniels, Leon Vickers married Fronney McMillen, Lewis Vickers first married Lucy Lott and then married Emma McEachin. George Vickers, Melissa Vickers married Dr. Howell and later married Thomas McMillen. Henry Vickers married Bessie Joiner, William Vickers married Bessie Paulk. Jacob Vickers married first, a Miss Lott and then married Rebecca Daniels. Rachael Vickers married Lott Paulk and Minnie Vickers married Ollie Paulk.

Henry Vickers married Ellen Sears and had the following children: Mary Jane Vickers, Elias Vickers, Rebecca Vickers, William Vickers, Hiram Vickers, Ely Vickers, Hattie Vickers, Micajah Vickers, Amanda Vickers, Ellen Vickers, Lister Vickers. A second time Henry Vickers married Kattie McMillen. Wiley Vickers married Betty Lott. Wiley Vickers married the second time Eugenia Parker and had the following children: O. J. Vickers, Calvin Vickers, Matilda Vickers, Mattie Vickers, Henry V. Vickers, B. L. Vickers, Eva Vickers, C. E. Vickers, and Gordon Vickers. Wiley Vickers married Betty Gaskin, third wife, and had no children.

William Vickers married Francis Lott and had the following children: Richard Vickers (Bud), Elie Vickers, Matilda Vickers, W. II. Vickers, Rebecca Vickers, William Vickers, John Vickers and Michael Vickers.

Mary (Polly) Vickers married Hampton Sears and they have the following children: Wiley Sears, Mary

Sears, Hiram Sears, Sol Sears, Rosa Ann Sears, Hamp Sears, Beedy Sears, Ollie Sears, and Matilda Sears.

Elijah Vickers married Annie Sutton and they have the following children: William Vickers, Johnnie Vickers, Flem Vickers, Leonard Vickers, Bennie Vickers, Blannie Vickers, Minnie Vickers, and Rachael Vickers.

Micajah Vickers married Harriet Sears and they have the following children: Leander Vickers, Bartley Vickers, Micajah Vickers, Liller Vickers, Rebecca Vickers, Onnie Vickers and Hattie Vickers.

Micajah Vickers married Viola Starling, his second wife, and they had the following children: Fannie Vickers and Dorsey Vickers.

Ely Vickers married Lucy Lott and they had the following children: Henry Vickers, J. J. Vickers, Mattie Vickers, Elisha Vickers, Warren Vickers, Micajah Vickers, Dan Vickers, Ely Vickers, Willie Vickers and H. E. Vickers.

Matilda Vickers married Dan P. Lott and they have the following children: Reason Lott, Mary Jane Lott, Lucy Lott, Rebecca Lott, Dan Lott, Daisy Lott, Minnie Lott, Ely Lott, Henry Lott, Mattie Lott and Aliff Lott.

Mary Jane Vickers, daughter of Wiley Vickers, married John Grantham and had the following children: Betty Burkett, E. L. Grantham, C. H. Grantham. Rebecca married Williams, D. L. Grantham, Johnie Grantham; Nancy married Wolff, Minnie Grantham, Dewey Grantham; Mary married Boggan; Ethel married Bell, Glennis Grantham and Lucile married Moore.

J. J. Vickers married Miss Sumner and had three children: Bronz Vickers, Howard Vickers and Emory Vickers.

E. L. Vickers married Mary Lott and have the following children: Olden Vickers, Rebecca Vickers married Burl Summerlin and had many sons and daughters.

REPRESENTATIVES.
1. J. M. THRASH, 1927-28-29-30.
2. WILLIAM GASKIN, 1880-81.
3. ELIAS LOTT, 1911-12.
4. CALVIN A. WARD, 1905-6-7-8.
5. JOHN M. LOTT, 1873-74.
6. J. W. QUINCEY, 1919-20-21-22.

Ely married Lizzie McGovern and had many sons and daughters.

It is worthy of note that Rebecca Vickers, who married Jesse Vickers and who later married Ely Vickers was left a widow with many sons and daughters. They all went to work and she reared all her children in credit. She founded Hebron Church and was the central figure in that church as long as she lived. She sat in a homemade chair, hickory and rawhide bottom, for many, many years. When she died this old chair was placed up against the wall near the pulpit and remained there for many years.

It is also worthy of note that Rev. John (Jack) her oldest son was a prominent preacher in the Primitive Church. At last the Hebron Church was divided on some question of doctrine and Jack Vickers became the leader of one of the factions and for many, many years the members of Hebron Church were known as "Jackites."

The Lott Family

The Lott family came to Georgia from Maryland. There were three brothers, Mark, Arthur and one whose name I do not know. They settled, first in Bulloch County and then came on to Montgomery County. Arthur Lott was a prominent man in that day and went to the Legislature several times. Later on most of the family went to Pearl River, Mississippi. One of the brothers, Mark Lott, remained in Montgomery County and later died there. His widow, Delilah Lott, and several children came on to what is now Coffee County and settled exactly on the spot where the old graveyard at Lone Hill Church is now located. And strange to say that the same people who settled there about the year 1815 are buried within a few feet of where they built the first home. At the time the home was built Coffee County had not been laid out and that part of the county was Telfair County.

The first generation of the Lott family, as we know them were: Mark, Arthur and one other. Neither one of these ever lived south of the Ocmulgee River. Delilah Lott, the widow of Mark Lott and her family were the first to cross the Ocmulgee River.

The children of the second generation are the children of Mark and Delilah Lott, as follows: Daniel Lott, Joel Lott, Mark Lott, Betsie Lott, Pennie Lott, Polly Lott, Fannie Lott, and Sallie Lott.

Daniel Lott married Lucy Peterson the first time and Fannie Gaskin the last time. By his first wife, Lucy Peterson, they had the following children: Mark Lott, Elisha Lott, Joel Lott, Daniel Lott, John Lott, Arthur Lott, Betsie Lott, Hester Lott, Pink Lott, Narcissus Lott, and Martha Lott.

Following children by his second wife who was Fannie Gaskin: Jesse Lott, Elias Lott, David Lott, and J. S. Lott. Mark married Charlotte Gaskin; Elisha married Pollie Moore; Joel married Bede Vickers; Daniel married Nancy Wilcox; John married Mary Jane Wilcox; Arthur married Eliza Carver; Jesse married Mary Douglas; Elias married Tempie Douglas; David married Elizabeth Byrd; Betsie married John Paulk; Hester married Elias Moore; Pink married Benajah Pearson; Narcissus married Billie Meeks; Martha married Jack Vickers.

Betsie Lott married Old John Peterson. Their children are: Sallie Peterson married Henry Cato; Eliza

Peterson married Matthew McGovern; Delilah Peterson married Youngie Vickers; Alfred Peterson married a Cato; Betsie Peterson married Henry Paulk; Hal Peterson married Martha Gaskin first. Hal Peterson married Martha Turner second; Joel Lott married Rhoda Davis; Mark Lott married Araminta Ward; Bettie married old man John Peterson. He had been married before and had a large family by his first wife. Pennie married Stafford Davis; Pollie Lott married Jackson Newbern; her children, Daniel, Jack, Mark, Bill, and Joe. All but Dan went to Alabama long before the war, about 1855. The girls are Delilah, she married Wash Roberts; Sallie married a Roberts. Daniel married Nancy Wilcox and has the following children: Mary J. Lott married Elias Hinson; Lucy Lott married Thomas Paulk; D. W. Lott married Joe Parker's daughter, Matilda and then Alma Bowers. John Lott (Bud) married Janie Kirkland and then the widow of Thomas Wilcox, who before her marriage to Wilcox was a Dedge. He then married Mrs. Z. I. Hatfield; Nancy Lott married Frank Hinson. Following are the children of Dan Lott and his first wife Lucy Peterson:. Betsie, married John Paulk and had the following children: John Paulk, Henry Paulk, (Rooks) Jodie Paulk, Lucinda Paulk. Hester Lott married Elias Moore and had the following children: Aaron, married a Doughtery; Arthur married a Sermons, Elias married a Meeks; Dannie married a Kirkland two times; Lucy married Fat Charley Meeks; Hester married Newt Pafford, her second husband; Betsie married Matt Doughtery and then married Jesse Pafford; Frances married Jim Overstreet; Polly married Alex Meeks; Rebecca married a Shepherd.

Pink Pearson, daughter of Dan and Lucy Lott, had one child, Bettie, who married Joe Kirkland; Narcissus married Billie Meeks; children as follows: Anna Jane Kirkland; Martha married Jack Vickers, the preacher and their children, John, Dan and Eli; Dede married Elmo Main, (Sis) Avie Jane married a Whitten. Children of Lucy Lott who married Eli Vickers. Said Lucy Lott, being a daughter of Elias Lott, had the following children: Jack Vickers, H. L. Vickers, W. R. Vickers, Micajah Vickers. Mattie, who married a Tucker and then married Jim Kirkland; Willis Vickers, Eli Vickers, Dan Vickers, Herbert Vickers.

Children of Elisha Lott, who married Polly Moore: are Polly Lott married J. P. Lott; Bettie Lott married Wiley Vickers; Dan Lott, Elisha, John and Joe. Sarah Lott married Speed Paulk, Virgil Douglas married Lucy Lott. Eli Vickers married Mattie Lott. Mary Jane married Johnie Grantham; J. J. Vickers, Elisha Vickers and Eli Vickers. Elias Lott, son of Dan Lott and Fannie Gaskin married Tempie Douglas and have the following children: Mary, who married Joe Pafford; Fannie, who married E. R. Cross; Allie, who married Jim Jardine; Robert, who married Hortense Perkins; D. W. Lott, who married Nettie Deen, and James Lott, who married Ruth Barnes.

J. S. Lott, son of Dan Lott and Fannie Gaskin, married Avy Peterson by whom he had the following children: Willie Lott, Laura, who married Jim Paulk; Mattie, who married W. C. Lankford; Bessie, who married Thomas Bailey; J. S. Lott's second wife was Sallie Luke by whom he had the following children: Eunice Lott, who married Dr. Alderman; Clinton Lott, who married Mary Sanders; and Stanford. Lillian Fillingim was a child by his first wife.

Daniel Lott married Nancy Wilcox and had the following children: Mary J. Lott, who married Elias Hinson; Lucy Lott, who married Thomas Paulk; John Lott, who married Janie Kirkland and then the widow of Thomas Wilcox, who before her marriage to Wilcox was a Dedge and then married Mrs. J. I. Hatfield. Nancy Lott married Frank Hinson. J. D. Lott, Arthur Lott, Dan Lott, Jesse Lott, William Lott, Elisha Lott, Wiley Lott, Becca Lott, Lucy Lott, Narcissus Lott, Mary Lott.

John M. Lott, who married Mary Jane Wilcox, had the following children: Wash Lott, who married Mary Ann Moore; Elizabeth Lott married Johnnie Moore, then Dan Peterson, and then J. M. Denton; Lucy Lott married Simon Douglas; Rebecca Lott married Dr. M. M. Hall and then Thomas Davis; Minnie Lee Lott married Frank Sweat and then John Moore; Mary Jane Lott married R. Holton.

Arthur Lott, son of Daniel Lott and Lucy Peterson, married Eliza Carver and had the following children: Daniel Lott, Elias Lott, Elisha Lott, Dr. J. J. Lott, and Arthur Lott, Jr. Eliza Lott married C. D. Kirkland; Lucy Lott married Alonzo Paulk; Rebecca married J. M. Milhollin and Fannie married Thomas Byrd.

Jesse Lott, son of Dan Lott by Fannie Gaskin, married Mary Douglas and had Mitchell Lott, Tempie Lott, who married Perkins; Fannie who married Dr. Googe and Maggie who married E. B. Moore and Dora, who married R. R. Perkins.

The Gaskin Family

Mr. David Gaskin, Sr., moved from the northern part of Coffee County to about three miles south of Douglas about 1820; they had the following named children: John Gaskin, who married Fannie Lott; Jimmie Gaskin, Fannie Gaskin, who married Dan Lott, Sr.; Patsy Gaskin, who married Hal Peterson; Martha Gaskin, who married Mark Lott; and one who married Godden Solomen; and Charlotte Gaskin married John Harper.

Hal Peterson had the following named children: Dan Peterson, Dave Peterson and Henry Peterson. They had the following named girls: Fannie Peterson and Bettie Peterson. Fannie married Brooks Paulk and Bettie Peterson married Richard Lott. Brooks Paulk had the following children: John Paulk, Elisha Paulk and Roy Paulk. Tish Paulk married William Vickers and another girl married Elisha Corbett. John Gaskin and Fannie Lott had the following children: Delilah Gaskin, who married James Pearson; Sarah Gaskin married John Tanner; and Betty Gaskin married Harrison Kirkland and later married John Trowell. Betty Peterson and Richard Lott had one child, a girl, Sarah, who married R. G. Kirkland. Mrs. Sarah Tanner had the following children: Berry, John, Staten, Joe, Dave, Mary, Elijah, Sarah and Eliza.

The Paulk Family

The beginning of the Paulk family in Coffee County was Thomas Paulk. He was born March sixth, 1812, died 1894. His wife was Nancy Henderson. She was seven years older than her husband. She died in 1901. She was the mother of Thomas L. Paulk and

Judge Elijah Paulk. These two old brothers, Elijah Paulk and Thomas L. Paulk were brave soldiers. They followed Robert E. Lee and Stonewall Jackson from the start to the finish of the war. Judge Elijah Paulk was Ordinary of Coffee County from 1881 to 1889.

Thomas L. Paulk represented Coffee County in the Legislature in 1905. Thomas L. Paulk married Symanthia Sears and they had the following children: Mary Ellen Paulk who married A. T. Howell, Olive Paulk married James Dent, Hiram Paulk married a Miss McDonald, Dan Paulk married Fannie Lott and Ida Paulk married George McCranie. Ola Paulk married a Whiddon.

Judge Elijah Paulk was born in 1843 and married Rebecca Lott. His children: Thomas J. Paulk married Cora Ketron; Joel Paulk married Malissa Newbern; Henry Paulk died; Bessie Paulk married Leonard Tanner; Narcissus married Moses Griffin; Daniel Paulk married Minnie King; Lila Paulk married Archie Harper; Micajah Paulk married Mary Jane Harper; John Paulk married Mary McDonald; Jessie Paulk married Sula Dickerson; Aleph Paulk married Osie Harper; W. H. Paulk married Bell Roe.

The Wilcox Family

The names of the pioneer Wilcoxes that came to Coffee County are as follows:

Tom Wilcox settled on the Ocmulgee River section. He married Miss McMillan. They had the following children: Jim, John, Tom, George, Mark, Frank, Cabb, Jasper, Jack, Elizabeth, (Peggy) or Margaret and

Nancy. Only one of the girls married. Elizabeth married a Johnson and lived in Appling County.

John Wilcox married Elizabeth Simmons and they had the following children: J. M. Wilcox; Marjorie Wilcox, who married Int Cook; Winnie Wilcox, who married a Clements in Telfair County.

John Wilcox, Jr., married Fannie Lott and they had the following children: Johnie, Dan and Betty. Betty married Major Blunt, Tom Wilcox, George Wilcox married a Nash. She lives in Brunswick. Maggie married Ive Girtman. They had three children: Jack, Tiny and Aliff.

Tom Wilcox, son of Tom Wilcox, Sr., married a Frier and they had the following children: Eliza, who married Willie Byrd, Winnie who married Dan Newbern. Tom Wilcox No. 2 and his families moved to Missouri in 1851.

George Wilcox married a Hall and they had the following children: Tom Wilcox, who married a Pickern, Mary Jane Wilcox married John Lott, Nancy (Puss) married Dan Lott, Mattie married Neal Curry, Rebecca married Dr. Lott, John Wilcox married Maniza Holten, Piety Wilcox married Lewis Yonn. John Wilcox and Maniza Holten had several sons and daughters.

George Wilcox or (Bud) married a Holten and had one child.

Mark Wilcox married a Lott and had the following children: Joe Wilcox, Lewis C. Wilcox, Fannie Wilcox, who married John Denton, Ellen who married J. R. Smith, Elmira, who married Joe Ellis.

Dr. Jeff Wilcox married Mary Anne Henson.

Tom Wilcox married a Dedge.

John Wilcox, Sr., whose second wife was Fannie Lott, has the following children: Johnnie, who married Eliza Harper and had the following children: Joe Wilcox, Dan Wilcox, married a Currey and had the following children: Maud and Annie. The boy was Buddie.

J. M. Wilcox married Mary Wooten. They had the following children: Mary (Sweet), Virginia (Pet), Tiny, and "Shug," who married William Denton. Marvin Wilcox married Miss Heald.

The second wife of J. M. Wilcox was Emma Pickren. They had the following children: William, Monroe and Kate.

Tom Wilcox married Elizabeth Gaskin. They had the following children: Fannie, who married Jim Edenfield. Cora Bell, who married John Vickers. Catherine, who married Willie Fortune, and Georgia, who married Wilie Boyd.

Jack Wilcox married a Rodenberry. They had the following children: Robert Wilcox and several other boys.

Frank Wilcox, Sr., married a Simmons. They had the following children: Jack, Henry and Lewis.

DeKalb Wilcox married Elizabeth Tanner. They had the following children: Pate Wilcox, Colonel E. K. Wilcox and two girls. One married B. H. Cribb.

The Ward and Hargraves Families

About the year 1800 Priscilla Gibbs Ward Hargraves ("Mother Jones") and her six boys landed in what is now Coffee County, Georgia, and settled on the Seventeen Mile Creek. "Mother Jones" was not the real name of this pioneer woman. Her maiden name was Priscilla Gibbs, of the State of Maryland, daughter of Abram Gibbs, who was a brother to the ancestor of William G. McAdoo.

Miss Gibbs was a fine looking and well educated young woman. Eary in life she married James Ward of Roberson County, North Carolina. As the fruits of her marriage with Ward she had three sons, James Preston Ward, Joab Ward, and Abram Ward. While these boys were quite small their father, James Ward, died and in the common course of human events Mrs. Ward was married to an Englishman by the name of John Hargraves. She had three sons for Hargraves, Abram, Jack, and Tom; hence it will be seen that her real name was Priscilla Ward Hargraves, but she was always known as "Mother Jones" after she came to Georgia. She lived and died under that name.

The story in the change of her name is a romantic one. When the Revolutionary War closed and our trade relations with England were resumed Mr. Hargraves, her husband, wished to return to England, and make that his home. To this proposition his wife interposed serious objections; but as the years went on, Mr. Hargraves was making his plans to return to England.

About the year 1800 his plans had matured and he was ready to take his wife and children to Charleston, South Carolina, and take passage for England. His wife refused point blank to go. Then he insisted that she let him take his three boys with him back to England. This she refused to do.

Mr. Hargraves, being fully determined to return to England and, if possible, to take his children with him, sought legal advice how he might get possession of the children, and take them with him. So he left on a trip of several weeks to Charleston, South Carolina, to perfect his plans for returning to England.

About this time immigration had started toward South Georgia. People were coming from Virginia, North Carolina and South Carolina, down by way of Augusta, Georgia, settling Burke, Montgomery and Tattnall Counties as far south as the Ocmulgee River.

Mrs. Hargraves conceived the idea that she could take her six boys and fall in line with these settlers, for the south, and forever lose herself and her children, in the wilds of this new country in the Wiregrass.

At the time "Mother Jones" came to Georgia there were very few white people in what is now Coffee County. All this territory was owned and occupied by the Creek Indians. Only a few brave pioneers had dared to cross the Ocmulgee River and settle on the south side. There was a small settlement on the south side of the river, consisting of McRaes, Ashleys, and others; but "Mother Jones" not only crossed the Ocmulgee and came on the South side into the territory owned by the Creek Indians, but she passed on by the settlement named above, and came on thirty miles south, built a little log home on what is now lot of land 317 in the Sixth District of Coffee County, Georgia, being about five miles east of Douglas, and is now owned by Judge Levi O'Steen. When "Mother Jones" arrived she had six boys, two horses and a two-horse load of such stuff as pioneers usually took with them to make a start in a new country. "Mother Jones" and her boys went to work building a log house, set it on the dirt, and put clay floor in it. The roof was made with boards about four feet long, carefully laid on small poles for rafters and on top of the boards was laid a good size sapling pole with weight enough to hold all the boards in place. They got their water about two hundred yards west from the house, from a spring, and they obtained fire by the old flint and steel process. Cotton, or cotton rags, were singed and placed in a cow's horn,

REPRESENTATIVES.
1. WILLIE VICKERS, 1886-1887.
2. C. E. STEWART, 1913-1914-1915-1916-17-18.
3. DANIEL LOTT, 1896-1897.
4. THOMAS L. PAULK, 1902-3-4.
5. DR. D. H. MEEKS, 1923-1924.
6. J. R. SMITH, 1859-1860-1868-1869-1870.

to cut the air off, and then with flint and steel sparks of fire were knocked on the cotton, and thus fire was obtained, and thus "Mother Jones" and her six boys began life as pioneers in Wiregrass Georgia, now Coffee County.

The Meeks Family

About the year 1820 Charles C. Meeks, Hymrick Meeks and Miss Tempie Meeks moved from Emanuel County to Coffee County and settled on a farm and built a water mill about two miles north of Nicholls. Of course there was no Nicholls at that time. Before coming to Coffee County, Charles C. Meeks married Miss Lydia Ryner of Emanuel County. They had the folowing children: Willoughby Meeks, Hymrick Meeks, Merritt Meeks, Billy Meeks, Simpson Meeks and Charlie Meeks. The girls were Eliza Ann Meeks, and Mary Ann Meeks.

Hymrick Meeks married Martha Davis, a daughter of Stafford Davis, Sr. Their children were Merritt Meeks, Stafford Meeks, Martha Jane Meeks, Sarah Ann Meeks, Lydia Meeks, Hymrick Meeks, Bryant Meeks and Elijah Meeks.

Merritt Meeks married Mary Ann Morrison, a sister of Rev. Daniel Morrison and had the following children: Malcolm Meeks, John Meeks, Mary Jane Meeks, Rev. Hymrick Meeks, Mary Ann Meeks, Merritt (Bud) Meeks, Frank Meeks, and Daniel Meeks.

Billy Meeks married Narcissus Lott and had the following children: Charlie Meeks, Mary Jane Meeks, Gray Meeks, Jesse Meeks, Billie Meeks, Laura Meeks, and Sarah Meeks.

Simpson Meeks married Mary Roberts and had the following children: Charles Meeks, Sarah Meeks, Gray Meeks, Jesse Meeks, Lydia Meeks and Laura Meeks.

Charles W. Meeks, the youngest son, married Lucy Moore, a daughter of Elias Moore, who lived in the extreme western part of the county. This family consisted of three sons and six daughters. It is worthy of note that Lucy, the widow of Charles W. Meeks, is the only surviving one of the second generation living, now well past eighty and the mother of Dr. D. H. Meeks. Lydia married A. F. Thomas, Mattie married a Mr. Lee, her second marriage.

Mary A. Meeks, a daughter, was married first to Gray Roberts. Her second marriage was to T. N. Cady, who was at that time Sheriff of Coffee County. To them were born two sons and three daughters.

Eliza Ann Meeks married C. W. Dedge and lived near the old home. To them were born three sons and four daughters.

Rev. Malcolm Meeks, a son of Merritt Meeks and Mary Ann Morrison, married Elizabeth Tanner and they have the following children: Melvin Meeks, Elisha Meeks, Charlie Meeks, Albert Meeks, Malcolm Meeks, George Meeks, Gray Meeks. The daughters are Abbie Meeks, who married Phillip Newbern, Laura Meeks, who married Leonard Burkett, Mae Meeks, who married Screven Cole, and Maggie, who married Joe Starling. Elizabeth Meeks married J. R. Gardner.

John Meeks, a son of Merritt Meeks and Mary Ann Morrison, married Rebecca Douglas, a daughter of Dunk Douglas. Their children are: Willie Meeks, Elisha Meeks, Lonnie Meeks and Jesse Meeks. His daughters are Mary Jane Meeks, Maggie Meeks, Tempie Meeks and Minnie Meeks.

Merritt (Bud) Meeks married Elmira Waters and have the following children: Gilbert Meeks, Marvin Meeks, Julian Meeks, Loyd Meeks, and Cora Meeks, Effie Meeks, and Fleeta Meeks.

Rev. H. M. Meeks married Mattie Hall and they have the following children: Dan Meeks, Frank Meeks, Burton Meeks, Leon Meeks, Spurgeon Meeks, Irsa Meeks, Albert Meeks, Lucy Meeks, Ethel Meeks and Frances Meeks.

Daniel Meeks married Carrie Gaskin. They have the following children: Wesley Meeks, Earley Meeks, Lula Meeks, Dorcus Meeks and Joe Meeks.

Frank Meeks married Linnie Duren and they have the following children: Mary Ann Meeks, Aleph Meeks, Annie Meeks, Bessie Meeks, Pearl Meeks, Ruby Meeks, Malcom Meeks and Shafter Meeks.

Rev. Hymrick Meeks, son of old Hymrick Meeks, married Bettie Kirkland and had the following children: Elisha Meeks, Oliver Meeks, Mintie Meeks, Penney Meeks, Mae Meeks and Fannie Meeks.

Mary Ann Meeks, daughter of Merritt Meeks and Mary Ann Morrison, married Joshua A. Dent. They have the following children: Walter Dent, who married Elda Lewis, Neila Dent, who married M. King and Ira Dent, who married Sarah Thrasher. Lula Dent died young.

Stafford Meeks, son of Hymrick Meeks married a Miss Waters. They have the following children: Frank Meeks, Andrew J. Meeks and Archie Meeks. Lila Meeks, who married Mose Kirkland. Viola, who married Jake Foreman. Mattie married Henry Davis.

Willoughby Meeks married Lizzie Taylor. They have the following children: Willoughby (Willie) who married Eliza Taylor. Redding married Eliza Tanner. Will married Nancy Taylor. Mack never married. Burrell never married. Angel married Ben Teston. Eliza Jane married Tal Taylor. Lydia married Zeck Teston. Delphia Ann married John Lassiter.

Warren G. Meeks is a son of Merritt Meeks and Emily Tanner. His brothers and sisters are Martha Jane, who married Bill Minchew; Mattie, who married Mich Lewis; Hymrick died young in life. Warren G. Meeks married Emma Newbern.

Mary Ann Meeks married Gray Roberts and later married T. N. Cady.

Her Roberts children are as follows: Georgia Ann, who married Staff Davis. Eliza Ann, who married Sam Lee. Sarah Ann, who married Rube Taylor. John married Barbara Denton. Jesse died young. Her Cady children are as follows: Mark married Minnie Cole, Tom married Christian Vining, Lilah married a Mr. Henson, and Zona married.

Eliza Ann who married C. W. Dedge had the following children: Mary Ann married Wesley Ricketson, Ellen married Asbury Boyd, Lydia married Tom Wilcox, Lula married a Mr. Mobley, Dr. James Dedge married Martha Wells and Joe was killed early in life.

Lydia Meeks married A. F. Thomas. They have the following children: Henry M. Thomas, Nellie Thomas, Ben Thomas, Andrew Thomas, Harley Thomas, W. J. Thomas, Ella Thomas.

Charles W. Meeks, who married Lucy Moore, had following children: Tennessee married Jeff Bennett, Mattie married a Mr. Lee, Eliza Ann married Tom Lee and she died soon after. Elias married Priscilla Denton, Roan married Cassey Bennett, Elisha died before he married, Dr. Dan Meeks married Rila Bagley.

Penney Meeks married Bunk Tanner and they have the following children: Walter Tanner, George W. Tanner, Marshall Tanner, William, Mattie and Idell, married Duddley Bunn; and Dora who married A. C. Blalock and Mamie who married Dave Gillis.

Charles F. Meeks, who married Dorcas Douglas, had the following children: Jeff Meeks, Amos Meeks and Mattie, who married Eland Brooker. His second wife was Mrs. Baker. They have the following children: Emmett, Clarence, Lois, Legrand, Dorsey, Truit and Kenneth Meeks.

Bryant Meeks, son of Hymrick Meeks and Martha Davis, married a Williams and they have the following children: George, Mattie and Aleph.

Elisha A. Meeks, son of H. Meeks, who has been efficient postmaster of Nicholls for sixteen years. Through his faithfulness to duty he has attained to prominence in his line of service and now fills the office of President of The National League of Postmasters of America, which office he fills with honor and distinction.

The Kirkland Family

The Kirklands are of Scotch descent and came to Coffee County from South Carolina about the year 1810. There were three brothers, a half brother and one sister. Mose Kirkland married Peggy Carver, settled on the east side of the Seventeen Mile Creek about seven miles from Douglas. Timothy Kirkland married a Holiday and settled in the southwest part of

Coffee County. Josh Kirkland married a Fender and settled on the east side of Seventeen Mile Creek about six miles from Douglas. The sister, Zylphia, married James Preston Ward and settled on a pine ridge about eight miles east of Douglas, between Otter and Tiger Creeks. The half brother was Archie Miller.

Mose Kirkland had the following named children: Mose Kirkland, Jr., Zenus Kirkland, Joshua Kirkland, Tim Kirkland, who was killed in the Civil War. Manning Kirkland, who was killed by the deserters about the close of the war. The girls were Roxie Ann, who married Joe Davis, Elizabeth married Elijah Tanner, Sr.

Josh Kirkland had the following named children: Josh Kirkland, Jr., J. C. (Kyler) Kirkland, and David Kirkland. The girls were Mrs. Duren, Alice, who married Kyler Kirkland, Creasy who married Doc. Smith, Josh Kirkland, Jr., married Margaret Fales, and Mose Kirkland married Eliza Tanner, Zenus Kirkland married Penny Gaskin, Tim Kirkland married Rebecca Thomas, Manning Kirkland never married.

Timothy Kirkland had the following children: Mack Kirkland, who married a Bailey, William Kirkland, who married Susan Hilliard, Joe Kirkland, who married a Pearsons, Ben Kirkland.

Zylphia Kirkland married James Preston Ward and had the following named children: Jackson Ward, who married Sallie Davis, C. A. Ward, Sr., who married Zylphia Ward, W. W. Ward married Sarah Ann Spikes. The girls, Sallie, Nancy, Amanda, Arminta, Priscilla, Elizabeth, Hester, and Desdemona. Sallie married Sam Thomas and moved to Florida before the Civil War. Nancy married a Mr. Yates and moved away and was lost sight of. She probably went to Florida. Amanda married Zeke Thomas and moved to Florida. Arminta married Mark Lott. Priscilla married Sam Denton, she was the mother of Jim Denton, John Denton, and Bill Denton, and died early in life. Elizabeth married James Graham. She is the mother of Mrs. Doctor W. F. Sibbett. Hester married Hamp Tanner. Desdemona never married.

Abram Ward, the brother of James Preston Ward, moved to Florida early in life where many of his generation now live.

James Preston Ward reared a grandson, John F. Ward. He married Sarah Hilliard. They had three boys: James Franklin Ward, Warren Preston Ward and John Ward.

Timothy Kirkland had the following children: Mac Kirkland married a Bailey, William Kirkland married Susan Hilliard, Joe Kirkland, who married a Pearson, Ben Kirkland, who married an Adams, Jim Kirkland married a Solomons, Harrison Kirkland and Ive Kirkland.

Joe Kirkland, who married a Pearson, had the following children: Kyler Kirkland, Benajah Kirkland, Jeff Kirkland, Lock Kirkland, Jud Kirkland and Doll Kirkland. The girls were Janie, Laura, "Dub" Doryann, Lucy and Elmer.

Ive Kirkland married Sarah Lott and has the following children: Lizzie Kirkland, who married Wiley Byrd, Jr., and Dora Ann Kirkland, who married Russell B. Leggett. William Kirkland married Susan Hilliard and has the following children: Mattie, who married Ben Summerlin, Doctor T. J. Kirkland, who married a Sears, Pate, who married E. B. Wilden,

Estell, who married Joe Gaskins, Leila, who married Decocrat Wynn, and Ella, who married John Surmans.

The Tanner Family

Green Tanner, Elijah Tanner and Hampton Tanner. These three brothers had two sisters; Betty Tanner, who married Jesse Carter and lived in Appling County. Elizabeth Tanner married Jim Taylor and also lived in Appling County.

Elijah Tanner, the oldest brother, married Emily Mimms and they had the following children: Melvin Tanner, Sr., Fred Tanner, Monroe Tanner and three girls; Lydia Ann Tanner, who married Warren Taylor, Betty Tanner, who married DeKalb Wilcox and Eliza Tanner, who married Redding Meeks. Betty Tanner, who married DeKalb Wilcox, has the following children: Pate Wilcox, who married Tempie Ward, E. K. Wilcox, who married Minnie Reliham; Fred Tanner married Margaret Davis, and they had the following children: Melvin Tanner (Supt. County Schools), Clifton Tanner, Elmore and Leon Tanner, Mattie Tanner, who married Josh Dubose and Minnie, who married K. K. Bledsoe.

B. H. Tanner, first sheriff of Coffee County, married Eliza Taylor and they had the following children: Elijah Tanner, John Tanner, Bunk and Lydia. Lydia married Mose Kirkland, Emily married Joe Trowel. Elijah Tanner, Jr., son of Hamp Tanner (who went to the Georgia Legislature), had the following children: Warren Tanner, (Bud married a Davis, Elizabeth married Malcolm Meeks, John Tanner (Mudge) married Hester Ward and the last time he married Bessie Paulk. Tom (Booge) Tanner married Miss Wall, B. H. Tanner married Rose Sears and had the following children: E. L. Tanner, Elie Tanner, Carl Tanner, Rilze Tanner, Hiram Tanner and Julian Tanner. John Tanner, son of Hamp Tanner, married Sarah Gaskin, and they had the following children: Berry H. Tanner, John Tanner, Staten Tanner, Elijah Tanner, Dan Tanner and Mary Tanner, who married John Youngblood. Bunk Tanner, son of Hamp Tanner, married Penny Meeks and they had the following children: (Babe) J. H. Tanner, who married Mary Denton, George, Walter, Marshall and Mattie Tanner, who married Nas Young.

Green Tanner married Elminie Hall and they had these children: Emily, married Merritt Meeks, Mary married William Gill, Lucyndia married John Burkett, Delilah Tanner, married Moses Kirkland, (Cylia) Mose, Rhuban (Coot) married Susie Nettles. Syndia Tanner married Martha Taylor, sister of Rev. Green Taylor. Manning Tanner married Zelphia Ellis. Barney Tanner married Mary Ann Davis. Thad Tanner married Vicey Girtman.

The following is a list of the sons of John Tanner, Sr., with their wives.

Berry Tanner married Nine Davis. John Tanner, Jr., married a Miss Youngblood. Dave Tanner married Mattie McClelland. Joe Tanner married Ida McClelland. Dan Tanner married Renna Thompson Godbold. Elijah Tanner married Betty Davis. Staten Tanner married Jimmie Belle Smith. John Tanner had two girls: Liza Tanner married Abe Owens and they live in Texas. Sarah Tanner married Archie Meeks.

Sheriff W. M. Tanner married Melian Thomas and they have the following children: B. W. Tanner married Ursula Dent, Lucy Tanner married Tom Wilcox, J. M. Tanner married Addie Cole, D. W. Tanner married Emma Ellis, W. M. Tanner, Jr., married Martha Jane Meeks, A. F. Tanner married Lou Baker, Maggie Tanner married June Baker; Mary Jane Tanner married Jeff Lewis, Eula Tanner married S. S. Baker.

Old man Russell Tanner married a Miss Taylor and they had the following children: Vicey Tanner, who married Jesse Taylor, Nancy Tanner, who married Henry Jordon. Dacy and Jinsey Tanner never married. Chappel Tanner married a Thomas, Russell Tanner married Maria Hand, William (Sheriff Bill) Tanner married Melian Thomas.

The Burkett Family

Billie Burkett and his wife came from South Carolina and settled on the Ocmulgee River, now known as Burkett's Ferry, about 1800. They have the following children: Two sons by his first wife; Bartillery Burkett and Robert Burkett. His second wife was a Miss Dyal. They have the following children: William Burkett, Enos Burkett, Texas Burkett, Dock Burkett and one girl, Missouri, who married a Mr. Wright. William Burkett married Sarah Powers, Enos Burkett married a Ryals. His second wife was Betty Grantham and they have the following children: Carleen, Wilma, Quincey, Lura, Marine, E. H. Mozell, Coolege and Betty Dean.

Texas Burkett married a Davis; Dock Burkett married a Miss Johnson. All these Burketts lived in Coffee County on the Ocmulgee River Section.

Bartillery Burkett married Viney Taylor and they had the following children: Bartillery Burkett, who married Tom Denton, Emily Burkett married Bill Taylor and they had the following children: Rev. Sebe Taylor and Nancy Taylor and she married Boss Burkett. Mary Jane Burkett married Joe Hays and they had the following children: Lyman Hays, Angel Burkett who married Joe Ward and they have the following children: Emma Jane Ward, who married Tim Kirkland, Jack Ward who married Percy Ward, who was a Peterson; Vinney Ward married Johnie Denton, Tom Ward married a Newbern, Calvin Ward married a Miss Carter, Sarah Ward married Will Martin, Gay Ward married Bud Young. Angel Burkett also had these children: Tom R. Burkett, who married Martha Ward, Leonard Burkett, who married Laura Meeks, and Mary J. Burkett. Penny Ward is not married.

John Burkett, son of Bartillery Burkett, married Lucinda Tanner and they have the following children: Bartillery Burkett, who married Carrie Woods, Lucinda married "Jug" Douglas, Johnie Burkett married a Martin, Lige married an Ellis, Linnie married Jule Wilcox, Emmie married Mark Hall, Minnie married Lyman Hays, and Mintie Burkett married George Pridgen.

Ellen Burkett, daughter of Bartillery Burkett, married John Thomas, and they had the following children: Bartow, Wesley, Tom and Mary who were twins, Tom Thomas married a Ridgon, Dave Thomas married a Lassiter.

Bartillery (Bud) Burkett married Mary Jane Meeks and they have the following children: Eliza married Matthew Towns; Sophronia married Jack Ellis, Ida married Joe (Bud) Ellis, Noah Burkett married Clifford Fortune, Elisha Burkett is not married, Preston Burkett married Annie Gillis; Nealey married Dewey Ellis, Naomi married Robert Hale, Gray Burkett married Ruby Cashwell.

Angel married a Lewis, Jack married a Courson and they have the following children: Maggie, Mary and John. Maggie Burkett married E. A. Meeks, Mary Burkett married Charlie Moore and John Burkett is not married.

The Carver Family

About the year 1810 the Carver family came to what is now Coffee County from South Carolina. There were two old men, probably cousins. One was Samp Carver and the other was Sammie Carver. Sampie Carver was the father of Rev. Bill Carver, well known Baptist preacher who lived in Coffee County, about the close of the Civil War. Sammie Carver had a sister named Peggy, who married old man Mose Kirkland, Sr. Old man Samuel Carver was the father of Sol Carver, Braz Carver, Gabe Carver, Jim Carver, Lige Carver, Silas Carver and John Carver.

Jim Carver, Sr., was the father of Joe Carver, Allen Carver, Pink Carver, Jesse Carver and Vincent Carver. Jim Carver had the following named girls: Boyce, who married William Gaskin, Eliza Carver married Arthur Lott, one married Hiriam Davis, Hulda Carver married Tom Minix, and Sarah Carver married Eliga Purvis.

John Carver married a Metts. He had two sons, Josh Carver and Jesse Carver. He had the following girls: Patsy, Bede, who married Joe Cato, Eliza, who married Jack Levins, Millic married a McCall, Mary married a Howard.

Sammie Carver, Sr., was the father of a girl named Nancy, who was the mother of S. M. Harrell, prominent farmer of Coffee County.

The Sapp Family

Enoch Sapp came to Georgia from Virginia and married Ruth Barr. Their children were: John Sapp, Henry Sapp, Joseph Sapp, Enoch Sapp, Levi Sapp.

John Sapp married Gemima Cato. Their children were: Henry Sapp, John Sapp, Dan Sapp, Dave Sapp, Sarah Sapp, Bettie Sapp.

Henry Sapp married Delila Cato. Their children were: John Sapp, Henry Sapp, Enoch Sapp, Mary Sapp, Sarah Sapp, Fannie Sapp.

Joseph Sapp married Sallie Booth. Their children were: Mary Sapp, Nancy Sapp, E. S. Sapp, M. C. Sapp, H. W. Sapp, G. M. Sapp, Christian Sapp, Tempie Sapp.

Enoch Sapp married Martha Smith. Their children were: Elias, John, Jim, Henry, Richard, Tom and Missouri.

Levi Sapp married Sarah Solomon. Their children were: William, Fannie, Joe, Tilden and Ruth.

Priscilla Ward (Jones) and Her Ward Boys

James Preston Ward was the oldest of the Ward boys. He was about fifteen years old when he came to Georgia. About the year 1813 he was married to Miss Zylphia Kirkland. She was the only sister of Moses, Timothy, and Joshua Kirkland, and the half sister of Archie Miller. With this marriage began the relationship of the Wards and Kirklands, and their generations. To them were born three boys and eight girls. The boys were Jackson, Calvin Augustus, and Walton W. Ward. The girls were Sallie, Nancy, Amanda, Arminta, Priscilla, Elizabeth, Hester and Desdemona. Sallie married Sam Thomas and moved to Florida before the Civil War. Nancy married Mr. Yates and moved away and was lost sight of. Amanda married Zeke Thomas and moved to Florida before the Civil War. Priscilla married Sam Denton and died early in life. Arminta married Mark Lott and lived and died in Coffee County. Hester married Hamp Tanner and lived and died in Coffee County. Desdemona, the youngest girl, never married. Elizabeth married James Graham and recently died at the age of ninety-four years.

Abram Ward, the second son of "Mother Jones," was named for Abram Gibbs, father of "Mother Jones." Early in life he moved to Florida and his generation now live in Bradford, Alachua, and LaFayette Counties.

Joab Ward, the youngest son, married a Miss Carver and had several sons and one daughter. The sons were, old man Billy Ward, a doctor and a Baptist preacher, who lived and died in Coffee County. Josh Ward and Abram Ward who moved to Florida long before the Civil War. Most of the Wards and their generations continued to live in Coffee County and many of the young ones are here now.

James Preston Ward reared and educated a grandson whose name was John Franklin Ward. He married Sarah A. Hilliard and they had three boys, James Franklin Ward, Warren Preston Ward, and John C. Ward.

James Franklin Ward married Minta Kirkland, Warren Preston Ward married Annie Canova and they had the following children: George, Frank, Preston, Annie, Neele and Ward; John C. Ward married Maud Wilcox.

I have already told you that "Mother Jones" had six boys; three Wards and three Hargraves; James Preston Ward was the oldest Ward boy and Abram Hargraves was the oldest Hargraves. All these boys lived with their mother where she first settled until one by one married and made homes of their own.

About the year 1824, Abram Hargraves married Rhoda Carver, the daughter of Samson Carver; they had four boys and six girls. The boys were John, Abram, Christopher, and Sydney. The girls were Mary, Teresa, Linnie, Lucinda, Susan and Feraby. Mary married Honorable W. M. Denton; Feraby married Major John M. Spence of Ware County, and died young; Linnie married George Moody of Clinch County, and lived to be very old; Lucinda married Thomas Sweat of Ware County; Susan married Jonathan L. Morgan and lived to be eighty-two years of age; and Teresa married Capt. Cuyler W. Hilliard of Ware

County. John Hargraves married a Miss Parthenia Morgan from Echols County; early in life he moved to Florida and died there in 1876. Abram Hargraves, Jr., married first Mary McDonald, daughter of Col. William A. McDonald, and had two children, Leon and Bartow. Leon was the father of Col. Leon Hargraves of Pearson, Ga. Bartow lives near Waresboro. He married Laura Williamson in England while on a business trip over there. Sydney married Miss Mary Lott. Christopher married Ellen Roberts.

Tom Hargraves married a Miss Beverly and lived near Millwood, in Ware County, Georgia. He reared a large family of boys and girls. Many of his descendents live in that county now.

The other two Hargraves boys, Jack and Tom, were twins. Jack never married. He settled in Ware County, near where Bickley is now located. He built the old mill-dam now owned by Hon. William Denton. He had a good farm there, owned slaves and operated a farm in connection with his water mill. He lived to be an old man and died at his home in Ware County.

Priscilla Ward-Hargraves died about 1846, and was buried on the hill where she and her boys landed more than forty years before. Her grave is not marked. The year 1914, Prof. Gibbs, of Tennessee, a relative of "Mother Jones," was here and sought to find the location of her grave. He had a family tree showing the relation between "Mother Jones," himself and W. G. McAdoo, on the Gibbs' side of the family.

The grave of "Mother Jones" is about one hundred yards southeast of the head of the Spring Branch near where the saw mill of William Dent was located in 1869.

Abram Hargraves

"Mother Jones" was right, when she decided that her husband, John Hargraves, who had deserted her while living in North Carolina, went back to England; by the time she and her six boys reached the Wiregrass Country, in Georgia, John Hargraves had landed at his old home in England, and was rapidly adding to his fortune already accumulated. In the course of time, "Mother Jones' " six boys married and made homes for themselves.

I have already told you that Abram Hargraves married Rhody Carver, and that they had ten children; four boys and six girls. Soon after Abram was married, he settled on a farm on the west side of the Seventeen-Mile Creek, about eighteen miles southeast of Douglas, Ga. Mr. Hargraves was a thrifty farmer, had plenty of land, and plenty of stock, and he also owned some slaves and in a short time he had accumulated considerable property. In fact, he was considered a wealthy man. Soon after he married, an inquiry came from the Bank of Savannah, Georgia, from the banks of England for information about Abram Hargraves; through them he learned that his father was dead and had left a large estate and that an annuity of several thousand dollars, in gold, was due him at once, and every year the same amount would be paid him through the banks of Savannah, Georgia; and so about once a year, Mr. Hargraves and some of his neighbors went to Savannah by private conveyance to sell their produce, lay in supplies for their farm, and at the same time Mr. Hargraves collected his interest. It required about a week's time to go to Savannah and return, with horse and cart. Sometimes they had trouble with water courses, which they had to cross.

A good many stories are told about Mr. Hargraves and his trips to Savannah. He had grown up among the Creek Indians in the Wiregrass Country and had many of their habits of life. He wore a homespun shirt, carried a shot bag over his shoulders, a powder horn around his waist, and did not, in any way, have the appearance of being a well-to-do farmer. It is said that on one of his trips to Savannah, Mr. Hargraves went to the stables to buy a horse; when he priced the horse the stock man looked at him and said, "I will sell you this horse for $100.00, with good security, or $50.00 cash." The man looked at Mr. Hargraves as he emphasized the word "Cash." Mr. Hargraves returned the hard look, as he said, "Cash it shall be," and ran his hand into his shot bag and pulled out fifty shining dollars in gold. There was plenty more where that came from.

Mr. Hargraves was a very industrious man, worked himself and made a good plow hand in the field, as long as he lived.

Another amusing story is told about Mr. Hargraves, it is as follows: It is said that Mr. Ivey Kirkland, at this time a prosperous merchant of Douglas, Georgia, went to see the daughter of Mr. Hargraves. Mr. Kirkland was diked up in Sunday style. Mr. Hargraves asked the young man if he would not like to go with him to the woods and see his fine hogs. Mr. Kirkland did not know how to refuse and so he went. Mr. Hargraves took him through the woods, through the branches, through the muddy bays, and at last back to the Hargraves' home where he was gladly welcomed by the young lady whom he was courting. Mr. Kirkland was a sight to behold. His shoes were muddy, and his pants torn. He looked more like a man who had spent a week in the woods, than like a young merchant from Douglas out courting a country girl.

The war came on and he and his sons-in-law did their duty in that trying time. When the war was over, a call came to Mr. Hargraves from the banks of England that $70,000.00 in gold had been placed to his credit in the bank and that it was up to him to go or send to England for the money.

A List of Some Old People of Coffee County Married More Than Fifty Years Ago

Jake Anderson and L. Bowen married June 2nd, 1874. William Adams and Susan Harrell married July 20th, 1879. Texas Burkett and Ann Davis married May 6th, 1873. Charles C. Burrows and Anna Solomon married May 19th, 1871. Joe Bailey and Mary Pearson married April 12th, 1871. Tharp Bailey and Mary A. Ricketson married June 4th, 1874. Wiley Byrd and S. S. Creech married February 23, 1873. Joel W. Brooker and R. M. Wall married May 21st, 1876. John W. Burch and Mary Harrell married April 21st, 1877. Wiley Byrd and Elizabeth Kirkland married January 11th, 1878. B. T. Bagley and L. C. Davis married April 15th, 1877. John W. Booker and Nancy E. Parrish married September 26th, 1878.

Abner W. Curry and Mattie Wilcox married March 18th, 1873. James Carver and Rhoda Tucker married August 26th, 1873. William Chaney and Mary Moon married November 21st, 1873. Silas Carver and Nancy Joiner married November 8th, 1873. David Cannon and S. Suggs married March 10th, 1874. Joshua Carter and Martha Davis married January 9th, 1876. Jabriel Carver and Mary Joiner married July 23rd, 1876. B. Cothern and Melvinia Vining married March 28th, 1878. George Chaney and Lucendia Ward married May 18th, 1878. Jesse Carver and Hariot Mixon married August 23rd, 1878. W. B. Courson and Mattie Ward married January 10th, 1880. L. Cowart and Nancy Gaskin married November 20th, 1879.

Q. Douglas and Lucinda Lott married March 17th, 1873. Mose Davis and Mary J. Meeks married December 11th, 1871. D. Davis and L. Wooten married August 14th, 1875. S. Davis and E. Hursey married April 29th, 1875. R. H. Dent and Eliza A. E. J. Trowell married January 26th, 1878. J. B. Day and Fannie Fussell married January 17th, 1879. Thomas Davis and Eliza Tanner married March 17th, 1879. Richard Davis and E. Gaskin married July 20th, 1879. James Day and Mary Lankford married March 29th, 1879.

Jesse Edinfield and Rena Spence married December 1st, 1873.

William T. Fussell and Elizabeth Roberts married November 26th, 1873. John Fussell and Ann J. Kirkland married April 25th, 1874. J. W. Flanders and Sarah Burch married August 21st, 1874.

C. O. Harper and Lucinda Lott married February 10th, 1871. Henry Harper and Sarah Vickers married March 17th, 1873. William S. Hand and Susan Simmons married February 7th, 1874. H. S. Harper and Mary Vickers married January 10th, 1874. J. Q. Hammond and A. P. Pickern married December 29th, 1875. Dr. M. M. Hall and Rebecca B. Lott married January 10th, 1875. J. F. Henson and Nancy Lott married May 29th, 1876. John Hargraves and Nancy Hulett married April 28th, 1877. Lovett Harrell and Mary Murry married February 26th, 1878. H. L. Hutson and Mollie Merritt married January 20th, 1879.

William Jowers and Delilah Paulk married December 21st, 1872. Joe Jowers and Thaney Ruis married February 26th, 1874. David Jordon and Mary Sears married October 13th, 1874. E. Jowers and Dicey M.

Ricketson married January 3rd, 1876. Elijah Jowers and Sarah Sapp married May 5th, 1877. Allen Joiner and Susan Adams married July 31st, 1878.

Mose J. Kirkland and Marjorie Wilcox married April 26th, 1878, Jeff Kirkland and Mamie Greer married April 24th, 1879.

Henry Love and Artie Took married May 8th, 1876. Thomas M. Lee and Eliza A. Meeks married January 7th, 1877. J. S. Lott and Avie Peterson married April 4th, 1877. John M. Lott and Eliza J. Kirkland married December 20th, 1878. Mark Lott and Amanda Ward married August 10th, 1877. David Lott and Elizabeth Byrd married November 5th, 1878. R. E. Lankford and Ellen Hutto married October 22nd, 1878. W. H. Love and Abbie J. Kirkland married December 2nd, 1878. Elisha Lott and R. Vickers married January 10th, 1880.

Hiram Mancil, Jr., and Mary Arnold married April 18th, 1874. John Metts and Rhoda Boyd married November 28th, 1874. M. Metts and Ellen Bowen married January 26th, 1875. Eugene Merier, Sr., and S. A. Wilkinson married July 22nd, 1875. A. S. Minchew and Mary E. Denton married November 6th, 1875. Benajah Mills and E. Pearson married October 4th, 1872. Rev. Malcom Meeks and Elizabeth Tanner married April 6th, 1874. John J. Meeks and Rebecca Douglas married March 4th, 1877. Elias Metts and Nancy Bratcher married January 7th, 1878. John Minchew and Rhoda Ricketson married April 27th, 1879. C. F. Meeks and Dorcas Douglas married April 20th, 1879.

E. H. McClelland and E. Anderson married December 4th, 1874. W. S. McKinnon and Abbiegal Taff married June 24th, 1878. B. E. McLendon and Josephine Sears married November 2nd, 1880.

George W. Nelms and Nancy Smith married September 10th, 1874. J. Newbern and Mary A. Woods married March 9th, 1875. L. Newbern and Elizabeth Douglas married September 5th, 1877. A. Nolan and Elizabeth Overstreet married July 16th, 1877.

J. M. Odum and Nancy Hinson married March 23rd, 1877. James O'Mally and Ida Taylor married April 8th, 1879.

S. D. Phillips and Samanthia Wilcox married April 8th, 1874. C. S. Parker and Elizabeth Summerlin married November 18th, 1874. David Peterson and E. Byrd married December 18th, 1874. Paul Pallicer and R. Youngblood married December 6th, 1875. John Pridgen and Elizabeth Wooten married November 29th, 1875. L. Passmore and Jane Smith married May 15th, 1875. Elisha Purvis and Sarah Carver married July 17th, 1875. Lucius Paulk and Elizabeth Vickers married December 31st, 1877. John R. Paulk and L. Purvis married March 6th, 1880.

John Royals and Elizabeth Roberts married January 17th, 1873. James S. Royals and Levicey Bailey married January 23rd, 1874. John W. Robert and Dora A. Royals married December 25th, 1873. S. Ricketson and Mary Smith married September 21st, 1875. Sam Register and Emiline Hutto married October 16th, 1876. William Roe and Sarah Ann Sears married August 24th, 1878. Gray Roberts and Sarah J. Wilcox married December 19th, 1879. John Roberts and Barbara Denton married December 25th, 1879.

John Solomons and S. Ann Royals married December 25th, 1872. Elisha Summerlin and Delilah

Solomon married January 1st, 1872. Henry Solomon and Sarah A. Hutto married May 30th, 1871. M. Summerlin and Elizabeth Hill married December 9th, 1873. R. S. Smith and Symeria Gaskin married December 27th, 1873. Levy Sapp and Sarah Solomon married February 9th, 1874. Mathey Spivey and Adline Bennett married April 25th, 1874. R. R. Stevens and H. E. Ricketson married July 22nd, 1875. John Spivey and E. McLendon married February 2nd, 1876. William Summerlin and Amanda Sears married November 17th, 1875. J. T. Spivey and Lydia Remis married August 18th, 1874. George Sears and Julia O'Neal married May 14th, 1878. George Sears and Elizabeth White married March 12th, 1879.

D. G. Thomas and Mary Taylor married March 1st, 1873. John L. Tyson and Martha Ricketson married July 8th, 1864. John T. Tucker and Nancy Pickern married July 9th, 1874. Richard Tucker and Roxie Wooten married November 21st, 1874. Jacob Tucker and Easter Pickern married July 9th, 1874. B. W. Tanner and Mary A. Davis married December 20th, 1874. J. W. Tanner and Hester Ward married May 18th, 1878. G. W. Tanner and Eliza A. Taylor married April 13th, 1879. John A. Taylor and Martha Thomas married July 24th, 1879. Berry H. Tanner and Pennolope Davis married December 11th, 1879.

J. J. Varnedore and Elizabeth Davis married November 21st, 1873. Banny Vining and Martha Crosby married April 16th, 1874. Dennis Vickers and Mary Carver married November 6th, 1876.

W. J. Wright and Missouri Burkett married May 6th, 1873. D. S. Walls and Rebecca Brooker married August 16th, 1873. Bryant Wood and Elizabeth Anderson married May 7th, 1873. J. H. Wall and D. E. Brooker married June 18th, 1874. Rowan Wood and Mary A. Hutto married December 29th, 1874. G. W. Wood and Nellie Anderson married December 16th, 1874. M. Wood and E. Ricketson married October 18th, 1875. J. W. Windfield and Mary A. Wright married January 30th, 1873. D. S. Wall and Annie Brooker married March 6th, 1873. John A. Waters and Elizabeth Meeks married February 27th, 1877. James L. Walker and Dollie V. Watson married December 20th, 1879.

Pioneers of Coffee County
South of the Ocmulgee—Going to Market—Building Roads—Names of Streams

When the pioneers settled in the Wiregrass Country, in the year eighteen hundred, there were no counties laid out in this part of the state; no lots of lands had been surveyed and there were no roads.

All south of the Ocmulgee River, reaching nearly to the coast on the east, to the Florida line on the south, and on to the Chattahoochee River on the west, was one great stretch of pine woods and wiregrass, with here and there a lone pioneer. There were no roads through the country and no bridges over the streams.

When an immigrant, coming south, crossed the Ocmulgee River, he investigated the country until he found a place that suited him and built his little home, without reference as to who owned the land. In the course of time, trails and settlement roads were made from one place to another; there was a road out from Burkett's Ferry, on the Ocmulgee River, leading south.

Settlements were far apart at this early time in the history of Wiregrass Georgia; there were no towns and no places to trade, except Savannah, St. Marys, Centerville, and perhaps a few little stores situated up and down the Ocmulgee River.

Captain Thomas Wilcox, and Captain Aaron Brantley ran as the captains on the river boats and supplied some of the people in this section of Georgia with their merchandise and trade supplies.

When it became necessary to go to market, a group would get together, with perhaps a half dozen horse carts, and make the trip. It required a week or more to go to Savannah and return. It was also necessary to make this trip when the weather was dry, in order that the streams of water would be low and passable. A little later on in the history of this county, they had what was called flats, and on them they loaded their horses and carts, and with a long pole pushed them across the streams. The pioneers often blazed the trees, selecting the best routes from one place to another, and always selecting shallow places in the creeks as fords where they might cross when the water was not too high. There were so few people in this part of Georgia, and so little travel, that very little attention was paid to roads.

About 1812 to 1815, the Blackshear Road was built, extending from Jacksonville, in Telfair County, to Camp Pinkney, on the St. Mary's River, where old Centerville was afterwards located. The road was opened by the State troops, commanded by General David Blackshear. The road passed over the grounds where Douglas and Broxton now stand. Thomas Wilcox, grandfather of Dr. Jeff Wilcox, of Willacoochee, Georgia, was a soldier and helped to build this road. The road was built during our second war with England, for military purposes.

General Blackshear named many of the streams of Coffee County. The county had not been surveyed or named. Only the wild woods and the Creek Indians, with ever now and then a lone settler, were here. Some of the creeks named by him are the Five-Mile Creek, the Nine-Mile Creek, the Seventeen-Mile Creek, and the Twenty-Mile Creek. The Creek Indians named most of the large streams and their names remain with us to this day.

Indian Names

Ye say that they have passed away,
  That noble race and brave;
That their light canoes have vanished
  From off the crested wave;
That, 'mid the forests where they roamed,
  There rings no hunter's shout;
But their name is on your waters,
  Ye may not wash it out.

HON. W. G. BRANTLEY   ALLEN M. SPENCE

SOLICITORS SUPERIOR COURT

HONORABLE W. G. BRANTLEY, Solicitor-General of the Brunswick Circuit for many years, and afterwards went to Congress.
ALLEN M. SPENCE, now serving as Solicitor-General of the Superior Courts of Waycross Circuit.

Erwin Spivey

Erwin Spivey
"Gordon's Bull"

Erwin Spivey, known by the Armies North and South as "Gordon's Bull," was in Company E. 26th, Georgia. Mr. Spivey had a tremendous voice, loud, wild and weird. He could squeal and yell and bellow like a bull and be heard for miles around. He trained his voice in such a way as to give it "Carrying Power." He was the talk of both Armies. He belonged to Gordon's Brigade, which was a terror to the Northern Army. The Yankee Army could recognize the strange voice of Erwin Spivey and they knew that Gordon was after them. When the Yankees would hear him it is said that the soldiers would look at each other and say, "Boys, there is trouble ahead. Gordon's Brigade is on the move and Gordon's Bull is giving the alarm." It is said that many of the weak-kneed Yankees would break ranks and run for their lives when they heard the yell of "Gordon's Bull."

Captain Jefferson Wilcox

CAPTAIN JEFF WILCOX

He was born March 20th, 1860. His father was Mark Wilcox and his mother was a Lott.

He attended the Southern Medical College in Atlanta, Georgia, and graduated with second honor in a class of 37 young men in the class of 1883. He was the first native of Coffee County to receive a degree of Doctor of Medicine. August 16, 1883, he married Miss Marian Hinson, daughter of James Hinson of Coffee County, Georgia. There were three children born to that marriage, Ira E. Wilcox, who is a prominent business man of Birmingham, Alabama, and J. Mark Wilcox, who is a prominent attorney of West Palm Beach, Florida.

On December 1st, 1888, he located in Willacoochee, Georgia, his present location and where he has remained ever since. He was elected Mayor of Willacoochee in 1891. He was elected Representative of Coffee County to the Legislature in 1892. In 1896 he was elected to represent the 5th Senatorial District in the State Senate.

At the outbreak of the war with Spain he recruited a company of volunteers at his own personal expense.

He tendered their service to the Government and President McKinley commissioned him Captain and placed him in the 3rd regiment U. S. Vol. Infantry, where he served through the Santiago Campaign and was honorably discharged from service January 10th, 1899.

October 22nd, 1923, his companion who had stood by him all of these years was taken to her eternal home. He married Mrs. Annie Belle Parker Adams of Orlando, Fla., eldest daughter of the sainted William Parker.

The great American Republic and the Cuban Republic decorated him last year for services rendered in the Spanish-American War.

Dunk Douglas

(Communicated)

Dunk Douglas

Editor Breeze—I have just learned of the death of my fatherly old friend, Dunk Douglas. When mother was left a widow and her three little boys needed a father's help, we found a never failing friend in Mr. Douglas. He made the first pair of shoes I ever wore. He helped in a large measure to build the school and church where I first attended school and church. He built the church house at Lone Hill where I joined the church. The first public confession I made of Christ, he was the first to bid me God-speed. He taught me how to work. Impressed my young mind with the dignity of labor. He idolized the honest man, and laziness with him was a crime.

Dunk Douglas was no ordinary man. He had a good strong logical mind and a good memory. He was a good story teller and a good conversationalist. He never lost the thread of his story and knew just when to laugh. He could tell stories all day and then tell a good one after he lay down at night.

Dunk Douglas was a good farmer and a fair mechanic. He made what he needed for his own farm and made plows and plow stocks for the neighbors. In a word, he was "The professor of odd jobs," for the whole country, and for many years after the war our neighbors would have missed his services very much.

Dunk Douglas was one of the most hospitable men I ever knew. I think there was a time when he fed more men and horses free than the ordinary hotels of the country fed for pay. In any matter of business he was close and exacting. He paid his debts and expected the other people to do the same; but he tried to help every one in need of help. All the public workings, such as fodder pullings, log rollings, etc., he always got there soon and put in a good day's work, and was especially helpful in seeing that others did a good day's work, too.

Dunk Douglas was a good man with a strong personality. He was a good husband and a good father and a good neighbor indeed. I have known him, on many occasions, to stop his own work and help a neighbor. He was kind and forbearing and slow to resist an insult or an injury. He had unbounded faith in God, but he lacked confidence in men. He did not believe in any secret societies and often denounced clans, and combines of every kind.

In religion Dunk Douglas was an enigma. No one could fully understand him at this point. On three different occasions I was very much concerned about his religious life, and at each time I tried to help him all I could. He joined the church late in life but that does not show that he was not a child of God. He had a spiritual mind and loved the word of God.

His life was an exponent of the "pure and undefiled religion," and when Dunk Douglas stands before the judgment seat of Christ I am strongly of the opinion that he will hear the welcome plaudit, "Come ye blessed of my father and inherit the kingdom prepared for you, from the foundation of the world, for I was hungry and ye gave me meat, I was thirsty and ye gave me drink, I was a stranger and ye took me in, naked and ye clothed me, I was sick and ye visited me."

I do not write this as an obituary, but I have only given expression to a few thoughts of the man as I have seen him all my life. And now that he is gone, I desire with his family and friends to drop a tear and a flower upon his grave, trusting that our faith in Him who is the resurrection and the life will some sweet day bring us all together again.

Ward's Scrapbook, 1896.

Doctors and Medicine

In the early days we had a few doctors. People would wait till the sick were half dead before they sent for a doctor, perhaps thirty miles away. The sick used all sorts of remedies. Oil and turpentine were the favorites. Red oak bark was used as an astringent. Elderberry used

DR. STAFFORD DAVIS
a celebrated cancer doctor who lived to be 106 years old

both as an astringent and a purgative. When you wanted an astringent, scrape the bark up, and for a purgative scrape it down. "For cuts and to stop bleeding use cobweb." That is the spider webs hanging about the walls covered with smut. Sweet gum and mullein were used for fevers. Pepper tea for colds. For sprains and bruises use clay and vinegar. For bee stings use tobacco. For snake bites use whiskey and a poultice made of salt, tobacco and onions.

Parched corn will make coffee and so will parched sweet potatoes. Collard leaves were used for headaches—warm and bind to the head. Bleeding for pneumonia was used in first stages. For burns use eggs and flour mixed. Many people thought fire could be talked out. Warts, cancers, moles, etc., were conjured away, so they said. When choked, beat the patient in the back hard. Ginger tea was used as an astringent in case of stomach trouble. Tina, Sage and Rosemary teas was a remedy that never fails for colic, caused by eating too much. For bilious colic take a tablespoon full of salts, in five minutes take same dose and wait five minutes and if no relief then take another dose and in five minutes you will be relieved. It never fails. To use hot water will give more immediate results.

Stafford Davis was a celebrated old cancer doctor. People came to see him from all parts of the country. They thought he did them good. They also wrote him and he gave them a sort of "absent treatment." He was known far and near. He lived to be 106 years of age. Before he died it was said that he had transferred his "Gift" to Joe Ward, his grandson.

Old Billy Ward was a Homespun doctor and made his medicine from the woods. He knew enough about the vegetables to get results as astringent, purgatives, etc.

Every locality had its good man or its good woman, who could be sent for in time of sickness, and could be relied upon to go. Also every community had its coffin maker who worked free. Call in neighbors to help him. Many old men selected their coffin planks and laid them in the lofts to dry.

Old Man Billy Ward

In going from Baxley to Douglas you cross the Seventeen-Mile Creek at the bridge at Reed Lake. Just on the other side to the left, is a little log house. There is where Uncle Billy lives. He is now nearly seventy years old and lives all alone by the side of this big old creek where the "Hoot" of

BILLY WARD
Pioneer Doctor and Baptist Minister Before the War.

the owl and the "Chip Willow" of the whippoor-will greets his ear, but these wild, weird surroundings, no doubt, are congenial to his strange nature. He has raised a large family of children, but none are now with him. He will not live with them but prefers his little hut alone where he can brood over his past life and have all the world to himself.

In his better days he was doing well, had plenty and was a kind neighbor. He was a blacksmith, preacher, and a doctor, and a useful man in our beat. By some means or other he did not go to war and was one of the few men left in our community during that dreadful period. He used to come to our house to kill beef. Our cows were not used to seeing men folks in those days and they hated them more than dogs. But Uncle

Billy knew how to fool them. He put on a sun bonnet and an apron, and then he could keep them still long enough to shoot one.

He had plenty of cows himself but seldom had beef. He said if he knew which cow he would lose in the winter he would kill her in the summer and thus economize. He was not a stingy man, but seemingly curious, and so he is yet. He hardly ever sent corn to mill like other folks, but did his own grinding on a steel mill. I have often seen them gather corn from the field and grind it for dinner.

I never saw a table cloth on the table but once, and then Monroe Wilcox was there. They had a big turtle for dinner. I was a small boy but they let me eat at the first table and I enjoyed the cooter hugely.

Uncle Billy was a kind old man to the sick and was often called to the bedside of the suffering. He believed in moving pains by hard rubbing. By some accident or other one of his hands had been burned, his little finger was stiff, just half closed. It was badly in the way about rubbing, because it scratched more than it rubbed.

Uncle Billy had no use for shirt buttons on his shirt for he never buttoned one; still he had a fancy for ladies, and would do and say many funny things while in their presence. His wife, he called "Old Doman," poor old thing! I never saw her laugh, but she always wore a broad smile when Uncle Billy was about. She always looked like she was ashamed in his presence.

I have never heard him preach, but those who have heard him say there was a lot of fun in it. He could draw some amusing pictures and make very striking illustrations. Here is a sample: "If all the water was in one place and all the trees in one tree, all the men in one man and all the axes in one axe—Then if the big tree stood by that big water and if that big man should take that big axe and cut down that big tree in that big lake of water, whoopee! wouldn't it make a splash."

He never had family prayer, and never asked a blessing at his table, and has now given up preaching altogether. He never doctors anything now unless it is his cat or his pig. All of his property is gone, his wife is dead and his children all grown. Poor old man. I am sorry for him, but he doesn't want any sympathy, mine nor yours, and he doesn't think any more of me for writing this article either. But his life is a curious one and provides much food for thought. When you pass his home you will more fully realize what I have told you.

Ward's Scrapbook, 1885.

Tribute to Monroe Wilcox

I see by the last issue of your paper that another good man is gone. Monroe Wilcox is dead.

> "Friend after friend departs—
> Who has not lost a friend?
> There is no union here of hearts
> But that we find an end."

He was my friend and your friend and everybody's friend. Coffee County never had a more useful citizen than he, as doctor and preacher, singing master and school teacher and Christian neighbor. His field for usefulness was wide.

He was a self-made man in the true sense of the word. He educated himself. He read many good books and had a practical knowledge of the sciences, history, theology and medicine.

His influence for the good was widespread and lasting. At one time every office in Coffee County was filled by men who had been to school to him. As a local Methodist preacher he was indeed a model. Like a weeping prophet, he went from place to place, preaching, praying and singing. He seldom led a prayer meeting or addressed a class of Sunday school children that he did not weep over them as he warned them of the awful consequences of a sinful life. The next moment, with happy face and streaming eye, he would sing some glad, sweet song. I can see him now as he appeared to me in 1875, hymn book in hand, and hear his sad sweet voice as he tenderly reads, "How sweet the name of Jesus sounds in a believer's ear."

His first sermon was preached at old Lone Hill Church, in 1872, from the text, "Remember thy Creator in the days of thy youth." Under that sermon and on that day this writer joined the church. His song and his sermon and his very presence was always a help to me in my Christian life. I think I knew him as well as any one, for it was my privilege to live in his home and attend school. Twice a day he read the Bible and had prayer with his family. Often he was called to see the sick and visit the dying. His presence brought hope and comfort.

But he is gone. How much we shall all miss him! There was but one Monroe Wilcox. Is there any one anywhere who can take his place? Let us who knew the man profit by his life. May the memory of his words, his sweet songs and his weeping face inspire us all to be faithful until one by one we cross over the river to be forever for the Lord.

W. P. WARD.

From Ward's Scrapbook, 1897.

Indians Rob Dr. Parker's Home

DR. CALVIN GORDON BERRY WASHINGTON PARKER
Pioneer Doctor, Indian Fighter and Leading Citizen.

About the year 1836 William Parker, (Short-Arm Bill) as he was called, and the father of C. G. W. Parker, and later a well-known doctor, was living in Berrien County on the old Patterson place. One winter day when Mr. Parker was away from home, several Indians appeared at the foot of the hill, at a spring, where the family got water. It is said that the Indians began to beat on logs, thereby attracting the attention of the people. It appears the Indians meant to rob and not to murder, but as there were no men at home the women ran through the field, a back way, a distance of five miles to the home of Dread Newborn. The Indians robbed the house, broke open a trunk and got $300 in cash, cut the feather beds open, emptied the feathers out and took the ticks with them. A company of men soon collected together, under the command of George Peterson, Dread Newborn, William Parker, and others. The Indians were overtaken at the Allapaha River and three were killed, others made their escape but were followed and overtaken at the St. Illa River, at what is now known as Indian Lake, about two miles northeast of the town of Axson, Ga. They were all shot and killed, except one squaw; it was reported that she was captured and shot. Dread Newborn, the son of Dread Newborn, who followed the Indians, informs me that the Indian woman was kept in prison for a while and then by direction of the government was returned to her own people. About this time a whole family by the name of Wilds was killed by the Indians, near Waresboro, Ga. One little boy, Reuben Wilds, made his escape. Of course there are a great many Indian stories, but the narratives I have given you are facts testified to by living witnesses and most worthy tradition, for the first time they are put into history.

Old Churches in Coffee County

Old Hebron Church

Founded By That Great and Good Man, Elder John Vickers—Mother Vickers' Chair—The Present Ministers of the Church—Other Matters of History

High up on the hill, near the Satilla River, on the public road, midway between Douglas and Willacoochee, stands old Hebron Church, one of the old landmarks of Coffee County. Like Jerusalem of old, she is beautiful for situation. This church was built about 1870 by the friends and followers of Rev. John Vickers, a great and good man now gone to his reward.

The church building is one of the largest and neatest in the county and reflects great credit upon the membership of the church and others who aided in the construction. The building is nicely painted on the outside and has good, comfortable seats.

One of the first things that attracts the attention of a stranger on entering the church is an old-fashioned leather-bottomed chair hanging upon the wall of the building. This chair has a history. It is the chair of old "Mother Vickers" of sainted memory, mother of Rev. John Vickers, the founder of that church. This is the same chair that she occupied in church for several years. When Mother Vickers left this land of troubles and heartaches and went to be with her Lord whom she loved and served so long, she exchanged this old country chair for a seat in glory among the angels, and this old chair was left vacant, and now hangs upon the wall, a constant reminder to children and friends that she has gone up higher. As this editor sat and looked at the old chair, he thought what a sermon it preaches to all who enter there. The mother fought a good fight, kept the faith and is now gone to her reward; but this empty chair is calling, calling, calling children and friends, sinners and all. If it were my mother's chair, I would long to live the life she lived, and walk in the way she walked and would never cease to pray till her God was my God and I had the witness in my heart that we would all meet again.

>Oh, that chair, our mother's chair
>Preaching sermons on the wall;
>Listen to mother, who left it there,
>Oh, heed her call, heed her call.

The graveyard at Hebron is one of the best kept in Coffee County. Many good fathers and mothers of Israel are buried there. Among them we noticed the names of Lott, Vickers, Purvis, Paulk, Lindsey and others. Many nice and costly tombstones mark the last resting place of these beloved dead. The one at the grave of Rev. John Vickers, who died in June, 1900, is especially beautiful.

The history of Hebron Church is a most interesting one. Rev. John Vickers, during his lifetime, was the central figure of that branch of the Primitive Baptist Church. When he first grew to manhood, he joined the Primitive Church and was, by them, licensed to preach; but a division among the members, on points of doctrine, very soon culminated in a split in the church. Rev. Vickers contended that salvation was conditional, while the old line hardshells claimed that salvation was by election and unconditional. Rev. Vickers wrote a tract giving his views of the plan of salvation in which he called the old line Baptists "fatalists" and contended that he and his followers held the true Primitive Baptist doctrines. In his faith he lived and died. The church, as a denomination, has not grown very fast, but has been blessed of God in doing great good. They have had much to contend with to maintain their doctrine and practice, and deserve great credit for what they have done and are doing. They should be encouraged to press on in their good work. There are many good men and women in that neighborhood of Hebron who are not members of any church, but who ought to be, and they will never be satisfied in any other church and therefore, ought to joint that church and help push the work of the Lord in that locality. Yes, mother has left a vacant seat. Who will be the first one to go in and sit down?

Ward's Scrapbook, 1905.

Arnie Church

Many of the pioneer citizens of Coffee County were believers in Primitive Baptist doctrine. They had churches in many places in South Georgia and some in Coffee County. One of the oldest churches in Coffee County is Arnie Church. It is situated about ten miles southwest of Douglas. This church was organized about 1886 by Elder Mobley and others. Elder King was one of the first pastors of that church. Among some of the members of that old church were the Morris', O'Steens', Douglas', McKinnons', Vickers' and others. This church has been a landmark among the

Primitive Baptists of Coffee County. It is situated among a class of good farmers. They also have a good school near the church and are a progressive people. The Primitive Baptist, as a people, are conservative in all matters. They are not quick "To go after strange fire to burn on their Altars." They have always stood like a stone wall between the church and all worldly institutions. They believe in a strict separation of church and state, or we might say the church and the world. There are no better citizens in Coffee County than the Primitive Baptists and their sons and daughters. They are strict to meet all their obligations, financial and otherwise, and are truly loyal to the Primitive Baptist Church.

Some of the pastors were Elders Parrish, Tomberlin, Stallings, O'Steen, Elder Weatherington and others.

Mormon Church

The Church of Jesus Christ of Latter-day Saints, or the Mormon Church, sent missionaries from the West to Coffee County in 1898.

Among the first Elders to appear were Nephi Henson and Elder Brewer. Many citizens of the county were excited over the appearance of the Elders. Some regarded them as messengers from Heaven, gave them shelter and lodging, remembering that Scripture says, "Be not forgetful to entertain strangers: for thereby some have entertained angels unawares." Others regarded them as emissaries of the devil, wrecking homes and carrying away women.

The first converts to the Mormon religion were Calvin W. Williams, Dan P. Lott, Joseph J. Adams and families. Elder Ben E. Rich was one of the first presidents of the Southern States Mission. He helped to establish the church in Coffee County. He was succeeded as president of the Mission by Elder Charles A. Callis.

Coffee County has been a fruitful field for the Mormon Church, it having grown to a membership of more than seven hundred. There are two churches in the territory—Cumorrah Church in Coffee County, and the Utah Church in Atkinson County, formerly Coffee. Traveling Elders have been preaching regularly in both of these churches since they were built.

The church and elders have grown more in favor with the people as the years have gone by. The majority of the Mormon people engage in agriculture. They are encouraged by the leaders to make the fields green with good crops. They stress as an essential part of their religion, "good health and clean bodies."

They believe in temperance and education.

Sand Hill Baptist Church

Sand Hill Church is situated about seven miles east of Douglas and was organized by Thomas P. O'Neal. Some of the ministers were: G. W. Newbern, Henry Dent, Gilford Lastinger, Rev. P. W. Powell and others. Some of the members of this church fifty years or more were: Henry Dent and his family, Thomas Dent and his family, Daniel Gaskins and his family, Franklin Ward and others.

A large association was held on the grounds where the church now stands in 1875. Preachers and people gathered from all over the country. Services were held under a brush arbor. Some of the ministers who attended that meeting were: G. W. Newbern, Johnie

Taylor, Gilford Lastinger, Thomas P. O'Neal, Elder Barber and W. R. Frier, Sr., father of the Editor Frier of the Douglas Enterprise, was clerk of the association. James Vining, S. P. Gaskins and others preached.

Lott Memorial Church

(Communicated 1924)

I attended the old Lone Hill Church last Sunday, the first Sunday in the New Year. I joined that church fifty years ago; I love to go there. It has been "Lone Hill" since 1854. The name of the place ought to be changed to meet the present day conditions. The sweet memories that cling about the old name may be embalmed and perpetuated in the new name.

I submit the "Lone Hill" Church name be changed to the "Lott Memorial Church." Some of the reasons are as follows:

When the Lott family moved to this country about the year 1810 they settled right on the spot where the church now stands. They were the pioneers of our present civilization. They cleared the land, built the houses, made a good and lasting impression on this part of Georgia. When they died they were buried at the Lone Hill Grave Yard and they continue to bury the Lotts and their generation there. Many of the best citizens in that locality are related to the Lotts. The old "Lone Hill" means nothing and stands for nothing. If the name is changed, as I suggest, it will be building a monument to the Lotts and will point the young generation to that heroic band who first settled there and whose children and grandchildren largely built Lone Hill and made it what it is, what it has meant to me and to hundreds of others who joined that old church and attended their first Sunday schools there. It will be placing a premium upon the lives of those saintly ones who wrought so well in the long ago. It will be like a clarion call to all the Lotts and their generations to again join their scattered forces and to make the "Lott Memorial Church" the best country church in this part of Georgia. The church could not fail with the two Dan Lotts—Elias' Dan and Arthur's Dan, John Peterson, Sampie and Monroe Smith, E. R. Cross, Willis Newbern and their families and many others. They have the talent to do anything necessary to be done to make a big, successful church. The woods out there are full of fine people who, no doubt, would be glad to fall in line with the proper leadership and build up a great church choir and a great church. My heart thrills at the possibility of such a movement. I submit the question—shall it be the Lott Memorial Church?

Ward's Scrapbook, 1910.

Lone Hill Methodist Church

Lone Hill Methodist Church is situated twelve miles northeast of Douglas, Ga. This church was organized at the close of the Civil War. It was the plan of the pastor of the church to have preaching once a month, Saturday and Sunday. It is said that the preacher came to church on Saturday, once upon a time, and that not a soul came to meeting. He came at 11 o'clock and waited until twelve or one and still no one came. He left the church and went to Aunt Fannie Gaskins for dinner. He told Mrs. Gaskins his experience and said it was the most lonesome place he ever saw. He repeated that it was a Lonesome Hill and so the church had a name from that time on—"Lone Hill."

The old members of this church were the Lotts, Newberns, Douglases, Wards, Smiths, and many others. One of the first Sunday schools in Coffee County was organized in that old church, and the superintendent of the Sunday school was a woman—Mrs. Clem Brooker. She was a good superintendent; she had tact, and sense. The Sunday school was very prosperous under her management. After her death, R. S. Smith was elected superintendent and acted for many, many years.

Some of the old preachers who served that church were: David Crenshaw, John E. Sentell, John L. Williams, J. D. Maulden, J. D. Anthony, W. J. Flanders, William F. Roberts, A. M. Williams, W. F. Hixon, H. C. Fentrass, A. H. Bazmore, Ben L. Sentell, R. M. Booth, J. M. Wilcox and David Blalock.

The Old Carver Church

The Carver Baptist Church is situated about six miles south of Douglas, Ga. This old church was built about the close of the Confederate War. Old Billy Ward, Gilford Lastinger, Elias Walden, L. D. Geiger, George W. Newbern, et. al., were the preachers.

Among the old members were: John Carver and family, Aaron Anderson and family, Ashford Yeomans and family and many others. This old church has had a hard struggle to live all through the years. When the old log house gave way, Mr. Willie Vickers very kindly built a frame house and gave it to the community with the understanding that all denominations might preach there. This writer remembers having attended this old church soon after the war. He does not remember the preacher nor a single person who attended the church that day, but remembers one thing, and that was a dog fight right in front of the pulpit.

The Old Elizabeth Church

Elizabeth Church is located about two miles west of Hazlehurst, Ga. This church was named for Elizabeth Wilcox, the mother of Rev. J. M. Wilcox, of precious memory. The church was established long before the Confederate War. Some of the first ministers who preached there were: Revs. Dupree, Graham, Thorpe, and others. Some of the early members of this church were: the Hinsons, Friers, Dents, Dyals, and others.

Midway Methodist Church

Midway Methodist Church was situated about five miles south of Hazlehurst, Ga., and was built several years before the Confederate War. Some of the ministers were: Daniel Morrison, Wilson, Lowe, and others. Some of the members of the old church were: Jim Hinson and his family, Joshua Smith, the father of old George and old Tom Smith, Wiley Hargroves and family, and others.

Gravel Hill Methodist Church

This church was organized long before the Civil War. Some of the members were: Mrs. Caroline Ashley, Matt Ashley, Nathaniel Ashley, with their families, and others. This was a Methodist Church and had the same preachers that preached at Midway Church.

Pleasant Grove Baptist Church

This church was located two miles northwest of Hazlehurst. Some of the old preachers were: Rev. Thorpe, Josh Frier, and others. Some of the members of that old church were: the Birds, the Pridgens, the Paces, and others.

Mount Zion Methodist Church

This church was located about ten miles south of Hazlehurst, and was built before the Civil War. This being a Methodist church, the ministers who served old Midway Church also preached at this church. Some of the members of that old church were: the Wilcoxes, the Taylors, Josh Smith and his family, Peter White, and others.

Rehoboth Primitive Baptist Church

Rehoboth Primitive Baptist Church was organized in the home of William Bagley about the close of the Confederate War, by Elder Cornelius Buie. Some of the first members were: William Bagley, Ben Bagley, the Moore family, and others. The church remained in the home of William Bagley for a year or two, and then a church house was built about two miles north of Bickley. It is of special interest to know how the church was located. Elder Cornelius Buie was a blind man and was a great preacher. He asked the Lord to make known to him where the new church was to be located. He was led, as he thought, to blow a trumpet and listen to what direction the sound went and where it seemed to locate, and after trying this plan for many times and blowing in many directions the sound of the trumpet seemed to locate at the same place every time, and so he decided that he was led by the Lord to locate the new church house at that place, and so a few names of them got together and built a log house and called the church "Rehoboth." The workers and builders on the church were so few until the logs were put in place by ropes. The old church house had a floor of hewed logs called puncheons.

After many years the old log house became dilapidated and the church members and their friends built a new meeting house out of sawed lumber. A few years ago, about 1915, a new church house was built about two miles southeast of this old church, where regular services are now held.

Elam Primitive Baptist Church

Elam Primitive Church is located about two miles northeast of Nicholls, Ga. This old church was constituted about the year 1865, soon after the Civil War. Some of the old members of that church were: Charles Meeks and wife, Redding Meeks and wife, Squire Dedge, Seab Holton and wife, William Cole and wife. Elder Richard Bennett was one of the first pastors of the church. This old church has been a landmark in Coffee County for many years. A fine class of citizens live in that neighborhood now and many of them have lived there for many years. It is now one of the leading churches in the Alapaha River Association.

Roberts' Methodist Church, South

The old Roberts' Methodist Church is located about two or three miles northeast of Kirkland. This church was organized about the year 1866. The first friends of the church were: old man Jack Roberts and his family, old man Rob Roberts and his family, old man Elias Moore and his family, old man John Moore and his family, Hiriam Mancil and his family, Timothy Kirkland and his family, Mac Kirkland and his family, Benajah Pearson and his family, Jim McKinnon and his family, Seth Durham and his family, Hiriam Sears and his family. Dennis Paulk and his family sometimes attended this church. Among the children of old Rob Roberts are the following: J. Wesley Roberts, Jimmie Roberts, Elder Dan Roberts, Jesse Roberts, and Mary Ann, who married Col. Corbitt. One among the first preachers of this church was Elder Harvey.

Royals' Methodist Church

The old Royals' Church is situated about half way between Douglas and Pearson and was organized soon after the Confederate War. Many of the families and friends who attended the old Roberts' Church also attended the Royals' Church.

There is also an old cemetery there where many of these old citizens are buried. The old Royals' Church is still in operation. Elder Ben Finley was one of the first preachers. Daniel Morrison, H. C. Etheridge, J. D. Anthony, W. H. Thomas, M. C. Austin, William F. Roberts and other ministers preached there.

Mount Pleasant Church

One of the oldest Baptist Churches in Coffee County is Mount Pleasant Church, located about six or eight miles east of Broxton. About seventy-five years ago the church was organized by G. W. Thorpe. (Wash.) Some of the pastors of that church more than fifty years ago were: George Newbern, W. M. Carver, and W. E. Morris. Old man Joshua Frier was one of the deacons in that old-time church, and when no preacher was there he would hold the services. Another deacon in that old-time church was William Creech. Wiley Byrd, Sr., Ben Minchew and family, Joe Garrett, Archie Miller were members of that church.

New Hope Church

Another old-time church is New Hope Church near Ambrose, Ga., which was constituted about 65 years ago. Johnie G. Taylor, George W. Newbern were pastors. Some of the old members were: J. R. Smith, S. D. Phillips, Squire Jowers, Eli Jowers, and others.

Mount Zion Baptist Church

Another old-time church was Mount Zion Baptist Church, situated ten or fifteen miles south of Douglas. Some of the earlier preachers were: George Newbern, Johnie G. Taylor, W. E. Morris, Gilford Lastinger, William Carver. Some of the old members were: Douglas Gillis, J. P. Wall, Brooker, Cicero Gillis, Arthur Gillis, and others. One of the special features of Mount Zion Church was the old-fashion singing.

Oak Grove Church

One of the old-time churches in Coffee County was the Oak Grove Church. Oak Grove Church was located about a mile northwest of the town of Pridgen. William Roberts, Dan Morrison, Rev. Blalock were the old preachers. Some of the members were: Capt. J. W. Boyd and family, Murdock McRae and family, some of the Fussells, and others.

Midway Methodist Church

Midway Methodist Church was organized by Greene Taylor in 1864. He was a great camp meeting preacher. Midway Church is situated about four miles east of where West Green is now located. The members there were: W. P. Taylor, John Burkett, Aunt Vina Burkett, and others.

Bethel Church

Another old church in Coffee County is Bethel Church. It was situated near the home of old man John Lott about fifteen miles northeast of Douglas. Its members were: John Lott and his family, Dan Lott and his family; and the preachers were: J. D. Anthony, Rev. Maulden, and others.

The Catholic Church

The only Catholic Church in Coffee County was built at Willacoochee, Georgia, about the year 1870. The group of Catholic Irish who came from New York to construct the Brisbane Railroad built this church. Among the names of the old members are McGoverns,

Nolans, McDaniels, Spiveys, Neugents, and perhaps some others. As Coffee County people have married into these Catholic families, some of them have joined the Catholic Church.

The church was located first at Willacoochee, Georgia. It was later on moved near Mr. John McGoverns.

These Irish Catholic people are among the best citizens of Coffee County, and we are glad that "The Brisbane Railroad" left us this group of good citizens.

Old School Houses

About 1865 a school was organized in the neighborhood of the Meeks settlement. The building was a plain log house, and had been used for a residence. The chimney had fallen down and the opening was turned into a door six or seven feet wide. The seats were made of logs with pegs underneath which served as legs for the log benches. Mr. A. F. Thomas and Miss Emma Pickern taught school at that place. Miss Pickern later became the wife of Rev. J. M. Wilcox. The building had a dirt floor and later was used for many years as a church. The school and church have been moved to Nicholls and some of the same material is now being used. Many of the Meeks generation attended school and church in that old-timey house.

Old Schools

One of the old schools before the war was the Hinson School. This school was out near Hazlehurst, Ga., and was taught many years by James Smith. Other teachers there were: Joe Wilcox, Lafayette, and

Tillis. This school was patronized largely by the Hinsons and the Smiths.

The Girtman School was probably one of the best schools in Coffee County at that time. This school was taught by Rev. Thorpe. The school was operated all the year for three years. The Girtmans, Hinsons, Pickerns, Creeches, and many others attended the school.

The Kirkland School

The Kirkland School was located about five miles south of Sand Hill Church, was in operation more than fifty years ago. The building was a log house situated on the old Waresboro road near the farm of Z. W. Kirkland, Sr. One of the first teachers who taught there was "Babe Moore." Another teacher who taught there was Rev. Malcom Meeks. Some of those who attended that old school were the families of Z. W. Kirkland, Sr., Mose Kirkland, Sr., Josh Kirkland, and others. Rev. Meeks was a splendid teacher for his day and time. He had splendid order in his school room. The writer of this article was one of his students, and so was Elder Hymrick Meeks and David Kirkland, and others.

There is no sign of the old school house, nor is there any sign where it stood. The only sign of that dear old school is a few old gray heads scattered over Coffee County.

Big Court, October Term, 1869

Superior Court in Coffee County was called "Big Court" by the natives. The court I am telling you about gives you a very good idea of the conditions of our courts at that time in Coffee County.

"Big Court Set" on the fourth Monday in October, 1869. The weather was frosty and fair. The days were warm and the nights were cool. By ten o'clock in the morning of the first day of the court people were coming in from all directions. Some walking, some riding, some in wagons and very few had buggies. There was not a hotel in Douglas. A few homes gave meals and lodging, but most people brought their provisions and cooked it on the ground. They built up a fire near their carts and wagons and slept under the carts and wagons. Old man John Spivey, with ten or twelve little Spiveys, kept a little store right where the present court house now stands. He sold ginger bread, hot coffee, and canned stuff.

At the time, there was not a railroad nor a bridge in Coffee County. When the streams were too full, it was to go around—or to go through. Carts and wagons were taken across on "flats." Those on foot "cooned" over on logs. The principal case to be tried at this term of court was a case of hog stealing. The sentiment against hog stealing, sheep stealing and cow stealing at this time was very strong. They did not think so much against a man fighting just a little bit; in fact, he might cut his neighbor into doll rags and he would not be despised so much for a crime of that sort as he would be for stealing a pig.

I will now tell you about the case at bar. The Judge on the bench was a little bald-headed man named Harris. The Solicitor-General was a tall, slender little man with big brown eyes. The Sheriff and his Deputies all wore their hats in the court room to show that they were officers of the law and had a right to command order in the court. All the witnesses and jurors were sworn with their hands on the Holy Bible and everybody else spit on the floor.

Old man John S. was on trial for stealing a hog. It was alleged that he had stolen a hog from W. W., his brother-in-law. When the case was put on trial it developed that the hair, hide and ears of a hog were found in the woods. Mr. W. discovered that the ears were in his mark. The hair had the color of his hogs. It further appeared that a hole had been dug in the ground about as big as a barrel and about half as deep and that this hole in the ground had partly been filled with water. The water had been heated by heating large rocks and plunging them into the water. This was the plan of the rogue to get the water hot enough to scald the hog. But the rogue failed to make the hair slip and so he skinned the hog, and took the meat home.

All the evidence being in, the lawyers went to the jury to make the arguments in the case. There was old Vernon E. McLendon, who had a face like an eagle, with eyes like an owl. He was a good lawyer and made a good speech. And then came old Colonel Dasher, he was as tall as a fishing pole and always wore a big beaver hat and a long-tail coat. During his speech he would sling his arms around like sticks tied to his shoulders, a regular scare crow. The jury brought in a verdict of guilty. The Judge fined the prisoner one hundred dollars with cost of the court. Mr. W. W. had heard the plea of the lawer telling about the sorrows of a poor man who had no meat, no hogs in the woods and nothing to buy with. In fact, Mr. W. was moved to tears, paid the fine and all the cost of the court and took his brother-in-law home with him.

It is said that the city of Rome was built upon seven hills. The city of Douglas was built on ten hills, and during these terms of big court every hill had a fire light on it. Where the jurors and witnesses and litigants camped it was a beautiful sight to see these camp fires burning on the hills round and about. Often they had coffee together, and other drinks as well. There was one good old man, "Peace to his memory," who would walk around these camp fires if perchance he might find someone who needed help and if it so happened that someone had too much to drink, was sleepy and had fallen over to rest in sleep, this good old man would often take a brick, or a box, or a saddle blanket, and put under the poor man's head that he might rest in sleep until the coming of day. This saintly man was Riley Wright.

Old Time Singers
(Communicated)

A revival of singing schools in Coffee County has set me to thinking. The "All-day sing and dinner on the grounds" is doing untold good to our young people. They are singing out the frolic and singing in a better day. I bid them all God Speed.

But the singing school is not a new thing in Coffee County. We had them in the "Days of long ago." The first name that comes to my mind is J. M. Wilcox of precious memory. He taught me some of the first songs I learned to sing. He loved to sing and was a successful teacher. He had a sad, sweet voice. He loved to sing minor pieces, with sweet and sad sentiments and often wept as he sang. He told me that he was saved by music, and it happened in this way: His parents were not religious and he spent his Sundays in the river swamp. But when he learned music he left the swamp and spent most of his Sundays at church and other places where he could sing. His life was a blessing to Coffee County, and while he sings above we who loved him continued to sing here below.

Another one of the old-time singers was Hiram Sears. He was a student of music. He took a periodical called "Musical Million," and contributed many articles to its columns.

The first sing I attended was taught forty-one years ago by William Stewart at the old Bethel Church near the homes of John Lott, Mark Wilcox, Dunk Douglas, and others. I tried to have a reunion of the old class at our singing convention in 1924 but they were so badly scattered I could not get them together.

In the early seventies several of Monroe Wilcox's students taught singing schools. I remember Joe Day, John Solomon, L. Passmore and many others whose names I do not recall.

About 1875 Tom Davis, "Singing Tom" as he was called, came to Coffee County from Montgomery County and taught several singing schools. He was a live wire. He generally taught in some country school house. He would take four long seats and make a pen. He stood in the center, with tenor on one seat, the bass on another, the alto on another, and the treble on another. He gave the key note sound all around, and then as they sang he walked around and around. When a part, like the bass for instance, seemed weak, he would jump like a cat to the bass seat and join in with the bass and pull them out of their trouble, and so on with all the parts. The writer of this article is largely a singing by-product of the teachings of "Singing Tom."

A little later Marcus A. Pafford appeared on the scene as teacher, and now the woods are full of them, and all good singers. Our country convention was a demonstration of what the singing school will do for the child and young people. The devil will never get them while they sing. There will be no singing in the bad world. All the singing is "Up Yonder" when the roll is called.

And now a note of warning. Do not neglect the "Old-time Songs." It is all right to sing the other kind, but teach the children a few tunes with the metres so they can start the tune in church and prayer meeting when called upon to do so.

And now as you all join in the chorus I will say good-bye for this time.

W. P. W.

Ward's Scrapbook, 1905.

SUPERIOR COURT CLERKS

1. A. W. HADDOCK, 1914-16. 2. CLEON FALES, 1926-1928—now serving. 3. J. R. OVERMAN, 1906-08-10-12. 4. SIMON P. GASKIN. 5. CYRUS GASKIN, 1885. 6. DAN W. GASKIN, 1897-99-1901-02-04. 7. SESSION FALES, 1906-1920-1924.

Some Old Graveyards

One of the oldest graveyards in Coffee County is the Ward graveyard, situated on lot of land 364 in the 6th district, being the place where Jim Tanner now lives, about seven miles east of Douglas. Some of the people buried there are: Old man Mose Kirkland, the father of Zene Kirkland and Josh Kirkland. He was buried there before the Civil War. Also old "Daddy" Ward and old "Mammy" Ward, the father and mother of the old Wards of Coffee County. They were buried there in 1849. Also the mother of W. M. Denton, a prominent citizen of Ware County, is buried there. She was buried there about 1845. She was the daughter of old James Preston Ward, the father of all the Wards in Coffee County. B. H. Tanner, Sr., the first sheriff of the county, was also buried there.

Very few people are being buried there now. Those who have loved ones there continue to clean off the graves about once a year.

Sandhill Graveyard

The Sandhill graveyard, at Sandhill Church, is only about fifty years old. However, there are many old citizens of Coffee County buried there. Among them old man William Dent, Daniel Gaskins, Sr., Thomas H. Dent, and others.

Lone Hill Graveyard

The graveyard at Lone Hill Church is more than fifty years old. Many of the Newbern family are buried there. The family had menengitis in 1870 and six of the family died in a week. The father and mother and four sons. Mrs. Dunk Douglas was buried there about the close of the Confederate War, and many other old citizens are buried there.

Mount Zion Graveyard

Another old cemetery is Mount Zion, about three miles north of Kirkland, Ga. This place was once in Coffee County and many of its old citizens are buried there. Mack Kirkland and his wife, who are the father and mother of Mrs. B. Peterson, are buried there. William Kirkland, an old citizen of that side of the county, was buried there.

New Hope Church Graveyard

The cemetery at New Hope Church, near Ambrose, Ga., is more than fifty years old and many old citizens are buried there. Among them J. P. Sweat, J. J. Jowers, Phillips, Days, and others.

War Times and Hard Times

In 1861 a horrible war broke out between the North and the South. Our men went to the battle front and our women and children, from necessity, went to the fields. For every man who took a gun there was a woman or a child who took a hoe or a plow and went to the fields. The men lost the fight for a separate union, but the women won for home and loved ones. They lived hard, it is true, but none of them went naked or starved. The spirit of the Wiregrass was the spirit of 1776. Their hardships as frontier men made them hardy and independent.

Matt Ashley organized the Fourth Georgia Cavalry and tendered their services to the South. Later in the year Company "C" 50th Georgia was organized with John M. Spence as Captain and J. K. Hilliard as Lieutenant. Captain Spence later became a Major and was the only man who went from this section of the Wiregrass country to be thus promoted. Later on many men volunteered and were sent to other companies.

Historians have told us about the men at the front, but not much has been written about the women and children at home. The men at the front were no more heroic or self-sacrificing than the women and children at home, who kept the wolf from many a door at home, and gave inspiration to the men at the front. They went to the fields by day and at night spun the thread and wove the cloth to clothe themselves and their children; and many of them sent clothing to their husbands at the front. When no salt could be bought to salt the bread, they would dig up the salty dirt in the meat house and boil the salt out of it and use it. When no coffee could be bought they would parch corn and sweet potatoes and use that. They did not consider it hard times to live without flour and sugar and the like. They counted it a blessing to have the necessaries of life. And so it was.

I will give you some pen-pictures of Coffee County homes during this war, to illustrate the conditions of the times.

A Wiregrass Home in 1864, Scene 1

Some one has said that "God gave us but one mother," but with some it is different; she was both father and mother. When red war smote the land with shock of battle and with flood of flame the father went to the front and never came back. With three baby boys to rear and only a little farm to do it with, she ceased her weeping and went to work. The hand she might have given in marriage to some other man, has been worn out in honest toil for her children.

Just at the close of the war the country was filled with "runaway" negroes. The mother and her three little boys lived all alone. One dark dreary evening in the summer time, when the thunder roared and the lightning flashed, a big black negro walked up to the door and asked for something to eat. The mother gave him something and he left. He was hardly out of sight, when the rain poured in perfect torrents and darkness settled down as black as Egypt. The mother was much afraid the negro would return to find shelter and rob the home. She put the boys to bed and prepared for the worst. She fastened the door, got the hatchet and put it under her pillow, blew out the tallow dip and then kneeling by her bedside she committed herself and her boys to the Great Father of us all. We never heard of the negro any more, but the pale outline of that mother in the dim fire light, as she kneeled in prayer on that dark stormy night, has followed me through all the years.

A Coffee County Home in 1864, Scene 2

A pine-knot fire blazed on the hearth. A w i d o w puts her three orphan boys to bed. She is busy with her spinning as roll after roll is drawn into finest t h r e a d. The night is c o l d. Above the whirl of the wheel could be heard the moan of the cold wind on the outside. At last the b r o a c h is finished

"The wheel turns around and around, And the cotton is drawn out into the finest thread."

and she turns aside to make up the fire and see that the children are covered and warm. Two boys sleep on a bed made down on the floor and they get first attention. She puts her busy hands on their heads and then cautiously feels of their feet.

Turning away from these, she goes to her own bed where the baby boy lies asleep snug and warm. When each child has received attention she goes back to the wheel to spin and to think. The wheel turns around and around and the cotton turns into finest thread. She stares vacantly at the fire and occasionally at her work. Just four years ago, her husband went to the war and never came back. Great tear drops came to her eyes as she thought of him and kept watch over his boys. Her eyes grew dimmer and dimmer and the wheel turned slower and slower. Soon the wheel and the widow both stood still. A tired hand hung heavy on the wheel and a great burden on the widow's heart. Neither could move. The wind was still, the fire burned low and not a sound was heard. The widow prayed. The burden lifted from her heart, strength came to her hand, the wheel started, and music with the wheel. Song after a song she sang, and prayer after prayer she said.

Late at night mother and children were all asleep, but one little boy did not sleep till his mother lay down, he heard the busy wheel and cold winds outside; saw his mother's tears and heard his mother's prayers. The fire, the wheel—the woman—the boy. As long as I live and winter winds blow, will I remember the spinning wheel and my mother's prayer in the long, long ago.

A Wiregrass Home in 1865, Scene 3

John F. Ward was a member of Company C, Fiftieth Georgia. He died in March, 1863, and is buried in an unknown grave in Virginia.

The following lines were selected and dedicated to his memory.

"There's a grave on the hillside,
  A lonely, sunken grave,
Where grow the tall rank grasses
  Above the fallen brave,
Where summer's sun smiles warmly
  Where winter's snow lies deep,
Where, o'er the unknown dreamer
  Unbidden voices weep.

"There's a grave on the hill, O wind,
  Pass by with plaintive moan,
Bend low the grass above it,
  And sigh 'Unknown, Unknown!'
Stoop down, O heavy rain cloud,
  And drop a pitying tear,
If thou dost mourn earth's chosen,
  Oh, spend thy sorrow here!

"There's a grave on the hill, O Father,
  Thy searching voice shall yet
Rouse up the sleeping soldier,
  For thou dost not forget,
There's a lonely grave on the hillside,
  But, oh, before thy throne,
The humble shall be honored
  The unknown shall be known!"

The father sleeps in an unknown grave in Virginia, while the mother rests in the soil of Coffee County. On a plain marble slab beneath a Confederate Flag you will find these words:

> Sacred to the Memory
> Sarah A. Ward.
> Born May 3, 1834,
> Died October 25, 1918.
> Widow of John F. Ward,
> Company C, Fiftieth Georgia.
> Now sleeps in an Unknown Grave
> near Fredericksburg, Va.

A Tribute to the Women of the South

Everybody will concede that before the War Between the States, under the slavery system, southern womanhood was esteemed the highest type in the world. Social weakness and depravity among the women of the South from bottom to top were matters scarcely known. In this respect, the social civilization of the South was the age of chivalry preserved and perpetuated. Our women also were noted for their health and for a certain maturing of beauty more and more adorable and attractive as the silver threads appeared among the hair. How beautiful my dear old grandmother looked on the seventieth anniversary of her birthday and the fiftieth of her marriage. A few wrinkles were there, to be sure, but the proud head was crowned with a white fleece of honor and unapproachable beauty. Her eyes were as bright and clear as on that night when she looked into the soul of my grandfather and there read security and return for all her honor and her love, fifty years before.

The Women of the South

Not Homer dreampt, nor Milton sung,
 Through his heroic verse,
Nor Prentiss did with wondrous tongue,
 In silver tones, rehearse;
The grandest thing that ever yet,
 Moved brush, or tongue or pen,
A theme in radiant glory set,
 To stir the souls of men,
THE WOMEN OF THE SOUTH.

Who bade us go with smiling tears?
 Who scorned the renegade?
Who, silencing their trembling fears,
 Watched, cheered, then wept and prayed?
Who nursed our wounds with tender care,
 And then, when all was lost,
Who lifted us from our despair
 And counted not the cost?
THE WOMEN OF THE SOUTH.

Coffee County in War

Coffee County has done her full share in furnishing soldiers and fighting the battles of her country.

Coffee County was created in 1854. She sent her full share of soldiers to the war with the Seminole Indians in Florida in 1858.

In 1861 the Confederate War called more than 300 soldiers into service from Coffee County. 1898 we had the Spanish American War on our hands. In 1917 the World War made a call for men and supplies and Coffee County responded with more than 600 men. We were also asked by our country to cut sugar and many other things out of our diet in order that we might have these necessary things for our soldiers.

Coffee County has always fought on the side of victory except in the Civil War, and in that conflict the most horrible of all, we believe that some great principles of government were saved to our country.

JAMES K. HILLIARD

Clerk of the Superior Court—elected 1856-January 15th, 1858. Clerk of the Inferior Court January 15th, 1858, to January 10th, 1860. First Lieutenant of Company C, 50th Ga. Reg. He built the first hotel in Douglas.

English Gold

The Civil War ended 1865. Mr. Hargraves' two sons and two or more of his sons-in-law had been in the army. Conditions, generally, were so disturbed by the war that Mr. Hargraves did not make any special effort to get his money from England, until the war was over. Sometime in 1866, Mr. Hargraves held a consultation with his relatives and friends and it was

CAPTAIN CUYLER W. HILLIARD, Husband of Teresa Hargraves, daughter of Abram Hargraves who received $70,000 from his estate in England. Captain Hilliard made two trips to England for the money.

decided, that his son-in-law, Captain Cuyler W. Hilliard, and his son, Abram Hargraves, Jr., be sent at once to England for the money. It was regarded as a big undertaking, as well as a very expensive one, but there was much at stake and so preparations were made for the journey.

The first thing they needed was money to pay expenses; and while Mr. Hargraves was a well-to-do farmer, and had plenty of property, there was little money in the county at this time, by reason of the fact that Confederate money was dead and but little silver and gold could be had. After searching among friends and relatives of the family, money was found and strange as it may seem, Mr. C. A. Ward, Sr., loaned Mr. Hargraves $300.00 in ten cent pieces.

The next thing in order was to have prepared a power of attorney, and such other legal papers as were necessary in order that they might receive and receipt for the money in England. After securing the money and legal papers, Captain Hilliard and Abe Hargraves, Jr., went to Savannah, and there they took a steamer to New York and from New York they went to Lancashire, England.

Soon they found the place and location of the gold, but when they presented their papers and introduced themselves, the banker looked at them in a sort of inquiring way and said, "Your papers are all right, but who are you?" It seems that their identification was not sufficient to satisfy the bankers that they were the persons named in the power of attorney. The banker told them that the papers had been executed for several months and that where so much money was involved it was possible for the papers to be stolen or to fall into the hands of strangers, and in that way the bank would be deceived, and the money paid over to persons who had no right to it.

No explanation or argument by Mr. Hilliard and Mr. Hargraves could convince the banker that they were the proper persons. And so the only thing to be done was to return home and get proper papers of identification. Captain Hilliard returned to Georgia to get proper papers prepared and in due course of time returned to England. Mr. Hargraves had remained in England and married an English girl; and so, after proper papers of identification were presented, the business was adjusted. They began their preparations for their return home. What to do with so much money and it all in gold was a serious question. $70,000.00 in gold weighs about two hundred and seventy-three pounds. It was finally decided to place the money in a strong cedar box and take it on the ship with them. And so, Captain Hilliard and Mr. Hargraves, Jr., and his young English wife, took their box of gold on the ship and bid old England a long farewell.

In due course of time they reached New York. They took their box of gold to the hotel and as English gold with its pounds and crowns, would be a strange thing in Wiregrass Georgia, they decided to have the English gold exchanged for American gold. They bought a plain iron safe and into this iron safe they placed the American gold with its eagles and dollars, and set sail for Savannah, Georgia, then out to old Tebeauville, now Waycross, Georgia, and then out by private conveyance to the old Hargraves farm, a distance of forty miles, or more. This farm is about eighteen miles southeast of Douglas, Georgia, on the Seventeen-Mile Creek.

So much money in the possession of one man in Wiregrass Georgia soon spread to every home in the county.

I shall tell you more about this gold at another time. Many of his friends and relatives paid him a visit and to every near relative he gave a twenty dollar gold piece. Mr. Hargraves was a man who did not let money turn his head. He remained the same plain old man, following the same pursuits of life, feeding his hogs, fishing, looking after his mill and cattle, and giving the same attention to his farm now, that he did before receiving his fortune. In a short time he divided most of the money among his children. None of them receiving less than $5,000.00, and some of them more than that.

Wherever the money went, you would see a white house spring up, and those who occupied the home owned and used a horse and buggy—a very rare thing in Coffee County at that time (1873). The coming of this amount of money in gold at this time to Coffee County, so soon after the Civil War, when money was so scarce, made a great impression upon the people of Coffee County. Every one who was old enough to know anything at that time remembers well when Abram Hargraves received his gold from England.

The little iron safe that first held the English gold is now owned by Hon. J. M. Denton. It was sold by the administrators of the Hargraves' estate to Hal Peterson, and the administrator of the estate of Hal Peterson sold it to J. M. Denton.

Abram Hargraves, Jr., who went to England with Captain Cuyler W. Hilliard for the $70,000 of English gold. Also the wife of Abram Hargraves whom he married in England.

Regulators

No people in the South were more patriotic and enthusiastic in the Confederate War than the men and women of Coffee County. Many of them were the sons and daughters of sturdy stock from Virginia. Most of them had been reared on the frontier, had fought in the Indian Wars, and were fighters both by blood and by training. But conditions were all against them and by the fall of 1864, the Confederacy was falling to pieces. Sherman had marched through Georgia, burned Atlanta, captured Savannah and many of our soldiers who were at home on furloughs, were not able to return to their commands, and were compelled to remain at home. And as a consequence many true soldiers were called "Deserters." Others had lost heart and came home to stay, let the consequences be what they may. The Confederate Government needed every soldier in line at this time and details were sent to arrest all the deserters and take them back to the front. Many soldiers and details were killed by each other. In all this time of stress and trouble funny things would happen. I give you one instance: Old Bill Wall, as he called himself, was one of the fellows who remained at home. Mr. Benajah Pearson made complaint that "Old Bill Wall" and his bunch were eating his sheep and hogs. Mr. Wall heard the complaint and sent Mr. Pearson the following verses; which he composed for the occasion.

"If it is my choice to stay at home, and
    the woods in beauty roam;
Pluck the flowers in early spring, and hear
    the little songsters sing!

"Why, then, should I, for the sake of gain,
   leave my conscience with a stain.
A traitor! who could hear the name with
   no respect for age or fame;
Who, for the sake of a little gold, would
   have his friends in bondage sold?
I would rather take the lash than betray
   them for Confederate trash.

"You say they kill your sheep and cows,
You say they take your hoss and your plows,
You say they took your potatoes away,
You said they dug your grave one day.
All of this may be true;
It makes me sorry for you.

"Yet, sir, if I, these men betray and they
   were all taken away,
And they did not in the battlefield fall,
They would then come back and kill
   'Old Man Bill Wall'."

About the time the Confederacy went to pieces and for a few years afterwards there was much lawlessness in the country. And some of the best citizens of the county organized themselves into a band of "Regulators" for the protection of the country. They held the lawbreaks in check for a while and did a lot of good until our courts could be organized and put in motion. I will give you one instance of the character of their work: A widow and her three little boys lived on a little farm, in the wildwoods of Coffee County. A few years before their father went to the war and never came back. He was sleeping in an unknown grave, in Virginia. About noontime two men in a wagon drove up to the little home and told the lone woman that they were peddlers and wanted to get dinner and sell her some goods. But it seems they had another purpose in view, and when the insult came the woman grabbed a board and was in the act of striking the man nearest to her when they begged like dogs for mercy, got into the wagon and left. News of the occurrence spread in the neighborhood. As soon as dark came a fire was kindled in the neighborhood which meant danger was near. The "Regulators" jumped in their saddles and soon the clatter of hoofs was heard and the clans were gathering in defense of Southern womanhood. Far into the night a man came up to the house where the woman lived and called her. She went to the front cautiously thinking it might be the peddlers returning, but a voice called out in a friendly tone and said, "We want some matches please mam." The woman recognized the voice, but she asked who it is that wants matches? The man said, "We are two peddlers. Our wagon broke down on the edge of the creek and we need a fire." The woman recognized the man's voice and the man's walk. She knew he was a friend and he only told her that he was a peddler to let her know that they were there to defend her against any and all who might insult and attack her. And so these brave men, these Confederate soldiers, these Regulators lay around this woman's home at night to defend her and her little boys at any cost.

These were the times that tried men's souls. A county and a people that came through a time like that, were well prepared to overcome all difficulties.

An Ideal Wedding

In the fall of 1867 the announcement was made that Mr. Sydney Hargraves and Miss Mary Lott would be married in December. They were distant relatives. Mr. Hargraves, a grandson, and Miss Lott, a great grand-daughter of "Mother Jones." Miss Lott lived with her widowed mother, Mrs. Mark Lott, about ten miles Northeast of Douglas, and Mr. Hargraves lived with his father, about eighteen miles southeast of Douglas.

This marriage was celebrated in the usual way for the better class of country people in that day and generation. Preparation was made for the invited guests who were supposed to include all the near relatives and many friends of the contracting parties.

The best cook in the country was employed to superintend for a week at the Lott home, and supervise all preparations for the occasion. Also bake cakes, pies, and goodies of every sort.

A beef and several hogs, chickens by the score, and turkeys a plenty were used in the wedding supper. One cake of immense size called the "wedding cake" required the skill of a cake artist. It was supposed to have all the frills and furbelows which the last word in cake making required. A ring was placed in this cake and when the cake was cut by the wedding party, the person who received the piece of cake containing the ring, was said to be the next one to get married. Everything was done on a big scale, nothing was spared in time or money to make the occasion memorable. Not only was "the big pot put in the little pot," but all the pots were put on. A sugar boiler, containing sixty gallons, was made full of rice pilau. When the wedding day arrived, people came from all directions. They came in carts, wagons, on horse back, and many of them came a-foot. All of the Lott negroes, old Cap, Aunt Martha, Sam, Ann and all the others were there, nice and clean, spick and span, all lined up to see Miss Mary get married. As the evening passed and the sun was getting low in the west, the crowd gathered about the front yard. Some thing great was going to happen in that family pretty soon. The groom and his best man, each riding white horses, and his four attendants were hiding in the woods, awaiting the signal for them to appear. Miss Mary and her attendants were in readiness.

Just as the sun went down, the signal was given to the groom and his party. The feet of horses were heard rumbling in the distance. Soon the two white horses, leading, were seen and then all the others came in view, and with increasing speed they dashed up to the front gate. Those in the party were Sydney Hargraves, the groom; Lewis C. Wilcox, Daniel Lott, Mark Lott, Jessie Lott, J. M. Denton, and Jim Lankford.

When they arrived they quickly alighted from their horses and rushed into the house. They were met at the door by the bride and her attendants. The marriage ceremony was performed by Moses Kirkland, a Justice of the Peace.

After the usual formal congratulations, supper was announced. A large table had been prepared in the yard; dozens of candles on the table and around about furnished light for the occasion. In addition to candles, fires were built in the yard around the premises, to light up the grounds.

The wedding party had been provided with a table of honor. The other people ate at a long table. There was plenty for all, both white and colored. From supper time until ten o'clock was spent in a social way, talking with old friends and relatives, renewing old acquaintances and making new friends. At ten o'clock, dancing began. Old Lewis Lott, colored, played the fiddle for them. Uncle Lewis was in all his glory as he played the fiddle. He leaned back in his chair, patted his foot and yodled his voice in unison with the music and dancing. Old Captain "beat the strings" and business was lively.

The Infair

The next night the Infair was held at the home of the bridegroom, thirty miles away. Only people of wealth in those days could afford to have both a wedding and an Infair. The wedding supper was given by the bride and the supper at the Infair was given by the bridegroom.

Old Uncle Abe Hargraves had made great preparations for the Infair and it was in keeping, in every way, with the times and all that was expected of the occasion.

The Constitution and the Flag

During the Confederate War many people who were able and patriotic bought patriotic quilts and put them on their beds. Patriotic quilts were printed tops and quilted like other quilts. The patriotic quilt had printed in large letters a motto like this: "The Constitution and the Flag." This motto was intended to teach the household in that home that it was not the home of a rebel but on the contrary was the home of a patriotic citizen fighting in the Confederate army.

In old testament times the Jews wore quotations from their law on their arms and sometimes around their foreheads but it remained for the Confederate Soldier to wrap his babies and cover his bed with the emblem of his devotion to his country.

I wonder if one of those patriotic quilts can be found in Coffee County at this time, 1930?

Railroads in Coffee County

The Brisbane Railroad

The earliest project to build a railroad within the confines of Coffee County was that known as the Brisbane railroad, having the eastern terminus at Mobley's Bluff on the Ocmulgee river in the northwestern corner of the county and the western terminus was to be Albany on Flint river in Dougherty County.

The project was conceived in New York City in 1856. The survey was made in 1857 and was a bee-line between the two points and enroute touched two county seats—one was Irwinville in Irwin county and the other Isabella in Worth County. The survey and grading was in charge of a man by the name of Brisbane, from whom it took its name. He came here from New York City and with him a large force of Irish laborers who were to do the grading. The work of grading went well for more than a year. It was executed upon the idea that a locomotive could not pull a train of cars up a grade and the roadbed was perfectly level so far as it went. The grading was completed from Mobley's Bluff to a point beyond Isabella, said to have been within twelve or fifteen miles of Albany.

Brisbane and his New York co-projectors met with financial troubles supposed to have risen because of the threatened war between the North and the South. He failed to meet his payrolls and the men, finding themselves without money with which to provide themselves with food and clothing, were forced to quit and seek other employment.

Hon. Nelson Tift, the founder of Albany, became interested in the project; he was anxious for its completion which would unite the navigable Ocmulgee river with what could be made a navigable Flint river with this means of transportation; it appeared to him a very progressive movement and promised much to his embryo city—Albany. Hence he loaned much time and influence in an effort to straighten out the financial impediment and complete the road into Albany. The war came on and this splendid project had to be abandoned. It was so near and yet so far from Albany. Mr. Tift was a Connecticut man.

However, the failure of this railroad project was not without benefit to Coffee County. It left within its borders some very desirable citizens from the ranks of the Irish laborers. Lands were cheap, could be bought on credit and on the most liberal terms. Many of these young Irishmen became attached to the country and the people with whom they were thrown in contact. They decided not to return to New York but remain in South Georgia and wisely determined to buy lands and settle down to farming and stock-raising for which the country was admirably adapted. They prospered because they were thrifty and energetic. They settled along the line of the railroad they had attempted to build. Among those who settled in Coffee County are remembered the names of Neugent, McGovern, McDonald, O'Brien, Nowland and Spivey. Their descendants are still in this territory and have grown into a host of fine people and citizens.

The Douglas and McDonald Railroad

The first railroad locomotive to reach Douglas rolled into Douglas sometime in 1896, pulling a load of brick to build a schoolhouse, which was the first brick building built in Douglas. A tram-road had been in operation for some time between McDonalds Mill and Downing, a turpentine still five miles south of Douglas. And so when the city of Douglas began the construction of a brick schoolhouse the need of a railroad was felt, and so for that reason and for other reasons the tram-road from McDonalds mill, now Axson, was extended to Douglas. This little road gave Douglas its first outlet to the big wide world. We went to Waycross, Jacksonville, Brunswick, Savannah, etc., by way of this little road. And so I thought it worth while to add this little scrap of history to the story of the progress of Coffee County.

Origin of the Georgia & Florida Railroad and Development

Wadley and Mt. Vernon Extension Railroad Company built Douglas to Broxton 1901. Extended to the River in 1903, changed to the Douglas, Augusta & Gulf in 1905. Took over Ocilla, Pine Bloom and Valdosta Railroad from Pine Bloom to Nashville, Ga., and built from Douglas to Willacoochee and Pine Bloom in 1905 giving railroad from Barrow's Bluff on Ocmulgee River to Nashville, Ga., 59½ miles of road.

Sold to John Skelton Williams and Middendort, Williams and Company in May, 1906.

Red Bear Creek to river built by Douglas capital and Captain James, of Wadley, Ga.

First plan was to build to Ocmulgee River at Barrow's Bluff to secure cheaper freight rates by securing water connection with boats on river.

Originators planned to ultimately cross Ocmulgee River and connect with Wadley and Mt. Vernon Railroad, owned by Capt. James, extending from Wadley toward Oconee river and thence to Augusta. Chief Promoters Wadley, Mt. Vernon Extension Railroad Company; Capt. James, Wadley, Ga.; Capt. J. W. Miller, Macon, Ga.; B. Peterson, Douglas; John McLean, Douglas, Ga.; F. L. Sweat, Douglas, Ga.; W. W. McDonald, Douglas; J. W. Quincey, Douglas, Ga.; J. S. Lott, Douglas, Ga., and other citizens of Douglas.

The Georgia and Florida Railroad was organized by Mr. John Skelton Williams and associated during the early part of 1906. The shops at Douglas, Coffee County, Georgia, were built during the year 1909. The machinery equipment, etc., were set in the shop during the year, 1910, and when we moved into the shops it was a great day for the shop employees at Douglas, as we had been working outdoors entirely for about three years.

Below you will find a partial list of the officials and employees that were in service shortly after the Georgia and Florida Railroad was organized.

The first general manager was Mr. Cecil Gabbitt, who was later succeeded by Mr. J. M. Turner, who was placed in charge of construction and operation.

Mr. W. H. Alexander, Auditor, formerly employed by the D. A. & G. R. R.

Mr. B. F. Holdzendorff, Superintendent, formerly employed by D. A. & G.

Mr. Tinsley, Trainmaster, was formerly employed by M. & S. W. R. R.

Mr. R. L. Loftin, Trainmaster, employed by the G. & F.

Mr. J. E. Mathis, Master Mechanic, employed by G. & F.

During the years 1918, 1919, 1920 and 1921 the railroads were operated under the direction of the United States Railway Administration, and during this time all of the employees were enjoying the best rates of pay that had ever been known in the history of this railroad, or any other railroad, hard times were forgotten.

The road suffered a very serious loss during January of 1929 by the death of Mr. W. H. Dyer, who was superintendent of motive power, and Mr. M. T. Lanigan, Auditor, both of them having been very efficient executives for a number of years, and figured to a large measure in the development of the Georgia & Florida Railroad. Those who are assigned to the duties formerly supervised by these two gentlemen and others who came in contact with them cannot but miss their presence on the road at this time.

The road was very fortunate to have for its chief executive, Mr. H. W. Purvis, who is conversant with problems of transportation in every detail. He possesses the faculties and the talent to promote and develop plans.

Mr. George W. Crowder, of Douglas, Ga., succeeded Mr. Dyer, superintendent of motive power. No better selection could have been made.

Sand Hill Church

One of the first large religious meetings I ever attended in Coffee County was the Smyrna Association, held under a brush arbor where Sand Hill Church is now located, about seven miles east of Douglas. This Association was held about the year 1875. I know it was a long time ago, for curly-headed Hymrick Meeks, now one of the best homespun Baptist preachers in Georgia, was hardly big enough to wear socks. Elders George Newbern, Johnie G. Taylor, Rev. Blitch, Bill Carver, Thomas P. O'Neal and other ministers attended the meeting. The weather was fine and the attendance was large. The people came from all over the country. Several counties were represented. Great preparations had been made by the citizens of the neighborhood to entertain all who came. Hogs were butchered, beeves were killed and chickens slayed by the hundreds. Those who lived in the locality and who helped to entertain were: William Dent, Dunk Douglas, Dan Gaskins, Sarah Ward and others. The people came in droves, in all sorts of conveyances, and fell in at the nearest homes until they were all full and running over. Then others went to the next home and so on until all had a place to eat and sleep. At many homes, for lack of seats, the people sat around on the edge of the porches and let their legs hang off to the ground. Mr. Douglas entertained about seventy-five people at his home with horses to feed in proportion. You have never seen more open-hearted hospitality. The by-word was "Get down and come in and make yourself at home. Put up your horses and feed them." It was a great time. We met so many new people. All of them good and kind. They came fresh from good country homes, in love with their neighbors and all the world. I was a small boy, but I took in everything that came along. I often laugh today over things that happened then. Our lot was full of horses, some in the potato patch, some in the cotton patch and others scattered over the fields. While all these good old brothers were talking about the meeting with all their minds and heart on the association, one of the brothers called out, "Brother Jim, where is your horse?" Brother Jim, with a wave of his hand towards the field said, "I just turned my horse into the association." Well, we all laughed and kept on laughing for up to that good hour we had never seen a horse turned into the association. That association was a great meeting. It was the planting of Sand Hill Church and from that church several other churches have come. Many of the old preachers are dead and gone but the good work that was begun then still lives and goes on to bless the world.

W. P. WARD.

From Ward's Scrap Book, 1905.

Newspapers

The first paper printed in Coffee County was the "Pioneer," by William Parker and Fred Ricketson, about 1870. The paper was published at Pearson, Ga., and it was printed on a home made press. The roller was made of wood. The type was inked, the paper spread out upon the type and the wooden roller was rolled over the paper by hand. This paper was sold to a man named L. A. Lutes.

WILLIAM PARKER

About 1876 William Parker started the "Coffee County Gazette." In 1883 the paper was sold to W. P. Ward. In 1884 the paper was enlarged to a seven column paper and moved to Waycross, Georgia, and was called "The Waycross Headlight."

William Parker began the publishing of the "South Georgia Land Agent" at Pearson, Ga., in 1883. C. A. Ward and Pat Smith started the "Douglas Breeze" in 1888.

The Douglas Leader was started by A. B. Finley as a Populist paper.

Quincey and McDonald started the Douglas Leader, which was bought by J. M. Freeman and changed to the Douglas Breeze. In 1904, W. P. Ward organized a stock company and began the publication of The Coffee County Gazette. In 1906, The Douglas Enterprise and the Coffee County Gazette merged and became The Douglas Enterprise. Coffee County Progress was started in 1915 by T. A. Wallace and now the present editor is Fred Ricketson.

Coffee County News started in 1906 by S. H. Christopher and was sold to the Douglas Enterprise.

William Parker, a prominent merchant and business man of Pearson, Ga., and later of Waycross, Ga., was born and reared in Coffee County, Ga., and was educated in Palmyra, N. Y.

He edited and published the first paper in Coffee County—"The Pioneer." He later established the "Coffee County Gazette" and later in life he published the "South Georgia Land Agent."

Mr. Parker was a very devout Christian man and organized "The Christian Layman Association."

Where Uncle Jim Lives

JAMES M. FREEMAN

In a two-story house, half hidden by the pines at the foot of the hill, is where Uncle Jim lives. Everybody knows Uncle Jim. He writes the "Note Book" in the Douglas Enterprise and marries couples. I have passed his door nearly every day for twenty years and more. "Aunt Sally," Uncle Jim's good wife, often stood in the door and talked to me as I went by. But she is not there any more. She was old and sick and tired and God took her, and now, Miss Dollie, the good Angel of Douglas, presides over the home, and little Simmie, the granddaughter, came like a sunbeam from Heaven to help and bless.

Uncle Jim has lots to be thankful for. Nearly all the winds blow good to him. A peach tree came up in the chimney corner, like Jonah's gourd, to shut out the sun, and likewise a plum tree in the front yard. It bears fruit and makes shade, and is a restful place for the birds which so often come and sing for Uncle Jim. Uncle Jim holds court and writes the "Note Book" in his office at the court house, but he prefers to marry the folks under the plum tree; sometimes out of the sunshine and many times in the moonshine.

Uncle Jim is not strong enough to go to church at night, and so the good winds blew a Presbyterian church close by, and when the nights are cold he sits in his big chair and nods and smokes and hears the singing and the sermon.

Uncle Jim has the best friends in the world. They bring him so many good things, the biggest and the best of the fruits and flowers. To many of the children, he is a sort of uncrowned king. They think of him as they do Santa Claus, as some one who loves them and helps them. Uncle Jim has big gray eyes and they often fill up with tears of gratitude as some kindness is shown him. But Uncle Jim is getting old. The sun is getting low in the West and the shadows are getting longer. He cannot stay with us much longer. He has written his life and thoughts into thousands of the people of his generation, and ere long, perhaps, he may look out of his window, through the pines, up into the sky beyond the stars where Sally is waiting at the beautiful Gates. All the light will go out and Uncle Jim will be gone. The trees will cease to bloom and the birds will come and sing no more. So, if you wish to show him a favor or do him a kindness, do it now.

Ward's Scrapbook, 1910.

A Log Rolling, Quilting and A Frolic

Much of the land cleared soon after the war was done in the most primitive way. When a farmer decided to clear up a piece of land he split every tree on the land that would split into fence rails. The logs that would not split were cut up into pieces twelve or fifteen feet long to be burned at some convenient time in the fall or winter. The farmer gave a "log rolling, quilting and a frolic." The neighbors were invited to a big dinner and a "log rolling." The wives and daughters came to sew and to quilt. The method of rolling logs was to take hand spikes, prize up the log, and put about three hand spikes under the log with two men to each stick, one on each side of the log. Many a contest in strength was made in lifting logs. If the log was very heavy the men had to be very strong in their arms, legs and backs to lift. If the man at the other end of the stick was not likewise a very strong man, he could not come up with his end of the log and so he became the laughing stock of the crowd. It often happened that a small man was much stronger than a big man. I knew one little man who could lift as heavy a log as any man; the harder he pulled at his hand spike, redder and redder his face got, the veins in his neck bulged larger and larger. When a man claimed he was very much of a man and then wanted the light end of the load he would bluff the crowd by saying, "I can carry this and then some. Jump on my end of the log and take a ride."

While the men were busy rolling logs in the fields, the women and girls at home were busy making quilts and cooking dinner. One of the main dishes for dinner was a sixty-gallon sugar boiler full of rice and chicken and backbones. The largest dinner pot was full of greens and dumplings. When the greens were served on the largest dish a boiled ham was placed on top, while sweet potatoes, cracklin bread, potatoes, mudgen and cakes, two-story biscuits which were served in large quantities. When dinner time comes some one blows a big cow horn loud and long. All hands took a drink and went to dinner. All sorts of dishes are used on the table, broken cups, cracked plates, knives without handles, forks with but one prong, but they all had a good dinner and a bushel of fun while they ate. When the log rolling and the quilting is over, and the sun sets into the West, old Bill Mundy, the colored man, came in with his fiddle. A lot of sand was put on the floor and everything is cleared for the dance. The dancers get on the floor with their partners, the fiddler starts up "The One-eyed Gopher," and the frolic is on. The tune "One-eyed Gopher" played by the fiddler was a repetition of the words, "Oh, the one-eyed gopher, he fell down and couldn't turn over," etc. He would play it high, play it fast, and play it slow. When the dance is over the old fiddler kept on fiddling. They couldn't stop him. He said he had a contract with the boss men to play all night for five dollars and he said he couldn't break his contract. If he broke his contract it would ruin his business. He said he could make a new contract and that would do away with the old contract, and so they made a new contract. He charged them ten dollars to quit, but he decided to give them a farewell tune.

They got Sandy Moore to beat the strings while he played "Squirrel Gravy," and thus the frolic ended.

About the time the crowd was leaving, up came a bunch of rough necks to pick a fuss and a fight with some of the crowd. This was a bunch who never worked and had not helped with the log rolling that day, they only hoped to get a drink and a fight. The young men put their heads together and decided to play these fellows a trick. At the end of the house near the kitchen chimney a clay hole had been dug to get clay with which to build the kitchen chimney. The hole was deep as a man's head and about half full of water. The young men figured, if they should go around behind the kitchen and get up a fuss among themselves that the rough necks would run around to get in the fight. And so the fuss was started and the rough necks ran around the kitchen just as they supposed and fell heels over head into the clay hole. Every head of them got ducked and wet from top to bottom. They got thoroughly cooled off and there was no fight pulled off that night. And thus ends a "log rolling, a quilting, and a frolic" in Coffee County.

The Hour of Prayer in a Saw Mill

It is early twilight in the pine woods of South Georgia. The morning air is crisp and cool. The smoke goes up from a hundred shacks in the "Quarters" of a big saw mill.

"Big Jim," the whistle of the big mill, had sounded the signal for rising just one hour before. The fire in the slab pit that "burns forever and ever" casts a halo over the mill grounds around and about. It is now the hour of prayer. The big boilers are all hot and running over with steam. The log train fired up, pants and waits the word to go. Everything is ready. Everybody on time. A short blast of the whistle and the men hurry from all parts of the mill grounds. They gather in a circle-like group on the lumber docks. In the center of the group stands a man with a Bible in hand. All sorts of men and boys gather around. The engineer with cap in hand, the sawyer with his bill of lumber, laborers, white and colored, with dinner pails on their arms, and chop axes on their shoulders.

The man with the book, in slow and measured tones, read a part of Psalm 133, which begins like this: "Behold how good and how pleasant it is for brethren to dwell together in unity," etc. He lifts his hands towards heaven and prayed: "Our Father in heaven, we thank thee for the light of this morning and for the promise of a new day. We thank thee for all the blessings of life. Bless us this day with our homes and houses. Help us to do a good day's work, but most of all help us to be true to thee, and may the one purpose of our lives be to do thy will. Amen." You hear the shuffle of feet, the rattle of dinner pails, and the whiz of the escaping steam. The bells on the log train rings. The cry of "All Aboard" is given and the trains pull out for the many miles away. The steam in the big mill is turned out and the great fly wheel spins round like a top. The log carriage sweeps in position, the man with the canthook puts a log in place. The saw sings and clatters and moans and the real day's work began.

Out in the woods many miles away the men with chop axes are singing. Trees are falling and the pine woods present a busy and happy scene. Back in the mill quarters all day long you hear the women singing "Swing Low Sweet Chariot" and other familiar songs. Everybody busy and everybody happy. Plenty to do and plenty to eat. God's country in action—in South Georgia.

That happy time was many years ago. Change and decay come to all things. There is now nothing left of that old mill, but the sweet memory rests of those days, which, like sweet incense, floats back to you and me to bless and sanctify our lives. It was Walter Lott, of precious memory, who ran the saw mill, called the men together, read God's Word to his helpers, and offered prayer in their behalf. Now he is gone, and the big mill is gone and soon we shall all be gone. Let us hope that some sweet day our God shall gather us all with our songs and prayers to live with Him and our loved ones forever and ever.

The Georgia Colonel

So far as I know, Georgia is the only state in the Union where lawyers are called colonels. Some people think this is a mere captious name, but it is not. When a person has been sworn in as an attorney-at-law that person at once becomes a part of the court and a part of the machinery for enforcing the law of the land, and good reasons for which I shall now tell you.

As you know, Georgia was settled by General Oglethorpe. He was the first Governor of Georgia. He was a military man. In the organization of the State of Georgia, General Oglethorpe, the military man, impressed himself upon the state of which he was governor.

To be brief we will start with General Oglethorpe, the governor. Next to the governor we have the attorney-general, and next to the attorney-general we have the solicitor-general, and coming on down the line we have the courts, with their attorneys being a part and parcel of the court. The next office below a general being that of "colonel," and so by operation of law every person sworn in as an attorney-at-law is either a general or a colonel.

In order to show the military coloring in Georgia, the state is laid out in militia districts.

And each judicial system is fashioned after a military system with its governor-general, attorney-general, solicitor-general, and colonels; then it follows that a very large percentage of the power and responsibility of the courts is vested in the lawyers that practice in the courts.

In closing let me suggest this, if all the members of the court from the judge to the solicitor-general, and all the lawyers who are sworn officers of the courts, would line up with the judge and the solicitor-general and do a lot of team work together, I believe a long step would be taken forward in the administration of justice and in the enforcement of our laws and that soon our great country would be in deed and in truth "the home of the brave and the land of the free."

The Ordinary

So far as I know, Georgia is the only state in the Union that has an ordinary. The corresponding office in most other states is the county judge.

The ordinary has a jurisdiction all his own, and in addition he is the Judge of the Court of Ordinary. Many years ago his jurisdiction was so extensive and his duties so numerous that he was called the "Guardian of the County." But in late years Boards of County Commissioners have taken charge of all county matters. The work of the ordinary is now confined mostly to the administration of estates, guardianships for minors, pensioners, lunatics, marriage licenses, etc. The office is usually filled by mature men who have some knowledge of business and law. The ordinary is supposed to be able to advise widows and orphans, handle pension matters, and in all things make himself useful to those who happen to need his help. He needs to be a man with busy hands, a good head and a warm heart. We now have 161 ordinaries in Georgia —a noble band they are, working for little pay and trying to help and bless the needy and the helpless.

The ordinary has many hard problems to solve. The people who make much of the friction in life are the ones he has to deal with. Much of his time is devoted to an effort to disentangle the threads of human life—to satisfy and soothe the sorrows of human hearts. All sorts of people with all sorts of troubles come for his advice and help. The settlement of estates, the cry of orphan children, the lunatic, the crippled man, the pauper—old and sick, and all forsaken find the way to his office; in short, the needy of all classes who need a friend find their way to his office. The office of ordinary is not a moneyed office, but an office of real service. The ordinary is a man who can keep busy at something useful every day. He can give advice. He can write letters for those who can't write. He can examine records for those who can't pay him for his services; yes, and sometimes he can weep with those who weep. But I must stop my thinking along this line. The day is cold, but my heart is made warm by these thoughts, and so with a faith unfailing in the great "I Am" I take up my pen and begin a new year's work, leaning on the "Everlasting Arms."

Ward's Scrapbook, January, 1906.

Two Boys From Clinch

M. D. DICKERSON
Judge of Superior Courts of
Waycross District

W. C. LANKFORD
Now in Congress, 11th District of Georgia

About the year 1901 two boys came "from Clinch," but they are not boys any more. They soon fell in line with the progressive spirit of Coffee County and became among the best citizens of the county. One of these young men signed his name "Marcus D. Dickerson" and the other young man signed his name "W. C. Lankford." They came together from Clinch County to Coffee County and formed a partnership for the practice of law. When they wrote their names jointly they wrote it "Lankford and Dickerson, Attorneys-at-Law, Douglas, Georgia." These two young men came from two pioneer families from Clinch

County. They were strong in body and in mind. They had the training that a good farmer usually gives a good son. These boys were taught how to work. They knew how to build a rail fence and how to lay off a "straight row." They attended the "old field" schools of Clinch County, and that means they know how to "figure and spell." Such a foundation as that is a good foundation on which to build a successful life.

Marcus D. Dickerson was born in Clinch County, Georgia, February 12th, 1880. He attended school in Jasper, Florida, and Abbeville, Georgia. He graduated in June, 1901, from the State University. He came to Douglas in 1901 and formed a law partnership with W. C. Lankford. This partnership lasted for several years. He was appointed Solicitor of the City of Douglas in 1902, and was elected by the people in 1904 and served until 1908. In 1910 Mr. Dickerson was elected Solicitor-General of the Waycross Circuit, and in 1914 was re-elected without opposition. Mr. Dickerson married Miss Ethel Frink of Douglas, Georgia, January 18th, 1905. They have three children: David Dickerson, Will Dickerson, now a young member of the Douglas bar, and Miss Ethel Dickerson.

Mr. Dickerson was elected Judge of the Superior Courts of the Waycross Circuit in 1928. He is making an excellent judge.

W. C. Lankford was born in Clinch County, Georgia, in 1877, and came to Douglas in 1901 and formed a law partnership with Mr. Dickerson in the year 1901. Mr. Lankford was elected Judge of the City Court of Douglas, Georgia, and served for many years. He was regarded as a good judge, able, honorable, and upright.

In 1918 Mr. Lankford was elected to Congress from the 11th District and has been re-elected at every election since that time. Mr. Lankford came up from among the people and he continues to keep in touch with that great throng of citizens known as the "Common People." He studies their interests and knows their needs. He is always on the job in Washington, a roll call never finds him out of place.

October 17th, 1906, Mr. Lankford married Miss Mattie Lott of Douglas, Georgia, a daughter of Mr. and Mrs. J. S. Lott. They have three children: Chester, Cecil and Laura.

And thus ends another chapter in the lives of "Two Boys from Clinch." One is Judge of the Superior Courts, being the highest trial courts in Georgia, the other is in the Congress of the United States, the highest law-making body in the world.

Saw Mills and Lumber

In 1858, when the court house was built in Coffee County, in Douglas, there was not a steam saw mill in Coffee County. Old man Jack Ward had a saw mill run by water about the close of the war. The saw was an "upright" saw, and was a very slow process of getting lumber. The lumber out of which the court house was built was sawed up the Ocmulgee River and floated down to Barrows Bluff and then hauled out to Douglas with oxen. There were a great many little pepper mills in Coffee County run by water, but so far as I know they did not saw lumber. They were used entirely for grinding corn. The farmers all over the country would put a bushel of corn on a horse or mule and send it to the mill. It is said that an old farmer went to one of these mills in a big hurry for his meal. He waited and waited and the little mill went round and round. At last with a good deal of spirit he said to the miller, "Your little old mill grinds awful slow. I can eat the bread as fast as you grind it." Whereupon the miller pep up and said, "In how long could you do it?" The man waiting for his meal replied, " 'Til I perish to death."

About 1869, when railroads came through Coffee County, the big saw mills came with them. One of the largest mills in Coffee County was operated by The Southern Pine Company at Nicholls, Georgia. Another large mill was operated at Saginaw about two miles west of Nicholls. Another large mill was operated at Broxton, Georgia, by the Dorminey Price Lumber Company. After running at Broxton for many years the mill was moved to Douglas and remained here for several years.

About the year 1906 the Darby Lumber Company operated a mill at Douglas, Georgia. These mills were all of the large type and had tram roads reaching to the various sections of the country which brought logs to the mills.

When these large mills ceased to operate a lot of smaller mills were built all over the county. They had no tram roads and used mules to haul the logs.

Another large mill in Coffee County was operated at West Green, Georgia, and was known as The Garrant Lumber Company.

The lumber business in Coffee County was not a success. The cost production was high and the market most of the time was dull. It is estimated that less than ten per cent of the saw mills made a success. A large saw mill required something like fifty or a hundred mules, several miles of railroad iron for tram road purposes. Also two or three railroad engines were necessary to pull the trucks. In addition to this was the saw mill itself which required a large investment. When the wheels of the great mill were not turning, the expense of the investment with the mules and railroad equipment, all the laborers and high class mechanics was still going on. And as a consequence the mills could not make any money at the prices they had to sell lumber for.

I might say in passing that millions and millions in feet of the finest yellow pine lumber ever grown was wasted and scattered over the country and burned with fire. It was indeed a great destruction of the wealth of Coffee County.

At this writing, 1930, there are several small mills in Coffee County all cutting lumber of a very inferior grade, but it is the best to be had. New trees will grow in a few years large enough for lumber purposes, but the trees have no heart. They are sap and full of knots. We have lost the timber and will never see the like again.

The following saw mills were owned and operated at the times and places named:

Mill at Westonia, Georgia, operated by Jesse Weston in 1880. Capacity about 30,000 feet of lumber per day.

Saw mill owned and operated by Gray and Gatchel at Lelington, Georgia, in 1880, capacity 60,000 feet per day.

Mill owned and operated by B. B. Gray & Brother at Pine Bloom, Georgia, in 1881, capacity 40,000 feet per day.

The following saw mills have been operated in Douglas, Georgia:

The Ashley Price Lumber Company, capacity 50,000 feet per day.

The J. F. Darby Lumber Company, capacity 50,000 feet per day.

The Pat Darby Lumber Company, capacity 25,000 feet per day.

The Douglas Stave and Lumber Company, capacity 25,000 feet per day.

In addition to these saw mills there have been several small mills operated in many sections of the county since the year 1900.

The Pine Tree

By Eula Newbern Cottingham

THE PINES

"The groves were God's first temples, and in the presence of the tree one finds peace, quietude and inspiration."

Of the eighty well-established species of pines, one-half are American. Who knows and remembers forty different kinds of pines? No one, at least no one needs to. But what we do need to know is how to appreciate the full value of the Georgia long-leaf pine, for this pine taken from its large family ranks as second in value.

We must recognize our pine forest as the oldest, mightiest and sublimest thing living in Coffee County. The first comers to Coffee County found the lands densely forested. To make themselves houses, and to fit the land for agriculture, they had to cut down the forests. And, too, wood was needed for fuel, for furniture, for almost numberless things; and new uses constantly developed. In addition to all this, in every wooded region which has been settled, inestimable quantities of wood have been wasted—burned just to get it out of the way; such extravagance has been practiced until there is a sad lack of forest areas in many sections of our county.

The original forest of our county, if standing, would be of more value today than all our present industries and improvements combined.

This is a moderately accurate estimate of the value of one of Coffee's original forests. This forest contained four hundred and ninety acres; on this lot there are forty thousand long-leaf pines that should yield annually for four years nine hundred barrels of gum, from which tar, pitch, turpentine, and rosin are extracted. With the present low prices of turpentine averaging forty-five cents a gallon, and rosin eight dollars a barrel, the value of these by-products is enormous. Yet this great natural product was sold for an insignificant sum, for when the Carolina operators began looking in this direction (about 1890) for timber, the owners didn't realize its value. My father was among the first to sell; he didn't fully realize what he had done until the negroes came in with their box-axes, and as he expressed it, began to slaughter his beautiful trees. He wept, and for many days scarcely ate anything, but there was nothing to do but become hardened to the situation.

After the trees were boxed and drained of their gum, the great merchant saw mills began their operations. One of these were at McDonalds, one at Willacoochee, one at Hazlehurst, and later one of the largest in the county was placed at Broxton; and like great octopuses, they began reaching out their long tentacles in the form of tram roads, which gradually reached almost every timber tract in this county.

In times past the waste involved in gum gathering was serious, but improved methods have greatly reduced it and have put to good use many products which have formerly escaped in steam and smoke. In times past the waste in wood gathering was serious, but this too has been relieved, for it has been learned that every part of the pine is of value.

When I began this little story of the pine, I meant to name every product and every use of this valuable tree, but I find the task too stupendous. Suffice it to say that there are hundreds of ways in which pine lumber is utilized. It is being sent through nearly every vein of commerce to all parts of the world. Stumps and branches left in the forests after the woodsmen have done their work are now turned into slabs, laths, shingles, and bundles of faggots which are sold for fuel; stumps are taken to plants from which oil and many other products are extracted; and a wonderful invention has made it possible to extract ethyl-alcohol, the highest grade known, from sawdust. Pine needles are made into beautiful baskets and table mats. Pine cones make a most attractive interior decoration for winter.

I love to associate my child life with the huge pines that grew near my home. My childhood companion was a younger brother. Our playhouse was under the shadows of these pines; our playhouse carpet was the needles of straws which they gave us from their boughs. The shrubbery in our play-garden was green pine tops and sprigs of gallberry erected here and there. The fence around this attractive garden was made of pine cones. Never was the quiet of a cathedral like the solemn and sweet silence that filled all the wide spaces among those kindly trees; and in their towering tops the winter winds sing to me their wild harmonies on the wild winter nights. Nowadays it is the little cluster of pines outside my window in Ward Street Park that catches the winter winds and calls back to memory the music of those sweet and solemn nights—for the sounds of wind are solemn sounds, and the thoughts of youth are long, long thoughts.

We should have a love of patriotism for our pines. Seek to prevent the present generation from despoiling the future of that which is right. We do not wish to decree that no trees are to be cut, for the trees must be cut constantly to meet imperative needs. But there should be other forests growing up to take the place of those which are being cut down. There should be a campaign against forest fires, a frightfully destructive agency. It is estimated that since the settlement of the United States, fire has destroyed more timber than man. We know this is true in Coffee County. Every spring our forests are robbed of beauty and inestimable value by fires.

Not only has the pine a high commercial value, but it has its place in literature. It has been the theme of many beautiful verses.

Among them all none are more expressive than these two stanzas from the poem "The Pines."

"On the flanks of storm-gorged ridges our black
 battalions massed;
We surge in a host to the sullen coast, and we sing in
 the ocean blast;
From empire of sea to empire of snow we grip our
 empire fast.

Wind of the east, wind of the west, wandering to
 and fro,
Chant your songs in our topmost boughs that the sons
 of men may know,
The peerless pine was the first to come, and the pine
 will be the last to go.''

The pine tree is the largest money asset that Coffee County has ever had. For many years our farmers have given lots of attention to cotton as a money crop. Peanuts, velvet beans, sweet potatoes, etc., have figured largely in the prosperity of Coffee County. But the pine trees have produced more wealth than all these products combined.

Stills and Mills

When the pioneers came to Coffee County, they built their homes and all their houses out of pine logs. Their houses were covered with boards split from pine trees. They fenced their fields with rails split from pine trees. This condition of things remained till about 1870, when the first saw mill made its adventure into Coffee County. At that time Coffee County had the appearance of a great pine park. We had pine hills and pine valleys and pines everywhere.

The Brunswick and Albany Railroad traversed South Coffee County about 1870. The Macon and Brunswick traversed the northern part of Coffee County in 1869. Saw mills and turpentine stills sprang up rapidly all along these two railroads. In a few years nearly the whole of Coffee County was overrun with turpentine stills. The saw mills operated mainly along the railroads, but as the years went by tram roads were built throughout the county to haul logs to the saw mills and turpentine products to the railroads.

There never has been such a destruction of property as was wrought by the saw mills and turpentine operators. The trees which were too small for the saw mills were worked by turpentine operators as high as they could scrape the trees. When the mills and the stills had done their work of destruction, then came the cross tie getters and cut every tree big enough to make a cross tie. And now turpentine operators are boxing the saplings and blowing up the stumps. This period of time covered fifty or sixty years. The pine tree has made a great fight to continue to grow in this country, and in spite of hogs and fire, saw mills, and turpentine stills, we still have the pine trees with us. And we are beginning to realize that the pine will come back if we will only let it alone and give it some protection.

> "Woodman, spare that tree,
> Touch not a single bough,
> In youth it sheltered me
> And I'll protect it now."

Railsplitters

Before Coffee County was settled, Abraham Lincoln was a great railsplitter. He was not the best railsplitter, for in the Pioneer days of Coffee County we had many good railsplitters. We had no plank nor wire fence, and the only chance to clear land and make a field was to fence it in some way. The first fencing in Coffee County was done with pine poles. Two stakes were driven up in such a way as to make a cross near the top. The fence was built on these posts. A fence like that would keep out cows but would not keep out hogs. And so, as time advanced and it became necessary to enlarge their fields it was then that the "railsplitter" made his appearance. The only tools he needed was an ax and a maul, an iron wedge, half a dozen gluts and a good strong back. A good railsplitter could split a thousand rails in five days. He would generally begin his task on Monday morning and finish his thousand rails by Friday night. Soon after the Civil War, when the people raised a lot of cattle and sheep, it was necessary to have large pastures, and this required a lot of rails, and so there were a lot of men "professional railsplitters" as they could get a contract for splitting rails. The rails were usually ten and a half feet long and the usual heighth of the rail fence was ten or twelve rails high. Many of the fences were staked and ridered, that is to say, a stake rail was set on either side of the fence jam and crossed near the top and a good, heavy rail was laid on top of these stakes. Many of the farmers took a great pride in the looks of a rail fence. The worm rail, as they called it, was laid on the ground and then another rail was laid and then another one, and so on until the ground rail was laid as long as they wanted the fence to be. Then the fence was built up rail by rail, taking great care to make the corners just alike lined up by line and as straight as could be.

ORDINARIES
1. ELIJAH PAULK, 1881-1889.
2. ARCHIBALD MCLEAN, 1856-1861.
3. ELDER JOHN VICKERS, 1893-1895.
4. THOMAS YOUNG, 1877-1881-1897-1904.
5. WARREN P. WARD, 1904—now serving.

When a rail fence was well built it made a good, strong fence, and would remain for many years. There are a few of these old fences now, 1930. They have gone the way of all the earth. Wire fencing now is used extensively, and when properly erected makes a good fence.

I remember many of the old railsplitters in Coffee County soon after the war. Some white and some colored. Old Dock Ryals was a great railsplitter. John Smith was a good one. Several of the Lott negroes. Old Dick Bagley, and many others. They were in a class all to themselves. A man who had never learned how to split rails made a poor start when he first began. If he got a hundred rails a day he did well. Selecting the timber was one of the fine arts of railsplitting. The best rail was made as square as possible and made to contain as much heart as could be gotten out of the tree being used.

A Wheat and Flour Mill

Long before the Confederate War old man Jackson Ward operated a wheat and flour mill in Coffee County. The mill was situated on Otter Creek about ten miles north of Douglas. The mill was operated by water power. The flour was not very white but it was bolted and clean and made very good bread. In the olden days before the Civil War many of our people grew wheat from necessity, as flour was hard to get from the markets. Wheat has been grown in Coffee County since the war but it is said that the grain is soft and will not keep sound like it does in a northern climate. And so at this writing, 1930, no wheat of any consequence is grown in Coffee County.

A Carding Machine

One of the most unusual business enterprises operated in Coffee County, in the olden days, was a carding machine owned and operated by Mr. Joseph Kirkland. The power for running the machinery was furnished by an immense body of water known as the "Round About." It was an immense pond covering seven or eight lots of land.

At that day and time much of the cloth was woven in the country. Much of the cotton was picked by hand and also the carding and the spinning was done by hand. The cotton and wool was first carded into rolls and then put on a spinning wheel and spun into thread, and then the thread was woven into cloth. The carding was a big job and Mr. Kirkland operated a machine for carding wool and cotton. People from far and near had their carding and spinning done by his machinery.

Soon after the war the mill was burned down and thus ended the mill and its work. However, by this time thread could be bought from the stores and the mill ceased to be a necessity.

Snakes in Coffee County

We first met the snake in the "Garden of Eden." He is sometimes called a serpent. He came into the world with a lie in his mouth and until this day his mouth is dangerous. It may not be out of order to make a list of the snakes of Coffee County as they are known by the natives. The most numerous and best known snakes are: the Black Snake, the Coach Whip, the Water Moccasin, the Highland Moccasin, the Spreading Adder, the Rattle Snake Pilot, the Gopher Snake, the Chicken Snake, the Garter Snake, the King Snake. There are several varieties of Black Snakes and Moccasins. The big Cotton Mouth Stump Tail Moccasin is said to be poison and the bite of which will sometimes kill. The Ground Rattler is also poisonous. Its bite will sometimes kill. The only poisonous snakes that I know are those named, but there has never lived a human being but what is afraid of snakes and this has ever been the case since the old Devil turned himself into a snake.

Can Rattlesnakes Charm Birds and Animals?

It is thought by many natives of Coffee County that rattlesnakes have the power to charm or hypnotize birds and small animals such as they wish to eat. A great many incidents have been told me by responsible persons who have seen squirrels come down out of trees and go to the very mouth of the rattlesnake. Mr. Dan Lott, a well known citizen of Coffee County, a big farmer and a good business man, gives me a half dozen incidents or more where snakes have charmed birds and squirrels. But the most convincing case is where a cat in his yard was charmed by a rattlesnake. The cat was almost in striking distance of the snake when discovered and fully under the spell of the snake. Rattlesnakes have been so numerous in Coffee County and so many persons have been killed by them I thought it worth while to discuss this question of their power to charm animals and birds.

Rattlesnakes

The rattlesnake is the most deadly of all snakes. They are not so numerous as other snakes and have a quiet and peaceful disposition. They seldom get angry enough to fight unless they are imposed upon in some way. There are not so many rattlesnakes now as once. The coming in of turpentine stills and saw mills put a lot of workmen in the woods and they killed a lot of snakes. In an area of about half a mile square on the east side of the Seventeen-Mile Creek at the Reed Lake, sixteen rattlesnakes were killed in one season by turpentine hands. More than three hundred people have died in the United States within the last three years from snake bites. It appears that no sure cure has yet been discovered for the cure of the bite of the rattlesnake.

Probably two or three people die every year from snake bites in Coffee County. I know of but one person bitten by a rattlesnake to survive; that was Mr. Jasper Hand. One of the first men within my information who was killed by a rattlesnake was a man named Ellis; he lived up near the section of West Green, Georgia, and died before the Confederate War. Mr. Ellis lived on a farm. A storm came up and blew his fence down at night and he got up out of his bed and went around the field and was bitten by a snake in the dark and died. Mr. Thomas Paulk was bitten and died soon after the war. He lived near Lax and was hunting; a deer came along and he shot the deer and the explosion angered the snake and Mr. Paulk was bitten and died.

About 1870 a Mr. Guthrie was bitten at the home of John Lott, Sr. He lived three or four days but finally died. Another case was that of Mr. Vickers, son of Johnie Vickers, near Lax. He was bitten by a snake in the field. He lived only a few hours. Another very sad case was a little son of Mr. John Jowers. It seems that he was picking huckleberries in a swamp and fell off a log on the snake. He was bitten several times by the snake and died in a very short time.

Alligators

The word "alligator" is an old Spanish word (el lagarto) and means the lizard. During the war between the states and for many years after, alligators were numerous in Coffee County. There was one alligator or more in every pond in Coffee County. Alligators prefer to live in ponds with mud and stagnant water rather than live in streams with living water. They have caves generally under the root of some tree and coming almost to the top of the earth some ten or twelve feet from the mouth of the cave. The alligator does not always sleep with his head under the water but his house (the cave) is so constructed that he can keep his head above the water. Alligators do not grow very large in Coffee County. Six and seven feet long would be considered a large alligator. In the winter time alligators are dormant and do not travel nor eat. In the spring of the year when the weather gets warm they come out of their winter quarters and travel around for miles seeking for new quarters and perhaps for a new mate. When the alligator has selected his new residence he piles up a lot of leaves and brush about the root of some tree where the land is dry and lays eighteen or twenty eggs in the nest. Many of their nests are two or three feet high and three or four feet through. In due time the warm sunshine hatches the little gators and they start life in a mud hole.

The alligator is not so vicious as you perhaps have heard he is. I have never known an alligator to catch a man in Coffee County. The worse crime that he ever commits is to kill a hog.

As time went on there was a good market for alligator hides and that put a premium upon the head of every alligator. Thousands of them were killed for their hides. At this time, 1930, there are very few alligators in Coffee County. There are a few in the large streams and rivers. Alligators will fight for their young and so far as I have ever heard they are not dangerous except in defense of their young.

Catching Fish

When the war ended in 1865, the streams of Coffee County were full of fish. In the small streams we had cats, perch and pike in abundance. The larger streams had Jack (pickerel), trout (bass), cats and all the larger variety of perch. Fish multiply rapidly. The common fish in the streams of Coffee County grow to their normal size in about two years.

In the olden days people caught all the fish they needed with hook and line. But as the population increased they could not satisfy their greed and wanted all the fish in sight. When the streams got low in the summer time the fish were poisoned with walnut leaves, devil shoe strings and lime. But this did not satisfy their greed and so they began to use dynamite and thousands of fish were destroyed and wasted and the streams rendered useless for fish for many years. It became necessary to pass drastic laws to protect fish and the streams where they raise.

It is worthy of note that when the Creek Indians occupied this territory they did not destroy the fish and game but only used what they needed. All honor to the Red Men for taking care of this country for the White Man. It is a shame that the White Man has not taken as good care of the fish and game as the Indians did.

The game law at this writing, 1930, permits fishing with hook and line and it is to be hoped that all those who have an interest in preserving our fish will line up with the hook and line fishers and put the others out of business.

Some of the lakes on the Seventeen-Mile Creek beginning at the Isiah Lake and coming on south are as follows: Reed Lake at the bridge, the Ward Lake, the Black Lake, Turkey Lake, Flat Lake, Ford Lake, Garr Lake and the Belle Lake.

These are well-known lakes on this stream and known to all the old-time fishermen. Some of these lakes have nicknames. There is one lake called the "Mugger Lake," named for old man Billy Ward's wife. Another lake is big John Ward's smokehouse. He said he never failed to get a mess of fish at that place.

Wild Turkeys

During the Civil War fish and game of all kinds increased rapidly. This was due to the fact that nearly all the men were away from home, and there was but little hunting and fishing done. Then the guns were very poor and they could not be loaded rapidly and so the game had a chance to increase.

From 1865 to about 1880 there was plenty of game in Coffee County. The woods were full of big fox squirrels and there were plenty of deer and a good many wild turkeys. Wild turkeys are very hard to shoot. They are wild and will leave a section of the country where they use when they find out that they are hunted. They are perhaps the wildest of all the game. They use around big swamps and most always roost over deep water. One of the favorite ways of shooting turkeys is to go in their locality where they use late in the evening and hear them fly up to roost. Hunters call this "roosting turkeys." A turkey flying up to roost can be heard for half a mile and further if the wind is right. Having located the roost of the turkeys, the hunter goes near the roost next morning before daylight and as daylight comes he seeks to find the turkey and then creeps up close enough to get a shot. It often happens that the turkeys are roosting on some big cyprus tree out in the water and then the hunter does not get his turkey.

Another method used by hunters is to use a yelp. This is usually made by putting a stick through a wooden match box and scraping on a piece of slate; by opening and closing the hand the tone of the yelp can be changed to high and low like the yelp of the turkey. The hunter goes into the neighborhood where turkeys are supposed to use and about the coming of daylight he begins to yelp. The yelp is supposed to be the call of a turkey hen, to which call the gobbler answers with a "gobble, gobble." Soon the gobbler will seek the hen. If he is very far away he will fly to the place where the hen is located, and if he is near he will slip up to the place through the swamp and trees. The hunter has to be on the alert to find the turkey before the turkey sees him for when the gobbler sees the hunter he says "put, put," and gets away from there.

Another mode of catching turkeys which was used before the war when turkeys were plentiful, was to build a rail pen some three or four feet high and dig a hole under it plenty big for a turkey to pass through and then scatter corn in the pen, also outside the pen near the hole through which the turkey is supposed to pass. When the turkey goes through the hole, getting the corn as he goes through, he finds himself in a pen, and strange to say he cannot find the way out. He looks up all the time for a way to escape and never looks down. We have known as many as seven turkeys to be caught in one pen.

Before the war and during the war there were great flocks of turkeys on the Satilla River, the Ocmulgee River and the Seventeen-Mile Creek, and in fact there were plenty turkeys near all the large streams. An old hunter told me the other day that he has seen as many as twenty-five turkeys in one drove.

It is said that the flavor of the wild turkey is much better than the tame turkey, but in my opinion it depends upon whom is eating the turkey. To my taste the wild turkey has a strong, wild taste, and there is much more dark meat in a wild turkey than there is in a tame turkey.

Turkeys make their nests in the swamps and lay fifteen and twenty eggs. If the eggs are hatched under a hen or a tame turkey hen, the little turkeys will have a wild disposition and sometimes when they get scared around the farm they will rise and fly a mile and further.

There are very few wild turkeys in Coffee County now, 1930. There are too many hunters and hunters' dogs and high-powered guns.

Killing Deer

Speaking of the new game law reminds me that Coffee County had some game and some good hunters in the long ago. Old man Elijah Youngblood killed 999 deer in his time and longed to kill one more to make it a thousand. Big John Ward, "Uncle Jack's John," who is yet living, killed 891, "That he got, as he calls it, when telling the number killed."

In addition to these hunters, there are many others who have done some good little stunts in hunting. "Little Mark Lott," "Aunt Minty's Mark," killed three deer at one shot. It happened on this wise. Mark was sent to the woods to hunt a beef; while beating around the bush he spied a door standing at the root of a tree in a pond near by. He fired, and when the smoke cleared away there was a kicking of legs. Mark went to see how many legs the deer had and, lo and behold, he had killed three deer instead of one. The other two were lying at the root of the tree concealed by some huckleberry bushes.

Do not be surprised when you are told that this scribe killed two deer at one shot. He did it this way. Early one morning he went over to Otter Creek, a little stream near his home, seven miles east of Douglas, when he discovered several deer feeding on the hillside. He dropped to his knees and crawled up near to them and hid behind a tree. He prepared his gun to shoot and looked out from behind the tree. The deer had found him out and were all standing looking his way. One was looking straight at him. About thirty feet behind this one, was another one, looking at him. He fired and got them both. At breakfast he had two fine deer hanging up before the smokehouse door.

To further illustrate marksmanship, I will tell you how he killed another deer. He and Tommie Dent were out hunting and as the dog entered the little brushy head where Mr. M. Kight lives, out popped two deer, one about ten feet behind the other. He shot at the head one and killed the hindmost one.

During the year 1876 deer was plentiful in Coffee County. There was a drove of 13 which used in a string of ponds out between the old Dunk Douglas place and the old Dan Lott place. When the woods in the Ocmulgee River section filled up with saw mills and turpentine stills the deer left and came to Coffee County wild woods.

Along with many other friends of the long ago is passing the deer, turkey, fox, squirrel, doves and pine trees.

I love the new civilization in Coffee County, her thrift and enterprise, but when I think of its good old times, "I get mighty lonesome."

A Stormy Night on the Seventeen-Mile Creek

It was summer time on the Hargraves farm. The time was three o'clock in the afternoon, the hottest part of a hot day in Wiregrass Georgia. "Old Lazy Lawrence" was dancing on the fences and in the fields. Not a breeze was blowing; all vegetation was withered. Both man and beast were needing rain. It was hot, oh, so hot, and dry, so dry. The old dog was panting with his tongue out. He dug a hole in the dirt, hunting a cooler spot. The chickens fluttered in the sand and everything seemed to join in the pant for fresh air. Everything was suffering from the awful heat.

—*Courtesy John L. Herring.*

And the owl he say, "I cook for myself, who cooks for you all?"

Later in the afternoon, Mr. Hargraves called to Hen, his right-hand man and once his trusted slave, and said, "This awful heat means thunder and rain. It may storm before midnight. Now is a good time to go to the creek and "roost" some turkeys and catch some fish. Get the bullet moulds and mould some bullets.

Grease "Old Long Tom," fill the powder horn, put a new flint in the lock, polish the steel, and get a sack of corn to feed the hogs."

When they reached the creek Uncle Abe told Hen to get some wood and build a little fire at the lake and he would go around the bay and feed his hogs and "roost" the turkeys. Just at dark, Uncle Abe reached the lake and found Hen with a fire. Hen told him that he never heard so much fuss in all his life. The bull frogs, tree frogs, and "Katydids" and all sorts of crickets all seemed to be on dress parade and were singing and making all sorts of music. When I started to make my fire, Hen said, a Whippoorwill sung out, "stick-fire the-whiteoak." I wondered what he meant. About that time, another one from over the lake says, "stick-fire, the red oak." I said go away from you, "you bird of ill omen." I thought he might be dat bird what Mr. John read us about, what sat on the "Busted Palace" and said "Nevermore, Nevermore." About good dark, the old 'gater down at the mill lake, he ups and bellers like something bad was about to happen down there. But them plegged owls nearly run me crazy. One at the upper end of the lake would say, "I cook for myself, who cooks for you-o-o-oo all?" Then one at the lower end of the lake would answer back, "Tom Shickle-shackle and the devil knows who-o-o-oo all."

"Hen, you go down the lake to the 'cat hole' and I will try my luck here by this gum stump." Pretty soon Hen yelled out, "Run here, Mars Abe, I have got a big snake on my hook and can't get him off. He look like the snake that bit Adam and Eve." "That is not a snake," said Mr. Hargraves; "that is an eel and he is good to eat, go right on with your fishing." Pretty soon Hen gave another yell and said, "run here, Mars Abe, quick, I got a whale on my hook." "That is not a whale Hen, it is a large black fish." "My Lord, I thought it was the whale that eat Jonah," said Hen.

"Mars Abe, I want to go home, I'm sick of this hunting and fishing. I am afraid we will get cotch in a storm. I been afraid something bad was going to happen to us down here for before we left home, the rooster crowed in the house—bad sign—and last night the screech owl sot on the gate post, something bad bound to happen." "Hen, I do not believe in signs, go on with your fishing." "Old Peter did not believe in signs either, until he heard dat rooster crow."

In the meantime, the thunder roared deeper, louder, and closer. Flash after flash of lightning lighted up the lake and the swamp around and about. The trees cast shadows on the water like strange animals, hobgoblins, witches, and everything to make a man afraid. Pretty soon Uncle Abe heard a splash in the water, a break of limbs and brushes, and then a voice from Hen, something like this: "My Goade, Mars Abe, look at this thing. How many legs has the devil got?" "Plenty of legs to get you." "Mars Abe, look at dat thing, it sho must be the devil." "No, Hen, this is not the devil, it is a large Snapping Turtle." "Maybe so, but it sho looks like Snappen devil to me."

By this time the awful thunder clouds had covered the heavens above, shut out moon and stars and it was dark as Egypt, till flashes of lightning came and made everything seem more and more horrible. "Mars Abe, I am going home, I am. Cold streaks are running up and down my back. I don't want any fish, I am going home.''

Soon they were on their way home, and soon the rain began to pour. They hurried to an old fodder house at the old Kemp place and got into it just in time to save themselves from one of the most fearful thunder and rain storms that was ever seen in this country. The rain poured all night long. The earth seemed to quiver from the awful jars of the thunder. There was plenty of fodder in the old house. It was dry and made a good summer bed. They were surrounded with such things as would make them think of the end of the world, and the final judgment. Uncle Abe told Hen many of the secrets of his life; told him where he wanted to be buried and how he wanted to be put away. He gave him the plans for his funeral all in detail.

At last Hen talked out, got quiet and went to sleep, but ever and anon he would say over and over again in his sleep: ''Rooster crowed in the house, screech owl set out the gate.''

They spent the night in the old fodder house, got home for breakfast next morning sans fish, sans turkeys and sans everything.

Camp Meetings

Georgia is a camp meeting state and all the history of camp meetings has not been written. They come and go. Dooly County and Liberty County have camp meetings in operation and there may be others as far as I know. Also Tatnall County.

The Gaskin Springs camp meeting was started about 1895. Gaskin Springs is situated about two miles east of Douglas on the east side of the Seventeen-Mile Creek.

REV. GREEN TAYLOR

A distinguished camp meeting preacher before the war.

Mr. Joel Gaskin donated four acres of land to certain trustees named in the deed with the expressed provision that the said land was to be used as camp meeting purposes. The lands to revert to the donor when it ceased to be used for camp meeting purposes. This deed carried with it the right to use the water from Gaskin Springs for the camp meetings. A large pavillion was built near the spring. The pavillion would seat several hundred people. A bridge was built across the Seventeen-Mile Creek for pedestrians between Douglas and the Springs. Many families from Douglas, Broxton, and people from surrounding counties built houses, where their families moved and kept open house during the camp meeting times for ten days once a year. The camp meeting was under the supervision of the Methodist Church. The presiding elder of the Douglas church had charge of the camp grounds and selected the preachers. However, ministers of all denominations were invited to preach. Several services would be held each day. The first service was held at sunrise. The second service was held at eleven o'clock. The third service was held at 3 P. M., the last service was held at 8 P. M. Much attention was given to the singing of many beautiful gospel songs. Many special services were held for children. Sundown prayer meetings were held in front of the various cottages. All the tenters would gather up and go around together. Service would be held in front of each cottage until all the cottages were visited.

It was the purpose of the camp meeting management to have the best Gospel preachers in the country. When the weather was good people would come from other counties to attend the camp meetings. In old days the camp served a good purpose. The people and the churches were so sparsely settled that they had not much chance to attend church and the camp meeting was intended to furnish preaching to these scattered communities. But as the years went by the need for the camp meeting largely disappeared. It developed into a mere social gathering where people went to see their friends and have an outing for two or three days. Some of these old-time camp meeting preachers were very unique. M. C. Austin, for instance, on one occasion at Gaskin Springs was preaching on "Family Training" and the home life of the people. His remarks were directed mainly to that class of men who run around at night. He says you men know when Coffee County was the best sheep county in the state, that men had trouble with dogs killing their sheep. A sheep-killing dog is one of the most despised things in all the world and they are the hardest things to catch in killing the sheep. They know how to cover up their sins, but at last the preacher said, "The way to locate a sheep-killing dog was to look at his teeth; if there was wool in his teeth the evidence was satisfactory and the dog was killed." The preacher having laid the foundation for his argument then raised his hand high above his head and declared, "It is quite certain that some of you men have wool in your teeth."

In course of the camp meeting services, many special meetings were held. Some for children, some for fathers and mothers, and some for old people. All the special meetings were very interesting. I must tell you about the meeting for old men held one Sunday afternoon at the Gaskin Camp Meeting Tabernacle. A large group of old men seated themselves around the rostrum and many of them sat on the "Mourners Bench." One old brother read a scripture and several old-time hymns were sung and then the meeting thrown open for talks. Many good talks were made, but I shall tell you only about one which impressed me more than all the others. A very old man who had lived a Godly life and who was ripe for the tomb made a talk like this, as near as I can remember: "My brethren, the years of my life are more than three score years and ten. I have known what it was to be young and now I know what it is to be old. Many people discount old age and make light remarks about old age, like this: 'Old age is honorable,' yes, he said, 'Old age is honorable,' and it is more than that. It is God's plan for some of us to grow old. When a man gets as old as I am it shows that he has been wonderfully blessed by God. There is just one way to keep from getting old and that way is to die while you are young. I prefer living to be old rather than dying young. The secret of being old and being happy is to be reconciled to God's will about these things. God wants some of us to be old. He has a use for old men and women, if we will only realize that we are old and be reconciled to God's will and find our places in the world as old men and women and then try and fill the place that God has planned for ourselves. The reason that so many old men are grouchy and dissatisfied with life is because they are not willing for God's will to be done about their lives. They want to stay young and God wants them old, but when an old man trys to play young he makes himself silly and the laughing stock of sensible people. I am willing to be as old as God wants me to be and I am trying to find my place as an old man and to do God's will more perfectly in this world. I am not concerned about how much longer I live nor how soon I die, I am leaving all this in the hands of my Lord. He knows what is best and I am His."

"An old grouchy man once wrote some lines like this:

'The world turns over and over,
And the sun sinks into the sea;
And whether I live or die,
No one cares for me.'

"My brethren, these are not my sentiments and I do not think they are the sentiments of any Godly old people. I think the poem should be changed to something like this:

> 'The world turns over and over,
> And the sun sinks into the sea;
> And whether I live or die,
> It all looks good to me.'

"With an unfailing faith in Jesus Christ and this philosophy of life every old person could be happy and content and count it all a joy to be able to live a long and useful life."

The Language of the Birds

It is surprising how little we know about the birds who sing and play about us every day. They have a language all their own, and if you are familiar with the birds in Coffee County, you will know one when he speaks. The best known singer among all the birds, perhaps, is the Mocking Bird. He sings day and night sometimes, and there is no bird that can produce as many notes as the Mocking Bird. The Brown Thrush comes next. He sings beautifully, but does not sing very much. His place to sing is to perch himself upon the top most bough of some tree. The Robin is a good singer but they sing very seldom and we find many people who grew up on the farm who have never heard a Robin sing. The Robin is a very sweet singer but his songs are short and far between. Once upon a time just about sunrise a Robin, sitting on the highest limb of a dead pine tree in front of our home, sat there and sang for an hour. His notes were beautiful, but he sang in a sweet, subdued tone.

Every boy knows the language of a Bob White. They seem to say, "Old Bob White, are your peas most ripe?"

The field lark who sneaks around your fields in the early spring, pulls up your corn, will fly upon the fence or perch himself in some nearby tree and sing, "I have been here three years," and he means to say that he will stay just as long as ever he pleases.

Chickens also have a language of their own. The old hen will put on her best looks, walk up beside of her old man and say, "I have to do this and I have to do that, and I have to go barefooted." The dear old man puts on a surprised look and answers with all the dignity that he commands, "If I can't get a shoe to fit your foot, to fit your foot, how can I help it."

The Whip-poor-will says, "Stick fire to the white oak." And so with all the birds. They sing and talk.

Birds, Fishes and Fowls

No history of any country would be complete without its birds, fishes, and fowls. In naming the birds, fishes and fowls in Coffee County, I shall name only those generally known by the people of Coffee County.

Turtledove, Partridge, Lark, Bluebird, Tomtit, Bull Bat, Whip-poor-will, Buzzards, Eagle, Kingfisher, Catbird, Ricebirds, Jay Birds, Blackbirds, Sapsucker, many varieties of Sparrows, Humming Bird, Mocking Bird, Crow, Hawks—many varieties, Carrion Crow, Killdeer, Kingbird, Woodpecker, Redbird, Robin, Thrush, Swallows, Ducks, Snipe, Owls, Chick-a-dees, English Sparrows.

Fish

Fresh-water Trout, Mud Cat, War-mouth Perch, Red-eyed Perch and others, Red-belly Perch, Stump Knocker, Jack, Pike, Perch—several varieties, Mud Fish.

Fowls

Chickens, Cranes, Turkeys, Ducks and others, Geese, Guinea.

Trees

By Mrs. Lon Dickey

To think of the trees of Coffee County, as I knew them from about 1885 to 1900, is to bring a vision of an almost unbroken forest of long leaf yellow pine, boxed and scraped for turpentining, in some instances left untouched in their beauty and natural state. Long, straight roads led through them, and their cool, breezy aisles were filled with the music of the swaying boughs and the songs of wild birds flitting among them.

Besides the wealth in naval stores which it brought to the "Many Captains of Industry," these trees have provided houses and storehouses for its populace, fences for their flocks, bridges over the ever flowing, turbulent streams, and innumerable other things.

The Tree Family

There were many other species of the pine besides the long leaf, among them the short leaf, the pitch pine, the loblolly or low-field pines, and a dear little short leaf Christmas tree pine in the swamps and lowlands that closely resembled the celebrated spruce pine of northern climates.

Classed with these might also be the red cedar which might easily have been grown in commercial quantities, being the same that is used for making pencils, moth-proof chests, linen closets, and for ornamental posts and many purposes. There was also the white cedar, or arbor vitae, useful for many things, which was only for hedge and ornamental purposes.

The great bald cypress, with its creeping, angular knees, furnished a soft wood that has worked into shingles, barrel staves, fence posts, door panels, and construction of many types.

The "bay" in front of our home was not a body of water, but a thicket of evergreen trees with their great gray trunks and their glossy leaves lined underneath with silver that glistened in the sun when the wind stirred them. They bore fragrant white blossoms in summer, and in early spring the rose bays blossomed profusely making a perfect mass of pink blooms around the borders of the swamp.

The Sturdy Oak

I shall carry to my grave visions of sandy hillsides covered with great scarlet oaks hung with gray Spanish moss. In the spring they showed innumerable shades of green, tan and brown in their budding leaves and silky catkins or tassels. These colors intermingled with the green of the holly and cedar and the starry gleam of white blossoming dogwood, the misty rose and lavender of wild crabapple and Judas tree bloom, and the crimson of budding maple, made a scene to rest tired eyes and lift one's spirit.

But autumn changed these great oaks into one flaming forest after a long summer of dark, glossy green coolness, then laid a thick carpet of brown for the short cool winter. This carpet was swept away by the blustery March winds.

Then there were many species of useful trees in the oak family, tanbark, shingle oak, post oak, iron oak, pin oak, willow oak, and great barren oaks (the negroes called them "bar'n oaks," and I thought for many years that barns were made of them). Many of these oaks bore acorns which fattened the hogs and fed the squirrels, deer, birds, and other wild life.

The Basket Oak

The sweetest in my memory are the basket oaks, or white oaks. Splits were peeled from these and woven into baskets for cotton, laundry, and some of fancier type were painted for parlor wood containers and to hold magazines.

The little babies were often cradled in long baskets made of these, and often the little colored babies of former slaves were suspended in these from the drooping limbs of great water oaks to the edge of the fields, and as parents reached the ends of the rows they would set them swinging and croon their unforgettable songs to them as they hoed away, or resumed their cotton picking, corn gathering, or potato digging.

Many of these great old water oaks still stand, their great trunks dotted with pale green lichens and draped about with soft grey-green Spanish moss, and with wild birds flitting among their decaying branches. I would think that one of them might be cut down to within a few feet of the ground and covered with mortar or cement and some fitting memorial be written on it for the faithful old slaves who rest unnoticed in the old neglected cemeteries nearby.

Other Tree Families

The woods of my plantation home were thick with giant hickories bearing various sizes of nuts, one shaped like a top, another round and large, others small and sweet.

The wood of these hickory trees was fashioned into axe handles and parts for many useful farm implements, made into mauls, chairs, and many other things.

Great tree trunks of some kind, I think poplar, were fashioned into watering troughs for the stock, salting troughs for meat, feed troughs for the stables, and laundry troughs for the "wash house."

There was a shop with a bellows we loved to watch where various things were made, including tubs for sugar, lard, vats for syrup, there being negroes specially trained for this service, which passed out almost too early for me to remember, my most vivid recollection being of a casket made for a colored person.

The Black Walnut

We had many large black walnut trees, and though we used these only for their shade and the delicious black walnut meat for cakes, candies, and salted nuts, I see them being planted over vast acres now to be used for furniture, gun stocks, airplane propellers, and many important things.

Other trees of value which were purely ornamental with us, or handed down as a natural heritage, were great magnolias with their massive, fragrant white blossoms and pods of red seeds; sycamore with gleaming white trunks; tupelos with yellow tulip-like blossoms in spring and gold leaves in autumn; black gum, ash, holly, elm, beech, alder, cottonwood, hackberries, locust, maple, persimmon, false mulberry, poplar, swamp bay, willow, chinaberry, sourwood, thorntree, and evergreen or cherry laurel.

The woods of many of these are being used for making tennis racquets, golf sticks, baseball bats,

Pullman car interiors, automobile bodies, furniture, and many other things.

Our Chewing Gums

A grove of sweet gum trees furnished our gum supply. We scarred the great old trunks and with a knife or pointed instrument transferred the white syrup to our mouths, where it became a wad of gum.

And, although we "snitched" it from each other and fought for its possession, our old colored mammy never interfered and I never knew a case of "hydrophobie" or any other dreaded disease to be transmitted through the exchange.

These sweet gum trees were particularly beautiful in autumn, being a deep blood-red, and I learn that its wood is now used for "satin walnut" in veneering furniture, and for paving blocks, and many other things.

The Medicine Trees

A visitor on these grounds not long since told me that he counted thirty-six different varieties of trees in one acre and a quarter, so it is impossible to name them all, but I must touch on the "medicine trees."

The cherry trees yielded their bark for many medicinal uses; the root of the sassafras was much sought after in the spring, its delicious tea being one of my sweetest springtime memories, and creamy flowers in early spring were only surpassed in beauty by its leaves in autumn, being a mixture of gold, crimson and bronze set off with clusters of bright red berries.

The famous "black drink" handed down from the Indians was made from the yaupon tree, or cassena berry, called now swamp holly. This is much used for decorative purposes at Christmas times, its wealth of bright red berries making it particularly appropriate. Thus is "Liex vomitoria," and the drink is an emetic.

A great many of these great old trees bore great bunches of mistletoe, which was also popular in decoration.

Many pecans have been planted in place of the trees which stood in this old grove, and their flavor is said to be a superior one owing, it is thought, to their proximity to the great hickories and walnuts; in fact, the pecan limbs have been grafted into the trunks of the hickories in many instances.

Of the future of these I take the liberty of quoting Honorable Chase S. Osborn, former Governor of Michigan, whose winter home is at Poulan, about fifty miles away.

Value of Pecan Trees

Says Governor Osborn in this treasured sketch, "Why I Think Georgia is Perfect," published in a state paper:

"The value of the pecan as a nut-producing tree is appreciated, but its arboreal value is as yet little valued. Some day pecan trees will be planted here for their timber. A member of the hicoria family, the wood of the pecan is as hard as you can wish. Later we will utilize pecan tree timber. Then, there is another value attached to pecan trees. Do you wonder why South Georgia is so healthful, why your towns have so remarkably low a death rate? May it not be due to the fact that pecan trees, which abound here in millions consume carbon dioxide in unusually great quantities, giving forth again purest oxygen? Does that sound like a wild theory? Maybe, but I do not doubt that there is truth to it."

Other Values in Trees

Then there is the value of the last leaf crop to the building up of the soil. I recall an instance of some forty years ago at my plantation home. A visitor from the southwest remarked to my father that he did not realize the wealth that lay in the century of leaf-mold

SHERIFFS
1. W. M. TANNER, 1916-1928.
2. R. C. RELIHAN, 1928—now serving.
3. WILLIAM TANNER, 1889-1893-1895-1901.
4. W. W. SOUTHERLAND, 1901-1906.

packed away under the trees in the Ocmulgee River swamp, using them as fertilizer as florists and orchardists of other localities did.

Acting on the suggestion, my father sent wagons into the swamp and brought out several loads of this leaf-mold and had it worked into the vegetable garden. Then the fun began.

A certain wag on the place declared that the watermelon vines tore off all its young melons running around so fast and that the Irish potatoes played hop-scotch with each other after crowding themselves out of the ground. In truth, I never saw such vegetables and things as that ground produced, and fruit trees around where some of it was spread grew amazingly ahead of others.

It was my father's plan to follow the use of this extensively, but alas, after a rigorous winter in Atlanta, where he represented the 5th district as Senator, 1890-91, fell ill and was unable to carry out his plan.

A Bee Tree

My mind goes back to a spring morning when we enjoyed a bee tree cutting on our place. It was discovered by Mr. Duncan McLean who thereby shared its wealth of golden honey with our family, and there were a number of invited guests outside.

This was a great hollow pine tree which the bees had filled with honey known as the gall berry blossoms type. This gall berry bush is a species of the holly family, known as black, and its blossom yields a superior quality of honey, along with the bloom of the tyty bushes.

The pine was great and tall, and it required a lot of cutting before it gave up the ghost and crashed through the blossoming wild shrubbery, carrying many other small trees along with it. But the delightful flavor of the honey was worth all of them.

Down to Darien

When my father needed money, he took a group of colored farm hands into the river swamp for a number of successive days, then began preparation for drifting the great rafts of yellow pine logs to Darien to be turned into money. The negroes called it "Dairy Ann," and it was one of the burning desires of my young life to see that queer port of which they talked after their semi-annual excursion there with these rafts.

We sat on the river bank and watched them raft the great logs, while back in the great old kitchen were smells that I know I shall never enjoy again, home-made light bread, potato pone, parching green coffee, barbecuing pork and other meats, baking ginger bread and other things to eat on the journey.

Occasionally a steamboat passed by, fanning the drooping branches of the pale green sand bar willows, and stopping the work of pinning together the great logs as they rode up and down with the disturbed mud-yellow waters.

The Flowering Trees

After they had waved us good-bye and the last raft had disappeared around the bend, we went back to the house along a road lined with beautiful flowering locusts, wild plum trees, silky white tassels of the fringe tree, better known as "grandfather's beard," and festoons of vines covered with red trumpet blossoms.

In the old sand yard were great lagerstroemia trees, now called crape myrtle, with their light brown shining trunks and great panicles of crinkled and ruffled pink bloom, the accacies, the cape jasmine or gardenia with its fragrant waxen white bloom, the English hawthorn with its wealth of snowy white blossoms in spring and red haws in autumn, the mock orange or syringa, and many others dear to the heart of Coffee County home makers.

Know the Trees

Julia Ellen Rogers, who has compiled a wonderful tree guide, the study of which has helped me to describe many of the trees in this little sketch, prefaces one of her books with this:

"It is natural that trees, which are greatest in all the plant kingdom, should inspire in us the highest admiration. Their terms of life so far outrun the puny human span! They stand so high, and spread so high, and spread so far their sheltering arms! We bless them for the gifts they bring to supply our bodily needs, and for their beauty, which feeds our souls.

"To love trees intelligently we must learn to know them. We must be able to call them name by name, whenever and wherever we meet them. This is fundamental to any friendship. It is a fund of knowledge that starts with little, but grows more rapidly year by year."

Fast Becoming a Myth

There are many beautiful flowering trees and shrubs in Coffee County not named in this little sketch, and there are many that are of inestimable value to the industrial world which, if planted and cared for would bring wealth to land owners and prosperity to the county.

There are vast areas in this large county from which the trees have been taken, and if steps are not taken to protect the wild life, especially the wild birds that save them from extermination by destroying the insects and worms that infest them, many of these trees are in danger of becoming only a memory or a myth.

The wild birds scatter the seeds and have planted, no doubt, many of these beautiful forests as well as the wild flowers from which come the fine honey for which the county is noted. Do they not deserve our protection and our consideration? They are our natural heritage, ours to study, love, and protect, and to perpetuate. Birds and trees, "Useless each without the other."

A Member of the Confederate Cabinet

It is not generally known that at the same time Jefferson Davis was captured in Irwin County, May 10th, 1865, that John C. Breckinridge, a member of his cabinet spent a week at the home of Honorable Seaborn Hall near Graham, Georgia. When the Confederate Government went to pieces, a last cabinet meeting was held at Washington, Georgia. It was supposed that the Federal Government would make a desperate effort to capture President Davis and all his cabinet. And the cabinet was just as determined not to be captured. And so the members of the cabinet separated and each one looked out for himself. President Davis came by Dublin, Georgia, and on down to Irwinville where he was captured. General Breckinridge, leaving Washington, Georgia, came south and crossed the Altamaha River at Town Bluff and made his way to the home of Honorable Seaborn Hall in Appling County. Mr. Hall was well known all over South Georgia and had a wide reputation for hospitality.

It was thought by many that President Davis was going to Alabama to join the Confederate forces there, but if so, he never reached his destination. When the news of the capture of Mr. Davis reached Mr. Hall and Mr. Breckinridge, Mr. Breckinridge decided that he would leave the United States. So Mr. Hall, after entertaining him in great fashion for a week or more, took his distinguished guest in a buggy and went to Florida where he boarded a steamer and made good his escape. The entire trip was made by riding at night and hiding out at day. When the parting time came General Breckinridge was so overwhelmed with gratitude to Mr. Hall that he presented him his handsome gold watch as a token of his friendship and esteem. He also gave him a gold-trimmed saddle. Judge Elisha Graham of Baxley and McRae, Georgia, fell heir to the watch and wore it as long as he lived. It is supposed that Mr. Hall and General Breckinridge passed through Coffee County down through Ware County at old Waresboro and on to Florida.

It is also said that General Beauregard passed through this state on his way west. And it is also said that General Bragg passed through Coffee County about the same time that Jefferson Davis was captured, and gave some man at the court house in Douglas a five-dollar gold piece. And so it is that some of the great and some of the mighty passed through Coffee County in the most tragic history of the state.

The Negro Race

The negro race in Coffee County gave us but little trouble during slavery time, and they have made very good citizens since they got their freedom. Many of the slaves remained with their masters after they were freed. The Lott negroes, the Paulk negroes, the Ward negroes, the Vickers negroes, the Hargraves negroes, the Ashleys negroes and many other families of old negroes hung around the homes for their old masters and kept them as long as they lived. In 1860 the population of Coffee County was: whites 2206, colored 673. In 1870, ten years later, which covered the Civil War period, the whites 2614, the colored 678.

We would judge from this that Coffee County had less than a thousand slaves in it. The appraisement of the estate of Nathaniel Ashley shows that he owned 97 slaves, which were valued at $42,550. A list of their names and ages appears in Minute Book A in the office of the Ordinary of Coffee County. Several of these old negroes are living yet. The date of this appraisement was January 4, 1856. At that time old Ambrose Harris was sixteen years and Wade Harris was thirteen years of age. Wade Harris is still living, 1930.

Too much credit cannot be given to these old-time slave negroes who remained at home during the Civil War and helped to carry on the work of the country. There are very few instances where they were not true and faithful to their masters. The training the negroes received while they were slaves has been a great blessing to them since they were free. They learned how to work. Many of them were good carpenters, good blacksmiths and good farmers. For many years after the war they did the hard work of the country. They split rails and made fences, built log houses, worked on railroads and did other things. And there is one strange thing that I wish to speak about in connection with the negroes of Coffee County. They had a tact for the saw mill business. Many large saw mills in Coffee County had negro sawyers. I cannot think of any reason why a negro, with his thick skull, would make a better sawyer than a white man who is supposed to have better sense than a negro. Another thing I wish to say about the negroes of Coffee County, they never foment strikes and lockouts. They are mostly lawabiding citizens and respectful to the white race.

They have the gift of song and sing as they work. They are enthusiastic in their disposition, but their enthusiasm shows itself more in religion than riots and other unlawful conduct. Another characteristic of the negro is their disposition to be helpful and useful. If the house gets on fire or a horse runs away with a wagon, or if a car breaks down, or in case of an accident of any sort, a negro is the first one there is to help.

The old-time people, black and white, in Coffee County are living in peaceful relations and will continue thus to live so long as other people will keep their noses out of our business.

Grady's Tribute to the Negro Slaves

It has been noted repeatedly that history records no more remarkable illustration of loyalty to trust than that manifested by the negroes of the South during the Civil War. Often left behind as the sole support and protection of the families of the Confederate soldiers, not an instance is recorded in which one violated his trust. Of this remarkable record, Georgia's matchless orator, Henry W. Grady, said in his last great speech:

"History has no parallel to the faith kept by the negro in the South during the war, often five hundred negroes to a single white man, and yet through these dusky throngs the women and children walked in safety and the unprotected homes rested in peace.

"Unmarshaled, the black batallions moved patiently to the fields in the morning to feed the armies their idleness would have starved, and at night gathered anxiously at the big house to 'hear the news from Master,' though conscious that his victory made their chains enduring. Everywhere humble and kindly; body-guard of the helpless; the rough companion of the little ones; the observant friend; the silent sentry in his lowly cabin; the shrewd counselor; and when the dead came home, a mourner at the open grave.

"A thousand torches would have disbanded every Southern Army, but not one was lighted. When the master going to a war in which slavery was involved said to his slave, 'I leave my home and beloved ones in your charge,' the tenderness between man and master stood disclosed. And when the slave held that charge sacred through storm and temptation, he gave new meaning to faith and loyalty. I rejoice that when freedom came to him after years of waiting, it was all the sweeter because the black hands from which the shackles fell were stainless of a single crime against the helpless ones confided to his care.''

A Negro Funeral

"Good morning, Uncle Ben, how Uncle Ike doing this morning?"

"Well, he isn't so well; he didn't sleep so well last night, and den the sign is all against him. I heard my rooster crow before twelve o'clock last night and that is shore a bad sign. I was sitting up with Brother Ike when the rooster crew and I notis that he got worse off right away. Seem like his mind was disturbed about something. Can't you come over and sit up with us tonight?"

Uncle Ben was on hand the next night ready to sit up with the sick, and ready to see him die, for every negro likes to see a sad death. Not only was Uncle Ben there to sit up with the sick but there was a dozen or more of sympathetic friends gathered in the hut. A little fire burned in the hearth and a small candle burned on a dry goods box near the bed. Everything about the sick man was noted, and when he asked for a drink of water Sister Sealey Jones said, "I am afraid Brother Ike fever is rising, you see he is wanting water, and that is always a bad sign when you have a disease like that." And so with everything to discourage and nothing to encourage, Brother Ike turned over and bid this world a long farewell. The news went out that Uncle Ike was dead. His kinfolk, his pastor, and many of his friends called to see how poor old Ike looked when he was dead. By the rising of the sun the preacher, the clerk of the church, and the undertaker were all sitting around his bed. The clerk of the church was asked to write down the last words of the deceased. All the brothers and sisters were asked to tell something about Uncle Ike. All this was written down for the benefit of the preacher who was the pastor of the sermon. All next day the crowds came and went. The little candle was kept burning all day. Each friend or relative who came and looked on the sad face of Uncle Ike would make some kind of remark. One friend said, "Well don't he look the natural." Another one would say, "And ain't it such a quiet corpse too." While another one would say, "Well, what do you suppose he is thinking about right now."

The watchers came by detachments. The societies came in one group. The members of the church came in another group, and so on. When the plans of the funeral had been fully arranged the body was taken over to the church and laid in state during the night. The congregation sang funeral hymns and chanted Dirges with the saddest wails. Many prayers were uttered. Speeches were made. Groans weird and spooky filled the church and attracted attention round about. With the rising of the sun the congregation all stood up and sang "Sweet Chariot" and other songs, for they said, "Perchance the Holy angels will come at sunrise and take him to his home in his skies."

Eleven o'clock was the time set for the sermon. Brother Jim Crow, the pastor, made a few scattering remarks about the long and useful life of Brother Ike. He then read to the congregation the information written down by the clerk of the church. He then proceeded with his sermon something like this: Last night while I was sleeping I had a vision like Isiah the Prophet, the heavens were open and I saw the angels, the Ark Angels, the Cherbum and the Seraphin and all the other phims. I seemed to see Gabriel stand up and he say to one dem der phims, "Dis day heaven must be enriched. The glory of the Glory World must shine out in bright colors today. I seemed to see sadness on the face of the angels in heaven and it seems to have been because one child who belonged in heaven was not there. And Gabriel say to the angels, 'Fly down and fly over this world and see if you find any one who is worthy to open the Pearly Gates and come in to live with God's Glorified.' And as the Angel flew I saw him circle around over Douglas like an aeroplane fixing to land, and after while in my vision I saw him light. He went straight to the home of Brother Ike. He laid his hand on Brother Ike's foot and his foot went to sleep, and den he laid his hand on Brother Ike's lips and Brother Ike could talk no more. He put his hand on Brother Ike's eyes and Brother Ike went to sleep, and then he put his hand on Brother Ike's heart and it beat no more for Brother Ike was dead, and then there was shouting and singing in heaven. The little angels flew around the big angels and there was joy in heaven. The everlasting gates were opened and Uncle Ike went in as Hallulahs were ringing throughout the regions of heaven. Uncle Ike went in and took a seat with Abraham and Isiah and Jacob and Bob Douglas and Abe Lincoln."

The funeral being over, the congregation was asked to pass around and look on Brother Ike for the last time in this world, and also drop a nickel in the hat to help pay the funeral expenses.

Meningitis Epidemic

In February, 1870, Meningitis was epidemic in Coffee County. Old man Dan Newbern and his wife and four children died in six days. Old man John Lott lost two sons and a son-in-law, Mr. Moore. Old man Alfred Peterson lost some members of his family. Old man Jack Vickers, the preacher, lost some of his children. There were several persons who had it and lived. But most of them were dumb, deaf and blind.

There has never been as much excitement over any disease before or since as was over this epidemic. When the news went abroad that old man Dan Newbern and his wife and four sons had died within six days the people were dumbfounded and began to use all sorts of remedies. They made smokes around their premises out of pine tops, tar, pitch and other things. Turpentine and asafoetida was used in profusion on the persons and about the premises, where the diseases were located. It was thought to be very contagious. One case is noted that of Mr. Johnie Moore, who passed through the lane of old man Dan Newbern and he took the disease and died before he got home.

It is not known for certain how the disease got to Coffee County, but it is thought by some that the disease was brought here by strangers who were working on the new railroad between Hazlehurst and the river bridge. It is said that several negroes died there with the disease.

The county was in a most horrible situation and everybody was afraid of everybody else. But there is one instance that I wish to mention of a certain man, now deceased, who was a hero in that awful time of trial. When the disease broke out at old man Dan Newberns and he and his wife died, the family was like a bunch of sheep without a shepherd, they did not know which way to turn, no doctors nor any nurses nor any one who knew anything about the disease. It was at this critical time that old man Dan Gaskin, then a young man, and a relative to the Newberns, went to the Newbern home and took charge of things. At least one member of the family died in one day and once two members of the family died in one day. The sick had to be looked after and the dead had to be buried. Brothers and sisters had to bury their own brothers and sisters. Children had to bury father and mother. And so it went on for a week when six members of the family filled new made graves. No one will ever know the horrible situation endured by this family through the long winter nights. Scarcely any light in the house, with now and then one to be heard in the struggle of death.

It is said that a patient would be taken with a very high fever. His head would be drawn back and soon the patient would become unconscious and die within a very few hours.

At the cemetery at old Lone Hill Church, ten miles northeast of Douglas there stands six tombstones all in a row. They mark the last resting place of Mr. Newbern and his wife and four boys.

The Big Four

THE BIG FOUR

Reading from left to right; the two men standing, the first is Daniel Gaskin, the second man is R. S. Smith. Seated, reading from left to right, first man is Dan Newbern, Elias Lott.

Daniel Gaskin, Dan Newbern, R. S. Smith, and Elias Lott were known as the "Big Four." These men were about the same age and were all related. The mother of Elias Lott and the father of Daniel Gaskin were brother and sister. R. S. Smith married a sister of Daniel Gaskin.

Neither of these men was old enough to go into the Confederate Army. They were young men at the close of the war. They were all at home during the war and were worth a great deal to the widows and children of the communities where they lived.

Daniel Gaskins married Miss Aleph Hinson. They have two children; Bell, and Fisher. Mr. Gaskins was a good farmer and stock raiser. He was a large sheep owner and had plenty of hogs and cows. He was a hard working man and one of the best neighbors I ever knew. He was tax receiver in 1871 and tax collector in 1875 and County Commissioner in 1911.

Mr. R. S. Smith married Mary Gaskins, and had the following children: Monroe Smith, Sampie Smith, and Dr. John Smith. The girls are Mrs. John Peterson, Mrs. Levi O'steen. Mr. Smith was a very successful farmer. He was a hard worker and a fine man in every way. He was a member of the Methodist church and was a devout christian. He belonged to that old school of Methodists and had family prayer at his home every night. He was superintendent of the Lone Hill Sunday School for twenty years or more.

Daniel Newbern married Miss "Pet" Fussell. They have several children: William Newbern, Daniel Newbern, Jr., and Jesse Newbern. The girls are: Mrs. Micajah Vickers, and Mrs. W. T. Cottingham. Mr. Newbern was a good farmer and a fine man in every way. He was one of the few men who spent half his time attending his own business and the other half of his time he spent letting other people's business alone. He was tax receiver in 1878.

Mr. Elias Lott, the last man in the group, married Tempie Douglas. They have the following children: James Lott, Dan Lott. Girls: Mrs. E. R. Cross, Mrs. James Jardine and Mrs. Johnson. Mr. Lott is a wealthy land owner. He was a good farmer and stock man. He has always been a prosperous business man. He is a good hand to keep all his "Ducks in a row" and has many kinds of interest in Coffee County. He is now living and is more than 75 years old and is the only one of the "Big Four" now living. He was a member of the Georgia Legislature in 1911-12.

These men in early life, with their families, lived in the same locality and were always the best of friends. They assisted each other in every possible way. They always had plenty of this world's goods and some to spare. They teased and joked and had bushels of fun among themselves. When one passed through "The valley of the shadow of death" they all came to his rescue with money and sympathy and every needed help. They were an example of true friendship and relationship.

We shall never see their like again in Coffee County.

Friendship between men is said to be deeper and more lasting than friendship between women. Jonathan and David, characters from the old Testament, are given as examples of true friendship for man for man. An instance of Modern Times is the friendship between Damon and Pythias.

The friendship between the Big Four was a friendship like unto the friendship of those named above.

The Banking Business

The Union Banking Company of Douglas, Ga., is the oldest bank in the county. It was founded in 1898 and has continued to grow and expand up to this date, 1930. The Union Banking Company has branches in Broxton and Nicholls with plenty capital to do a real banking business. Two other banks were organized in Douglas but did not succeed. At one time in Coffee County there was a bank at Pearson, Ga., Willacoochee, Ga., and Ambrose, Ga. The bank at Ambrose has gone out of business. Willacoochee and Pearson have prosperous banks but they are now in Atkinson County, having been cut off from Coffee County with the creation of Atkinson County.

It is said the great success of the Union Banking Company is due to the men back of the Institution. The officers of the bank, the Cashiers and the Directors are men of character and good business qualifications.

J. M. ASHLEY

The Man Who Built the Union Banking Co.

Fraternal Orders

The first Masonic Lodge in Coffee County was established long years ago at Pearson, Ga. Several of its charter members lived near Hazlehurst and were faithful and regular attendants. The Lodge is still in a flourishing and prosperous condition. Lodge No. 163 is named Satilla, F. & A. M.

Broxton Lodge is No. 147 F. & A. M. Then the following Masonic Lodges: Douglas No. 386 F. & A. M.; Lax No. 556 F. & A. M.; Ambrose No. 658 F. & A. M.; Wilcox (at Douglas) No. 668. Only one Royal Arch Chapter in the county, which is Douglas Chapter No. 49 F. & A. M. at Douglas.

The Blue Lodges of the County are affiliated with the Eleventh District Masonic Convention which meets annually. The Royal Arch Chapter is also affiliated with the district convention, which meets annually.

We also have a tri-county Masonic Convention which meets quarterly, alternately with the different Lodges of the counties with which we are affiliated.

Satilla Lodge, No. 163, F. & A. M. was first established at a point on Satilla River, ten miles north of Pearson and six miles south of Douglas and, at the time, the only fraternal order in Coffee County. But soon afterwards members retired to organize lodges more convenient to them elsewhere. The date of its organization was prior to the Civil War. William Ashley was the first Worshipful Master.

Ladies' Clubs

Christian work has ever been the forerunner of civic and social organizations among women, and it is fitting that this should be in the history of Coffee County.

The Ladies Aid Societies of the town were strong organizations of the early church life here, leading ultimately to the broader work of Missionary Societies that have furnished inspiration, information and a social contact among the church women.

Mrs. Sadie Powell, Mrs. R. T. Relihan and Mrs. S. M. Roberts of sainted memory, Mrs. F. M. Appleby, Miss Dollie Freeman, Mrs. Hoke Davis, Mrs. E. L. Tanner, Mrs. Turner Brewer were among the faithful women of the Baptist denomination who steered the organization through the transition period to a larger work. Mrs. L. A. Hill, Mrs. C. N. Fielding, Mrs. J. A. Daughtrey, Mrs. A. W. Haddock, Mrs. J. S. Lott, Mrs. L. E. Heath, Mrs. C. A. Ward and Mrs. W. P. Ward, Sr., of sainted memory, were among the loyal workers of the Methodist Missionary Society in its early days. Mrs. J. W. Quincey and Mrs. M. D. Dickerson have through loyalty and sacrifice built up a strong Episcopal auxiliary, and a good auxiliary at the Presbyterian Church stands as a memorial to the work of Mrs. T. S. Hart, Mrs. Clara LaPrade and Mrs. W. P. Bellinger.

Mrs. S. H. D. Barnes was for many years the leading spirit in the Woman's Christian Temperance Union, organized in 1908.

The first civic organization in the town was the City Improvement Club, organized in 1907, with Mrs.

L. E. Heath president. This later became the Douglas Woman's Club with Mrs. J. C. Brewer president.

The United Daughters of the Confederacy was organized in 1906 and is still a flourishing organization. Mrs. W. W. McDonald was first president.

Three literary clubs, The Outlook Club, The Review Club, The Research Club, have been contributing factors to the intellectual life of the town.

One of the strongest and most helpful organizations of the town is the Parent-Teachers' Association of the Douglas High School, organized in 1925, with Mrs. T. H. Clark, as president.

Public Health Work

A full time health officer has been employed in Coffee County since July 1927. The general consensus of opinion amongst the tax payers appears to be that the money spent on health service has yielded an adequate return.

Here, as elsewhere, the health officer has two cardinal duties (1) The control of communicable diseases; (2) Elevation of the health standard, especially amongst the school population.

Our school population numbers over 3,000. Of these 31 per cent. were found under the standard weight, and 41 per cent handicapped through the presence of hook worm. Since the health work started in Coffee County there has been over 3,000 children treated for hook worm, and their parents given literature telling the source of infection and means of preventing re-infection.

Malaria is not a serious problem in Coffee County, however, the city authorities of Douglas don't take anything for granted. They appropriate money every year to carry on draining and oiling the streams and ponds in and near the city. By this constructive work Douglas is practically free from mosquitoes.

The evidence of physical defects in school children has been on a parity with that observed in other South Georgia counties. In this connection a notable task has been performed through the collaboration of Parent-Teachers' Association and the medical and dental profession. A series of tonsil and dental clinics have been held and a total of 275 patients operated upon.

A sentiment prevails in the county that something worth while has been accomplished in the way of public health. This happy state of affairs is in the main due to the spirit of the people. Perhaps there is no other section of the State in which there is a community more ready to back any project designed for the common good.

The Boy Scout Movement

It was evening in London. The day had been unusually foggy, even to such an extent that the street lights were turned on before noon.

Mr. William Boyce, Chicago publisher and traveler, was seeking a difficult address in old London.

ARCHIE BAGWELL

A boy approached and said, "May I be of service to you, sir?" "Yes, show me to this address."

At the desired location, Mr. Boyce tossed the boy a shilling. "Thank you sir, but I am a Scout and Scouts do not accept tips for courtesies."

Mr. Boyce became immediately interested in Scouting. He went to the office of Sir Robert Baden Powell, founder of the British Boy Scout Association and gathered all the information he could concerning Scouting.

In February 1909, he and some associates launched the movement in the United States. By 1926 over 3,-000,000 boys became Scouts. Statistics show that almost 50% of the present college men of America have been Scouts. Scouting now embraces 57 nations.

The Scout movement hit Douglas in 1918. Prof. C. M. Williams was Scoutmaster. Meetings were held in the school houses. Mr. Williams was succeeded by Dr. W. C. Bryan, who in turn was succeeded by Mr. F. C. Wilson.

In 1922 Fred Brewer became Scoutmaster and the Scout Hut was built on Pearl Street.

Rev. B. W. Smith and Archie Bagwell met a tragic and heroic death off Sea Island Beach near Brunswick, Ga., August 4th, 1926.

The scouts were taking an outing on the beach August 4th, 1926. They were all in bathing and were coming out. Mr. Smith, the Scoutmaster, remained in the water until the last scout was safe on shore. It was then discovered that he was in some sort of trouble and was drowning in the ocean. Archie Bagwell, age fifteen, stout and strong, went to the rescue of the drowning Scoutmaster and so they both went down and gave up their lives in an heroic effort to save the lives of others.

I think a monument should be built to both the scout and the Scoutmaster, but as this has not been done and probably will not be done, I am inserting the picture of one of these heroes that the memory of their lives shall not perish upon this earth.

Harold Adams next became Scoutmaster. He was succeeded by J. E. Crabb who was succeeded by Rev. M. P. Cain.

In November 1929, Prof. T. A. Clower became Scoutmaster. Under his leadership, the scout movement in Douglas reached its zenith. It is now the prize troop of the Okeenokee Council, and one of the best in the State.

History of the Bright Tobacco in Georgia

Tobacco has been grown in Georgia since the State was first settled, but not on a commercial scale until recent years. In 1910 only 2,000 acres of tobacco were grown. Most of this in Decatur County around Amsterdam. It was cigar filler and Sumatra wrapper types.

In 1914 through their agricultural and industrial departments the Central of Georgia, A. B. & C. and S. A. L. Railroads began to encourage the tobacco industry and to give the farmers assistance. Through the efforts of these roads tobacco was grown in Early, Stewart, and Wilcox Counties. The following year, 1916, Sumter County grew a little tobacco, and through the efforts of the A. B. & C., G. & F., and S. A. L. Railroads, and a few men who had moved in from the Carolinas the acreage in Coffee and adjoining counties increased. During this period tobacco prices were low and the farmers were slow to try a new crop that did not offer good opportunities for profit. In 1916 the tobacco acreage was materially increased in Coffee County and the counties adjoining.

In April 1917 a meeting was held in Fitzgerald, Georgia, for the purpose of discussing the advisability of establishing tobacco markets in Georgia. This meeting was composed of agricultural and industrial agents of the various railroads operating in South Georgia, of farmers and business men, and a tobacco warehouseman from South Carolina. This was the beginning of the permanent warehouse development in the

State. As a result of this meeting The Georgia Tobacco Company was organized at Douglas, and a warehouse was built. Through the aid of Georgia and Florida warehousemen as well as buyers, were secured from the leading tobacco companies. The second warehouse in Georgia was opened at Douglas, July, 1917. The sales that year were very satisfactory and compared favorably with those of the Carolinas. About 355,000 pounds was sold.

In 1918 the agricultural and industrial agents of practically every railroad operating in the southern half of Georgia made a special effort to induce the farmers in that section to plant more tobacco. Experienced tobacco growers were procured from North Carolina and South Carolina to supervise tobacco for the growers. Tobacco seed was distributed free to the farmers by railroad agents and tobacco warehousemen. As a result of this effort between 5,000 acres of tobacco was grown in 15 counties which prices ran about 34 cents, which was above the normal price. The average yield per acre was about 750 pounds, although yields as high as 2,000 pounds were reported. The same year, in addition to the warehouse built in Douglas, tobacco warehouses were built in Nicholls and Abbeville and markets established at these places.

In 1919 the Georgia State Agricultural College found it possible to employ a field agent to devote most of his time to this crop. The high prices obtained for tobacco and the damage done to cotton in 1918 by the boll weevil caused a wide increase in tobacco, so much in fact, that it was necessary to discourage the planting of a large acreage of individual farms. About 30,000 acres of tobacco were planted in 1919 in 45 counties which yielded 10,327,530 pounds of tobacco, which was sold at an average of $17.73 per hundred pounds. Warehouses were operated at Douglas, Abbeville, Nicholls, Fitzgerald, Blackshear, Nashville, Ashburn, Tifton, Vidalia, Hazlehurst and Valdosta. The counties that grew the largest acreage were Coffee, Wilcox, Berrien, Ben Hill, Tift, Irwin, Turner, Jeff Davis, Pierce and Lowndes.

Douglas led the State's markets in tonnage for the season, with 10,940,937 pounds sold there at an average price of 18.65 cents a pound, bringing $2,021,339.17. Nashville ran high in the matter of average price with 21.10 cents a pound, at which rate 7,623,089 pounds which brought an aggregate of $1,608,848.29.

Douglas sold more than twelve million pounds of tobacco during the year 1930.

It is worthy of note that this country was in the tobacco business as far back as 1619. When there was sent from London to the first colony, ninety women, "young and incorrupt" and two years later sixty more maids of "virtuous education, young and handsome" also seeking husbands under a forced social order. The first feminine arrivals were consigned to Virginia bachelors, each for a hundred and twenty pounds of native tobacco. The second group of English ladies was bartered for a hundred and fifty pounds of air-cured tobacco.

It is also worthy of note that in the early days of Virginia, tobacco was the currency of the realm.

Automobiles

There are now hundreds of automobiles in Coffee County. There are many kinds, including trucks of many kinds.

So far as we can learn, the first automobile in Coffee County was brought to Douglas by Dr. W. F. Sibbett about the year 1900. The name of the automobile was a Schat. It was a strange looking vehicle. It had high wheels and looked like an old-time buggy. The machine cost six hundred and eighty dollars. It was a strange looking sight on the streets of Douglas and on the roads of Coffee County.

It is strange what a great influence automobiles have had upon Coffee County. They have changed the habits of the people. Persons can now go as far in an hour as they used to travel in a whole day long. It has brought the people and their business closer together and has increased business to a large extent.

It is a question whether the automobile is an asset or a liability to the country.

Lawyers

Chastain & Henson, R. V. Chastain, Douglas, Ga.; Slater & Moore, Rufus Moore, John R. Slater, Douglas, Ga.; Quincey & Quincey, S. O. Quincey, Hately Quincey, Douglas, Ga.; Mingledoff & Gibson, George H. Mingledoff, John Gibson, Douglas, Ga.; L. E. Heath, Douglas, Ga.; Herman Barnes, Douglas, Ga.; Dave Sapp, Douglas, Ga.; Elisha Grantham, Douglas, Ga.; J. A. Roberts, Douglas, Ga.; Miss Clyde Wheeless, Douglas, Ga.; Kelley and Dickerson, Lawson Kelley, M. D. Dickerson, Douglas, Ga.; Will Dickerson, Douglas, Ga.; B. G. O'Berry, Jr., Douglas, Ga.; J. H. Williams, Douglas, Ga.; W. P. Ward, Douglas, Ga.

Doctors

Medical Doctors

Dr. A. S. M. Coleman, Douglas, Ga.; Dr. I. W. Moorman, Douglas, Ga.; Dr. Will F. Sibbett, Sr., Douglas, Ga.; Dr. Will A. Sibbett, Jr., Douglas, Ga.; Dr. T. H. Clark, Douglas, Ga.; Dr. John Smith, Douglas, Ga.; Dr. S. E. Vinson, Douglas, Ga.; Dr. B. O. Quillian, Douglas, Ga.; Dr. A. D. Bennett, Douglas, Ga.; Dr. Hughs, Douglas, Ga.; Dr. J. J. Lott, Broxton, Ga.; Dr. D. H. Meeks, Nicholls, Ga.; Dr. Hall, Nicholls, Ga.; Dr. Harper, Ambrose, Ga.

Dentists

Dr. Lewis Davis, Douglas, Ga.; Dr. M. H. Turrentine, Douglas, Ga.; Dr. M. H. Turrentine, Jr., Douglas, Ga.

Cotton Picking Time in Georgia

Sitting at my window this beautiful October day I see loads and loads of cotton coming to market. It makes me think of childhood and home when I was a little boy on the farm. Most of this cotton comes from country homes and much of it is picked by country boys and girls. They have worked hard all the summer, chopping, thinning, and hoeing the cotton, and now they have "picked it out," as we say, and it is now being sold; and I wonder, yes I wonder, what are all these boys and girls to get out of it?

Long time ago when I was a little boy on the farm my mother would tell me if I would be smart she would buy me something pretty when the cotton was sold. And all through the long summer days, as I worked I would think of something to buy. The first gun I owned, Brother Frank and I went partners. We "took in" the land and made the cotton and bought it all by ourselves. But the biggest thing I ever owned was an iron handle knife with "I. X. L." on the blade and on the handle. Uncle Dunk Douglas said it meant:

> "Iron handle and pewter blade,
> Sorriest knife was ever made."

But my knife was alright. I took it to bed with me when I went to sleep. That night I dreamed I lost it. I was so scared I waked up. I felt for my knife and found it and held it in my hand 'til daylight.

I wonder what the boys and girls are getting out of all this cotton? I hope all the fathers and mothers will be good to the boys and girls and get them all something nice. And let me beg this one favor. Let each boy and girl have some one thing that they wish most. Don't make them have what you wish and nothing else. Let them make one choice and then you get it, makes no difference what it is.

Writing these thoughts makes me hungry to be a boy again, out on the farm, free as the air, living in peace with God and all mankind and owing no man anything but to love him.

God bless the little boys and girls, the little cotton pickers of Coffee County. Fathers and mothers, give them a chance; they are worth more and much more than all your cotton. Give them a chance.

Their friend,

W. P. WARD.

From Ward's Scrapbook, 1905.

The Boll Weevil

The boll weevil made its first appearance in Coffee County in the year 1917. His coming was an epoch in the history of Coffee County. The farmers of Coffee County had never been hit so hard before. They were dumbfounded. They did not know which way to turn or what to do. Many of our farmers were not able to pay off the mortgages on their farms, and for lack of being able to make cotton their farms were lost. As an example of the awful destruction of the farming interests I will give you the figures of one of our best farmers, which will give you a good idea of what happened to all the farmers.

In the year 1917, the first year the boll weevil began his operations, the farm given you as an example produced 220 bales of cotton. In 1918, the next year, the same number of acres produced 116 bales of cotton. In 1919, the third year, the same farm only produced 16 bales of cotton, being almost a total destruction.

The farmers have tried many remedies to combat the boll weevil, but nothing so far has been a success. Early varieties of cotton and early planting with the use of lots of high grade fertilizers and rapid cultivation adds much in the production of cotton under boll weevil conditions. Dry, hot weather, with rapid cultivation helps in the fight.

This year, 1930, July weather conditions are favorable and the farmers hope to make at least half a crop.

So far as we can get information as to the history of the boll weevil in other countries, he continues his partial destruction of the cotton crops. The farmers continue their fight against the boll weevil but do not hope for his final elimination. But so long as the farmers can grow a half crop of cotton they will continue to grow it.

Storms

Coffee County and this section of Southeast Georgia is almost free from storms of every kind. So far as I can ascertain there has never been but one severe storm in Coffee County. I have heard of this storm all my life. I saw the track of this storm about twenty years after. There was not a tree standing in the path of the storm. It was in the fall season, about 1857, when a severe storm originated in the neighborhood where the country home of Mr. J. C. Brewer now stands, about three miles north of Douglas. The storm moved eastward almost in a straight line, passed on to the coast and into the Atlantic Ocean. The path of the storm was about one mile wide. A story is told about old man Dan Lott, who at that time was one of the biggest farmers in Coffee County and was well fixed with houses and fences and other things usually had on a big country farm. Mr. Lott had just left home on his way to Jacksonville, Georgia, to attend Superior Court. But the storm had passed over and there was not a roof on a house on the farm. The crib was blown away and the corn scattered for more than a mile. The cotton house was blown away and the cotton was scattered for more than a mile. It looked like a snow storm had passed over the place. The bed quilts were scattered for miles, some of them were hanging in the trees. Everything on the Lott place was in confusion and the big family all scared half to death. The old negro went after Mr. Lott and overtook him before he reached Jacksonville, Georgia. When he told Mr. Lott what had happened Mr. Lott said it was not so, that nothing could be as bad as that. But he turned around and went back home and found it much worse than the negro had pictured it.

No such storm has ever visited Coffee County since that time. We are perhaps safer from storms than any other section of South Georgia.

The Liquor Laws

By Act of the Legislature of 1878-9, page 388, a license for selling or vending spiritous, intoxicating and malt liquors in the counties of Wayne, Liberty, Coffee and Appling, was fixed at the sum of $1,000, and a bond was required given and an oath taken by the retailers, and the Act made it a misdemeanor for violation of its terms.

The Act of the Legislature approved August 18, 1881, Acts 1880-1, page 594, amended the previous Act so as to apply the license fixed in Coffee County to the sale of beers, ciders, bitters or nostrums, whether patented or not, and with or without name, which, if taken in sufficient quantities to produce intoxication.

The Act approved September 4, 1883, Acts 1882-3, page 567, amended the law further so as to fix the annual license fees in Wayne, Liberty, Coffee and Appling Counties at the sum of $10,000.

In 1885 the Legislature passed a general law, Acts 1884-5, pages 121-24, known as the local option Act, authorizing any county in the state to petition the Ordinary to call an election to determine whether liquors should be sold in the county. This Act was amended by the Acts of 1890-91, page 130, so as to attach penalties for violation of the Act.

A local act approved July 16, 1903, Acts 1903, pages 362-4, authorized the County Commissioners of Coffee County, and the Mayor and Council of the City of Douglas to open up and operate a dispensary for the sale of intoxicating liquors in the City of Douglas, and further authorized the County Commissioners to open up and operate a dispensary in any other incorporated town in the county having a population of four hundred or more. The Act contained a referendum requiring an election to put the Act in force, and when the election was held the Act failed of adoption.

Coffee County continued dry under the local option Act, until superseded by the Eighteenth Amendment of the Constitution, the Volstead Act, and the Enabling Act of the State of Georgia, under the Eighteenth Amendment.

A Strange Phenomenon

About the year 1914, in the month of August, there appeared a strange phenomenon in Coffee County. In a moment, in the twinkling of an eye, hundreds of acres of cotton plants were wilted in the fields. A rain had fallen about three o'clock in the afternoon but the clouds had passed away and the sun was shining. There was no wind blowing like the hot winds in the west, nor nothing to indicate that anything unusual was about to happen.

Mr. W. H. Vickers, a good farmer and a very reliable man, living about four miles south of Douglas, gives a good description of what happened on his farm. He was standing under a shelter and had a good view of the clouds and the fields. All at once the heavens seemed to light up as though a cloud had passed from under the sun, but the sun was shining all the time. The phenomenon did not cover the entire county but was in spots, perhaps worse at the Vickers farm than anywhere else. Many of the plants recovered and became normal, but many of the leaves twisted up and crimped around the edges and finally died.

This phenomenon does not compare with earthquakes nor with the falling stars of 1833, but it was a real phenomenon and is a part of the history of Coffee County.

Early Steamboat Navigation on the Ocmulgee

By Mrs. Lon Dickey

In the Centennial Edition of The Telfair Enterprise, published at McRae October 31, 1907, is the following bit of history concerning early navigation on the Ocmulgee River in Coffee County. Because of the fact that this territory was a part of Telfair County up to 1854, and the territories on the south side of the river were served in the same manner from the landings in the present boundaries of Coffee, as follows: Ashley's Landing, Barrow's Bluff, First Tub Lake, Manning's Lower Fence, Burkett's Ferry and Dodge's Boom. This article says:

In the Pioneer days of Telfair the only means the people had of transporting their products to market and obtaining supplies that could not be provided at home was by pole boats on the Ocmulgee, Altamaha to Darien, thence by sail to the markets, or by wagons, a distance of one hundred and twenty-five miles by dirt road to Savannah.

Pole Boats Built

Boats were built in the county, loaded with cotton and other farm products, drifted down the river to Darien where the cargoes were transferred to sailing vessels for Savannah and other ports. The boats were then loaded at Darien with cargoes of general merchandise brought by sail from Savannah, Charleston, and New York, and poled up the river by hand, requiring several weeks to make a trip. In times of high water it was often necessary to use a rope and windlass to pull the boats up the swift current at certain places in the river, so it can be readily understood that the up trip of a pole boat was slow and tedious, requiring much labor. In those days the freight on many kinds of goods was more than the prime cost; yet the people of this section were contented and prosperous though the cost of transportation was so high.

Introduction of Steamboats on the Ocmulgee

About the year 1827 steam navigation was introduced on the Ocmulgee. There is much doubt as to how high up the river the first boat ran. And there is no record at this late date as to the name of the boat and her commander.

The first steamboat on the Ocmulgee to run as high up as Macon was the "North Carolina," commanded by Captain Salter. The historical record and history of Macon and central Georgia, by J. C. Butler, gives the date of the arrival of this steamer at Macon as January 18, 1829.

On the trip of the steamer up the river, the Macon Telegraph, of 1829, said: "Many of the people along the river banks were alarmed at the smoke and noise. Some mistook the noise for a roaring lion; others for the sneeze of the elephant. Some thought it the hissing of a sea serpent, or the groaning of an earthquake. Others thought it was war, pestilence and famine, but the most general opinion was that it was the tariff coming in person to eat up our cotton and corn and to drink up the river dry and that was an infringement of the state's rights. There was a climbing of trees and picking of flints and had not the boat made its escape it would have been hard to tell what the consequence might have been."

The Steamboat "Pioneer"

The next boat to run through to Macon was the "Pioneer," built at Macon by Charles Day and James R. Butts.

At first, the steamboats ran only to Darien, but later regular line freight and passenger steamers ran through from Macon to Savannah. After the building of the Central of Georgia Railroad from Savannah to Macon in 1843, which furnished quicker transportation to the seaboard, steamboats to Macon were discontinued and Hawkinsville was made the head of navigation.

Before the war and for a few years after the surrender, there were some fine passenger and freight steamers on the Ocmulgee plying between Hawkinsville and Savannah. It was the only means of transportation for the merchants and planters along the river who made business trips to Savannah two or three times a year, but after the building of the old Macon and Brunswick and the territory adjacent to the river with the seaboard, navigation on the Ocmulgee began to decline.

Historic Incidents on the Ocmulgee

In the spring of 1861, just before the breaking out of the Civil War, the steamer "General Manning" on her up trip from Savannah to Hawkinsville, with a large cargo of general merchandise and a long list of passengers, was blown up at "Manning's Lower Fence," a landing a few miles below Jacksonville.

Many of the passengers and members of the crew were killed by the explosion of the boilers. Among those killed were Joseph Williams, Jacob Parker and John Harrell, all prominent planters of the China Hill neighborhood in Telfair County. The steamer was in command of Captain Taylor, of Hawkinsville, who was seriously injured and his son killed.

The "Governor Troup" Captured

Near the close of the Civil War, the steamer "Governor Troup" was captured by a band of deserters from the Confederate Army at Town Bluff, a few miles below the junction of the Ocmulgee and Oconee Rivers.

The "Governor Troup" was on her way down trip from Hawkinsville with a cargo of supplies for the Confederate army on the coast. At Town Bluff, where she had landed to take on wood, the band of deserters boarded her, took possession, placed guards over the pilots and engineers and forced them to run the boat to Savannah where she was delivered to the Union forces for a large money consideration.

The engineers of the steamer, Mr. Isaac Higgs, now a resident of Appling County, and Mr. Miller, late of Hawkinsville, conspired to blow up the boat with the deserters on board, but desisted on learning that some prominent men from Irwin and Telfair Counties were on board sleeping in their staterooms. The engineers intended saving themselves, in case that the boat was blown up, by taking refuge in the wheel house, the "Governor Troup" being a sidewheel steamer, they could easily have exploded the boiler.

The Steamer "Wanderer"

A few years prior to the Civil War, the noted steamship "Wanderer" landed a cargo of African negroes on the coast in the vicinity of Brunswick in violation of law, as years before Congress had passed a law prohibiting the importation of African slaves into the United States.

This cargo of Africans was smuggled in and a portion of them were shipped up to Ocmulgee and landed at Jacksonville, it being the object of the promoters of the enterprise to sell them as slaves.

But the authorities learned of the affair and sent officers to arrest the negroes as well as those having them in charge. Those landed at Jacksonville were captured, sent to Savannah, and either liberated or deported.

(Left) ARTHUR LOTT, who represented Coffee County in the Legislature 1900-01.
(Right) MAJOR JOHN M. SPENCE, Captain Company C., 5th Ga. Regiment, and later was elected Major of his regiment. He was also a member of the Constitutional Convention of 1877.

The Ocmulgee River Section

Plantation Memories

By Mrs. Lon Dickey

The Ocmulgee River section of Coffee County lies along the Ocmulgee River in the northern part of Coffee County. Before the Civil War this section was the wealthiest and most cultured section of Coffee County. The Ashleys who lived up there were big slaver owners. Nathaniel Ashley owned more than a hundred slaves.

A public road ran through this section and was known as "The River Road." Many beautiful homes were located along this highway which led from the section around Hazlehurst to Hawkinsville, Ga.

But it is not altogether of military heroes that I would write. For there are the character builders of Coffee County, those who believed in the study of the Holy Bible as a foundation of character.

The Boyd Plantation

There are two thousand acres included in it, and it lies three miles from the western boundary of the county, on the road from Hawkinsville to Hazlehurst.

The first accounts I have of it is that it was owned by one Hiram Swain, and was purchased by Cornelius Ashley, of Telfair County, for his son, Jonathan Ashley, who married Miss Elizabeth Shelton, daughter of Major Charles Shelton.

Major Shelton is buried at the Old Block House just across the river, and on his tombstone we read that he was born Nov. 16, 1787, and died July 19, 1871, nearly eighty-four years of age.

His descendants around Valdosta are numerous, but only two grandsons were born to him in Coffee County, Maxey and Ed Ashley, the former now living in Valdosta. His son, "J. M. the third," served in the World War from Lowndes County.

The Ashley Sisters

At the death of Cornelius Ashley his slaves were divided, and his daughters, Mary and Ellen, came over from Telfair County and made their home with their brother, Jonathan, who worked their slaves, twenty-five each, on this old plantation.

Mary married a Medlock, and Ellen married a Culver, from Culverton, in Hancock County. Her daughter, Burrows Culver, named for her Grandmother Burrows Maxey Ashley, married A. J. Comer and lived at Cordele in 1924.

There were other Ashley families along the river road all the way to Hazlehurst, and, as I understand it, Nat and Cornelius were the sons of old Dr. Bill Ashley, one of the first settlers of Telfair County. Matt Ashley, who organized the Fourth Georgia Cavalry, from Coffee County, was the son of Nat Ashley. His children were Dr. Bill Ashley of Ocilla, Marshall Ashley of Douglas, Mrs. J. J. Lewis and Mrs. William Hinson of Hazlehurst.

However, to use a right expression, their "family tree has become a forest," and it is not for me to try to unravel its history. Ashley River, on which are the famous Magnolia Gardens of Charleston, is named for one branch of their family.

Was Store Keeper

My father, Capt. Boyd, was a member of a family of twelve children, near Lumber City, and after receiving his education at Spring Hill Academy near there, he came over to "keep store" for his cousin, Jonathan Ashley.

Susan Caroline Ashley was my father's grandmother, and also, Elizabeth Shelton was his first cousin. And oh, the many happy and amusing experiences my father had with the slaves with which he used to delight us, for he was an excellent story teller.

My grandfather was James Boyd, born in Camden County, April 14, 1807. My grandmother was Mary Ann Monroe, born November 5th, 1811. They were married in Laurens County, Georgia, December 23, 1830. My grandfather died at his Telfair County home January 1st, 1884, and my grandmother came to make her home with us until she passed away March 25th, 1885.

Memory Goes Back

The question is often discussed, how far back into childhood can one remember?

I heard grandmother tell many delightful things concerning my father's oldest brother, Dr. Augustine Monroe Boyd, who had visited often at the home of Jonathan Ashley.

He received his medical education at the old Shorter College, which was then a medical college for men, located at Cave Spring, I was told. There he married Miss Eva Fitzgerald, October 3, 1854. Shorter was later moved to Rome.

He served throughout the War Between the States as surgeon for the Confederate forces, principally from Macon up to Virginia.

Goes to Mexico

At the close of the war he bitterly declared that the United States was no place in which to rear a family, with its free negroes, carpet baggers, and other undesirable conditions brought on by the war, so he took his family of several sons and a daughter to New Orleans, thence down to Tuxpam Bay, in Mexico, and at one time lived in Tampico. He died there July 21st, 1886. Although he tried to persuade the other members of his family to accompany him, my Aunt Ella Jane Boyd, for whom I was named, was the only one who went, having married Captain Archibald Hughes, of Mt. Vernon, in Montgomery County. She lived there eight years, but returned and died the last member of her family, December 28th, 1929.

But getting back to Coffee County. My father, Julius Warren Boyd, volunteered and joined a company at Jacksonville, and all the plantation and a great many people from other homes in Coffee went over to see them off. My father left as lieutenant, but on the death of their captain he took his place, Captain of Company H, 20th Georgia Infantry.

He served throughout the war without coming home, and was paroled at Appomattox Court House, Virginia, April 9th, 1865.

Off to Valdosta

With the slaves freed, all of the Coffee County Ashleys moved to Valdosta. Captain Boyd was left in charge of the Jonathan Ashley plantation, until the death of Mr. Ashley one year after settling in Valdosta.

Captain Boyd purchased it and, March 31, 1870, married Miss Marcella Smith, on the William Ashley plantation three miles further east.

On this plantation, right near the "Big House," are two old weatherstained tombstones that are very dear to me. Their inscriptions read: "Sacred to the memory of Joshua H. Frier. Died Feb. 28th, 1872. Aged 65 years, 9 months, and 28 days. None knew him but to love him."

"Narcissa Frier, died March 26, 1887. I love them that love me; and those that seek me early shall find me. Proverbs 8:17."

Things That Live

The stone was placed there by Mr. J. M. Ashley, of Douglas, who was surprised on receiving through her will this old plantation which had come to her, with its slaves, through her first husband, Capt. William Ashley, who died May 1st, 1839.

What would have been a mere pittance decided among others, was managed judiciously by its new owner, who traded it to Reverend Monroe Wilcox for a body of pines farther back from the river, and gave him the start in naval stores business that helped him to amass a fortune in and around Douglas.

Reverend Wilcox had also married a second time, and his wife, who was my mother's cousin, Emma Pickren, became another sweet memory to me as a neighbor. But just now it is of my great uncle and aunt, Joshua Frier and Narcissa Frier, that I would offer a few words in memory and appreciation.

Just a Tribute

She was first Narcissa Smith, and at the time of my Grandfather and Grandmother Smith, near Denton, took her three nieces, Narcissa, Annie and Marcella, and reared them, and as there were no schools that I ever heard of, except one on the adjoining plantation of Mr. Archibald McClean, they taught them all they ever knew. Uncle Joshua becoming one of my mother's sweet and sacred memories, for he was a gentleman of the old school and a loyal and devoted Christian.

The old school of which I speak was taught by a dear old gentleman whom my mother called "Uncle Tarrant," but she was never privileged to attend this old school but three months.

The eldest of these three orphan girls, Narcissa, married Mr. Aaron Frier and reared a large family in the lower part of the county.

An Old Doctor

Annie married Dr. James Allison Googe, whose father had come into the country from Holland. It was his second marriage, and they lived at Milltown and Homerville, and finally on one of the river plantations. She is buried at Oak Grove Church with one of her sons, Walter Googe. The others were Jefferson Lee and William Robert Googe, the latter being Dr. W. R. Googe of Abbeville.

Marcella married Captain Julius Warren Boyd, March 31, 1870, and eleven children were born to them at their plantation home.

A Church Founded

One of the first things my father did after his marriage to my mother March 31, 1870, was to begin a Methodist Church on his grounds. This was Oak Grove Church, and was not finally completed until along in the 80's, when Mr. Miles Wilson Howell, of Suffolk, Va., and Mr. John McLean began naval stores operations in that part of the country and contributed greatly in the upbuilding of the church.

Mr. "Tony Howell," as he was called, married my sister, Leila Boyd, in October, 1891, and Mr. John McLean married Miss Anne Latimer, daughter of Dr. Latimer, of Hazlehurst.

This church was burned sometime after my family moved to Fitzgerald in 1900, and later my husband gave lumber from his old saw mill at West Green and it was rebuilt across the road from the old site, some of the builders being A. M. Wilcox, Duncan McLean, Anderson McLean, and Mr. Dickey.

A Returned Soldier

I recall a very touching incident of my mother's girlhood days which she told to me, and which happened at an old church along the old river road beyond Rocky Creek, somewhere between there and Hazlehurst.

It was during the War Between the States, and my mother had seen two of her brothers march away to war, also two of them had gone from Bronson, Fla., which is way down on the Suwanee River in Levy County.

Her favorite brother, Neil Smith, had been wounded and had been reported near death in some far distant land, and she was feeling very sad and distressed when two of her friends, Miss Roxie Reed who later married Captain Tom Wilcox, and Miss Rebecca McDuffie who married Mr. Willis Dorminey, came to accompany her to this old church, which was nothing more than a shelter with a brush arbor built around it, though the elite of the land gathered there at these annual meetings in summer.

Sitting there listening to the old minister, with her face toward the east, she saw a soldier limping down the road in a tattered grey uniform, who, on reaching the crowd that rushed out to meet him when he collapsed from hunger and fatigue, turned out to be her brother, Neil Smith.

This brother afterward married Miss Nannie Smith, of Homerville, and lived in Valdosta a number of years, later moving with his large family to Nacadoschee, Texas, where he died.

Saw General Beauregard

Another war incident my mother remembered was of seeing General Beauregard and his staff of uniformed officers who stopped and had dinner at the home of her uncle and aunt following the surrender.

Needless to say, a great feast was prepared and after partaking of it the distinguished visitors drove rapidly away to the west along the old river road. She understood that they had been around Savannah and Charleston, and although I never saw anyone who knew of General Beauregard and his staff taking this route, my mother was quite sure this was he, and ever remembered the thrill she felt on seeing the beautiful, sleek black horses, their shining harness, and the glittering uniforms of the general and his staff, their courtly manners, and the sorrows they expressed over the surrender.

The Fussell Family

The great tract of land lying in Coffee County, coming from the west, was owned by the Fussell family. A granddaughter in this family married Mr. Daniel Newbern, and their children were: Emma, Winnie, Billy, Dan, Jesse and Eula. Two of these, Mrs. Micajah Vickers (Winnie) and Mrs. Cottingham (Eula) now live in Douglas.

Another granddaughter, Miss Mary Fussell, married Mr. Duncan McLean, and they still live on a section of these lands. Mrs. M. F. Head, who was Mary Ella McLean, lives in Douglas.

The new road leading to the bridge at Jacksonville Ferry passes through these lands, the old fields of which were among the most fertile and most diligently cultivated "Befo' de Wah."

Plantation Memories

About three miles out from the river, which is at Sapp's Still on this road, there is a ridge from which may be seen the blue hills of Telfair County across the river. At some points this is a beautiful panorama which spreads out before one on clear days. It is only of these plantations in this valley that I make mention.

The McLean Family

The next plantation to the east of my father was the Archibald McLean estate. These were Scotch people, and were great sheep raisers. A sheep shearing at their river home was one of the festive occasions of the eighties.

The tombstone at Oak Grove Cemetery has these two inscriptions: "Archibald McLean, born March 16, 1818. Died January 6, 1900." "Margaret Ann McLean, died February 4, 1888, aged 46 years, 4 months, and 11 days."

The latter was a daughter of Mr. Duncan McRae, of Telfair County, a member of the Scotch colony that settled that county in 1807. She grieved sadly over the death of their eldest son, Albert, who was killed in battle near Griffin, Ga., during the War Between the States, in 1864. He was a member of Company B, Artillery Battalion.

The other children were Flora Ella, Mary, John, Duncan, Anderson, and Frank.

The youngest, Frank, married Miss Ophelia Graham, of Telfair County, January 22, 1890, and their "Infare" at the McLean home following the marriage was one of the festive occasions of that period. She was a most lovable person, and was ever afterward a friend of my mother, a good neighbor and church member.

Their children were: Walter, Edna, Frank, Lola Mae, Roy, Jewell, Oscar, and John. Walter died early, and Frank was in service in the World War twenty-two months, eighteen of which were spent in France, while Roy was in service eighteen months, spending eleven months in France. They have been residents of Douglas for some years.

Reverend Monroe Wilcox

The first wife of Reverend Monroe Wilcox was Miss Mary Wooten, and her simple marker at Oak Grove has this inscription: "Mary Wilcox, born Feb. 28th, 1835, died June 16, 1887."

Their children were Augustus and Marvin, and the following daughters: Pet, William Hogan, of Mystic; Katherine, named T. L. Pickern; Elizabeth, named M. E. Yarbough, who died; and Cora, now Mrs. William Denton.

This good man served Oak Grove Church for many years, and his son, Gus, who died about 1926, kept the church and Sunday school going after all of the old river families had moved away, his family still being devoted to its welfare.

Beyond Rocky Creek

Next to the McLean estate was the plantation belonging to Aunt Narcissa Frier, formerly Mrs. William Ashley. Then came the treacherous and turbulent Rocky Creek, beyond which I know very little. There were the families of Wiley Byrd, Abraham Minchew, John Pickern, Colonel Manning, Colonel Hammond, Matt Ashley, the Paces, Taylors, Currys, Hinsons, and many others.

Colonel Manning married an Ashley, I think a sister of Matt Ashley. I heard people speak of the large number of slaves he owned before the war. There was considerable wealth on this portion of the river road, which, of course, was wiped out with the freeing of the slaves in 1863, and practically all of the old families drifted away from their plantations and left them in the hands of strangers.

Speaking of Rocky Creek, which was practically the dividing line of the two sections of the river road, one is charmed with the wild beauty of this stream, for it is one of ruggedness and mystery.

The Picnic Rocks

Its ruggedness begins with the great grey boulders of the picnic rocks, known in former times as "falling waters," for there was quite a water fall at this spot which was near the home of Major McNeill, one of the pioneer naval stores operators from Robeson County, North Carolina, who gave the place its name.

From there on to the Ocmulgee River, there were two great cliffs lining each side of a wooded stretch through which this stream flowed, great grey boulders with crevasses in them, and others poised perilously on top of each other just as though there had been a great upheaval there in the days gone by.

Dr. McCallie, State Geologist, once said that such conditions indicated oil beneath a surface. At any rate, it excites the wonder of visitors to see these great boulders balanced as though they might topple over, but never do.

The River Boats

I recall the steamboats on the Ocmulgee, some of them being the "City of Macon," "City of Hawkinsville," and "Lumber City," the latter being the property, I think, of Captain Eli Wilcox.

Captain John L. Day, of Lumber City, had a line of steamboats named for his children, the "Tommy Day," the "Ida Barrett," and the "John L. Day." Later he built a more pretentious boat and named it for his son who had died, "The Harry G. Day."

There was quite a celebration when this boat made its first trip up as far as old Jacksonville Ferry, which was almost opposite our plantation. The new boat was in charge of Captain Charley Phillips, and he treated the entire village of Jacksonville and its countryside to a free ride back to Barrows Bluff, on our side, for a fish fry.

Flowers Blossom Unseen

However, neither visitors nor natives venture very far in this wild solitude because it is known as a refuge for rattlesnakes and wild goats that scamper away at the sight of a human being.

Great magnolias, white dogwood, wild azaleas, grandfathers beard, Judas tree, crabapple, wild phlox, purple violets, and other woodland beauties, each spring blossom unseen along this stream, for it is in spring that it "goes on a rampage," and halts the motorist or traveler of any kind, for no bridge had been built over it when I last saw it.

During the War Between the States, those who would not fight hid out in the rocks, searchers almost catching a group of them once in a cave known as "The Billy Goat House," where their fire was found still burning. Heavy rains in recent years have filled in the caves to a great extent, and perhaps in years to come they may be hidden in drifting sand.

The Big Fish Fry

The fish were caught and prepared by Mr. Tony Howell and Mr. John McLean, whose naval stores products furnished the boats with chief cargoes.

Happy negro men fried the fish, cooked the bread, made lemonade with "Boughten Ice," families brought great hampers filled with good things to eat, and altogether it was one of the most notable and festive occasions of that period.

The big boat with its bright red roofs and fresh white painted sides, grey decks and big water wheel delighted my young mind as we all went aboard in line to inspect its plush carpeted cabin, state rooms, dining hall, and upper decks. It was one of the most memorable occasions people had enjoyed since "Befo' de Wah."

The Old House

This old house in which I was born was a double-pen log affair ceiled inside with wide, smooth boards, and weatherboarded outside, porch all the way across front, shed room and side porch, and previously the big kitchen had been set quite a distance from the house, in case of fire it was easier to save one or the other. There was a dining room adjoining the kitchen for good weather, and another indoors for unpleasant weather.

From time to time portions of the original dwelling had been torn away and the good lumber utilized in adding necessary rooms for our family. Lumber was not available then, all this having been sawn at Lumber City and floated up on barges, and all the bricks for the chimney and tall pillars had been made in Macon and hauled down in wagons.

Rooms were designated as "Cousin Lizzie's old room," "Mary and Ellen's room," the "Preacher's room," and the "Company room," and so on. Later a kitchen and "Blow way" were added and the old kitchen converted into a dairy.

The Cotton Industry

Raising cotton was still the order of the day when my father, Capt. Boyd, began his married life on the plantation. And although the old gin houses and storage houses had fallen into a state of decay when I first began to observe operations, the old loom house was in a fair state of preservation, and considerable weaving was done by my mother, aunts, and my oldest sister. There were wonderful bedspreads, heavy white cloth, and "Blue Jeans."

Working thread into "hanks" for the loom on the old warping bars was a delight to me. And the spinning wheel was ever a source of fascination to us. Carding bats of white, fluffy new cotton with which to pad quilts was, also, most intriguing, and gathering indigo for dye furnished us many happy excursions into the woods and blossoming hedges.

My father carried his cotton in wagons to market. It brought anywhere from four to six cents, which could not have helped much with our finances.

Old Slave Quarters

The old slave quarters had fallen into a state of decay, and many houses had been torn away to rebuild a sufficient number for our use, leaving a row of old wells and chimney mounds.

The slaves had literally played "Turn over the Fruit Basket" in their restlessness, so that the old ones moved away and we had a remnant of the Hatton and McArthur negroes from across the river, and the Hammonds, Mannings and others of our side.

An orphaned colored child reared by Aunt Narcissa Frier, and who was her little body servant up to the time of her death, lives in Fitzgerald at the present time, and is an excellent seamstress and is well educated. The majority of them were trained to be excellent cooks, laundry women and seamstresses.

The Ku Klux Klan

The Knights of the Ku Klux Klan has become a permanent, nationwide organization comprising millions of the best citizens of the nation.

The Douglas Klan No. 105 Realm of Georgia. Konklave assembled pledge and adopt the following resolutions as part of the program for the year 1930:

A firm defense of the Constitution of the United States and to assist in creating in the minds of the people a finer, better understanding and appreciation of what it means to live under the Glorious American Flag.

1. To aid in a strict law enforcement program.

2. To assist and co-operate with city and county officials in the apprehension of bootleggers, rum runners and whiskey makers.

3. To assist and support any movement which will furnish and provide healthful and wholesome recreation for the young people.

4. To defend, patronize, support and attend all Protestant American Churches and Institutions, particularly the Churches and Public Schools.

5. To uphold and defend the Holy Bible as it is written.

6. The unwavering devotion to our sacred duty as Klansmen.

"In the name of our fathers, for our country, our homes and each other."

The Douglas Cemetery

The Douglas Cemetery is one of the most beautiful in South Georgia. It is located about a mile north of the city. It is on high, rolling land. A great deal of attention has been given the cemetery by the ladies of Douglas. Several years ago the cemetery was planted with trees and shrubbery. Some of the trees are: Arborvitae, Juniper trees, but the most beautiful of all are the tall trees called Italian Cypress. They grow forty and fifty feet high. The limbs are very short and cling to the body of the tree. They are very beautiful and very scarce in South Georgia. The Douglas Cemetery has scores of them.

The ladies of Douglas have an organization, the purpose of which is to keep the cemetery clean and to keep everything in order on the grounds. This cemetery is not an old cemetery and is not as large as some other cemeteries in Georgia, but is so well kept and the tombstones are so beautiful and so varied that they lend a charming beauty to the grounds that few other cemeteries have. Perhaps it is the only cemetery in South Georgia that has a mausoleum. Those contained in the mausoleum are: John Marshall Ashley, born July 31st, 1861, and died October 28th, 1916. John Marshall Ashley, Jr., born February 4th, 1915, died October 24th, 1916. John Wooten Clements, born October 15th, 1848, died March 31st, 1925. Isabel McRae Clemens, born October 17th, 1851, died August 21st, 1929. John R. Slater, died Sept. 7th, 1930, age 38 years.

Other persons buried in the cemetery are: Joe F. Gaskin, Private 328 Inf. 82nd Division (World War), died October 13th, 1918. John Tanner, born January 8th, 1881, died March 1st, 1928. Harrison Kirkland, born January 6th, 1866, and died March 19th, 1929. Daniel Vickers, born May 28th, 1873, died July 7th, 1919. J. I. Hatfield, born December 14th, 1861, died August 7th, 1920. Oscar Rudolph, born June 13th, 1861, died May 26th, 1929. Alexander Jardine, born September 3rd, 1866, died August 4th, 1913. R. J. Cornelius, born 1887, died 1927. Mrs. Frances Overstreet, born May 6th, 1872, died January 17th, 1919. Alice Clemens Terrell, born April 7th, 1873, died August 26th, 1917. Boyce Gaskin, wife of W. M. Gaskin, born February 23rd, 1848, died October 4th, 1910. Fannie Lott, wife of Daniel Lott, born February 28th, 1815, died October 28th, 1897. Daniel Lott, died June 19th, 1872, age 77 years. Lucinda Lott, died March 17th, 1848, age 51 years. John M. Lott, Sr., born 1831, died October 6th, 1907. Mrs. Mary Jane Lott, born January 28th, 1837, died December 11th, 1910. Henry Peterson (Hal), died November 11th, 1878, 57 years of age. Martha Peterson, died February 11th, 1905, 76 years of age. Benajah Peterson, born April 10th, 1860, died August 1st, 1915. Minnie V. Sellers, born August 5th, 1859, died March 10, 1912. Willis McDonald, born July 8th, 1871, died October 15th, 1906. Annie Henson Kirkland, wife of V. W. Kirkland, born November 26th, 1859, and died September 8th, 1915. Frank L. Sweat, born March 19th, 1866, and died September 16th, 1915. B. H. Tanner, born March 17th, 1861, died December 24th, 1920. Rosa Ann Tanner, born October 27th, 1867, and died December 17th, 1910. Mother Brice was born October 2nd, 1846, and died September 18th, 1915.

David H. Kirkland was one of the first merchants in the town of Douglas. The Kirkland store stood about where the Chevrolet place now stands. He was born in 1835 and died February 15th, 1865. He was the first man who was buried in the Douglas Cemetery. George R. Briggs was born December 29th, 1839, died October 12th, 1924. Sallie Peterson, the wife of Henry Peterson, died 1891. Rev. C. W. Infinger was born August 22nd, 1856, died March 23rd, 1896. Tobitha T. Infinger was born December 27th, 1849, died January 1st, 1923. R. G. Kirkland was born October 13th, 1860, died March 22nd, 1920. John McLean was born January 5th, 1860, and died May 15th, 1909. Judge Calvin A. Ward was born December 20th, 1857, and died April 18th, 1926. Emma J. Ward was born February 18th, 1866, and died March 19th, 1921. Desdemonia Ward was born 1847, died May 3rd, 1902.

Dr. Henry C. Whelchel, born in Hall County, Georgia, in 1861, and died 1929. Maggie F. Goodyear, born April 15th, 1862, and died September 10th, 1926. Duncan S. Goodyear, born November 1st, 1857, died January 17th, 1929. Thomas Shelton Deen, born September 11th, 1855, died October 11th, 1901. Mary E. Deen, wife of T. S. Deen, born January 30th, 1856, died August 12th, 1918. Thomas S. Price, born 1870, died 1927. Lula Drew Price, born 1879, died 1927. Captain John W. Price, born February 31st, 1839, died March 5th, 1922. Sarah A. Ward, born May 3rd, 1834, died October 26th, 1918. Widow of John F. Ward, Company C, 50th Georgia. "Who now sleeps in an unknown grave near Fredericksburg, Virginia." A beautiful Confederate flag is carved on the slab covering this grave. Annie Canova Ward was born June 4th, 1867, died January 29th, 1926.

The Public Schools

Prof. Melvin Tanner
Superintendent County Schools of Coffee County.

In the early days of Coffee County and before the War Between the States, there were very few and very poor schools. Most of the teaching was done by a class of transient teachers whose learning was limited to the rudiments of the three R's—Reading, 'Riting and 'Rithmetic—and whose powers of discipline lay largely in their ability to wield the rod. During the four years of the war, practically no schools were operated. The period of reconstruction witnessed little change for the better. With the adoption of the State Constitution in 1877 provisions were made for a system of common schools for giving instruction in the elementary branches of an English education to be paid for through state appropriations made and authorized by the Legislature.

Gradually the school spirit in Coffee County began to rise. J. Monroe Wilcox, a local Methodist minister, a saintly man, and a progressive citizen, was elected County School Commissioner by the newly constituted County Board of Education.

The meager state income being the only means of

public support, the schools established were taught in country churches and in little log buildings erected through community co-operation. The school term was limited to three months, taught largely through the summer. Few teachers were paid more than twenty-five dollars per month. The Commissioner and Board of Education paid off annually, usually the first Monday in January.

Following the administration of Commissioner Wilcox, W. B. Tarrent succeeded to the office, followed by W. H. Love, Malcom Meeks, John Fussell, Jeff Kirkland, Melvin Tanner, J. H. Williams, J. G. Floyd, H. C. Roberts, and again Melvin Tanner, the present incumbent.

In the year 1900, Coffee, then the largest in area, 1123 square miles, of any county in the state, had eighty white schools and forty colored. The income for the support of this large number aggregated approximately $8,000.00. Five years later, 1905, the number of schools, white and colored, had been reduced to about eighty. The income by this time had grown to $12,113.41, all derived from the state.

About the year 1900 the city of Douglas, through Legislative Act, established an independent, or local system.

Broxton and Nicholls also established local systems which operated as independent units until 1927, when Broxton by vote of its citizens came back into the County School System. In 1929 Nicholls followed suit. Douglas continues to operate as an independent system.

Until 1911, the county schools had no income other than the state appropriation. In this year the citizens voted to levy a countywide school tax not exceeding five mills, the constitutional limit under what was then known as the McMichael Act. Up to this time no effort had been made to give high school instruction in the schools comprising the County System.

Through consolidation there are now five local tax districts in the county, viz: Ambrose, Broxton, Nicholls, Pridgen, and West Green. There are also two county line units—Lax and Temperance—that have voted local district tax. Nicholls District maintains a Senior High School on the state accredited list. The other local tax districts are maintaining Junior High Schools operating eight months.

More than four hundred pupils are enrolled in the high school departments. The income from all sources including district tax for school year 1929-30 aggregated approximately $65,000.00.

The public school system of Georgia and Coffee County was based on the Constitution of 1877. Before that time the schools were operated by the parents of the pupils. All sorts of books were used, some of which are as follows: "Webster's Blue Back Spelling Book," was used in all the schools. It was a great book. Full of information of all sorts. The principles of spelling and reading were taught in this book; in fact, it was a standard spelling book in the schools of that day. Among other books was "Smith's Arithmetic," "Smith's Grammar," "McGuffie's Readers," etc.

A slate and a pencil were used for working mathematics. Copies set by the teacher and sometimes Copy Books for writing were used. A black board was seldom seen in a school room. The main work in the school was to teach the three R's, Reading, 'Riting and 'Rithmetic. The three R's have now developed into "Rah, Rah, Rah." Another book in use at that time was the Confederate Speller. It was after the order of the Blue Back Speller, but not as large a book. Much of the reading matter was quotations from "Poor Richard." I will give you a sample as I remember it:

"He that will steal an egg will steal an ox."
"Never buy a thing because it is cheap."
"Pride goes before a fall."
"A rolling stone never gathers any moss."
"Early to bed and early to rise makes a man healthy, wealthy and wise."
"When Adam was created,
He dwelt in Eden's shade
As Moses has related,
Ten thousand times ten thousand
Creatures swarmed around,
Before any bride was made,
Or any Mate was found."
"God has a thousand musicians on every hill and ten thousand in every valley."

Teachers Coffee County Public Schools, 1930-31

Ambrose School

Mr. W. M. Melton, Mr. Thomas Gregory, Miss Alma Watson, Miss Ruby Smith, Miss Polly Fletcher, Miss Julia Harper, Miss Lydia Vickers, Miss Maxie Mixon, Miss Gussie Mixon.

Broxton School

Mr. D. Foster, Mr. J. W. McCallum, Miss Beulah Harden, Mrs. E. J. Newbern, Miss Hanna Neal Jones, Miss Lucille Keene, Miss Mattie Talley, Miss Zella Barwick, Mrs. Rubye Brown, Miss Frances Cason, Miss Irma Willis, Miss Gladys Kilpatrick, Miss Emma Blount, Mrs. J. W. McCallum, Miss Gladys DuBose.

Nicholls School

Mr. V. E. Glenn, Mr. Clement Carton, Miss Marion Laine, Mr. E. M. Thompson, Miss Beatrice Meeks, Miss Miriam Anderson, Miss Alice Parker, Mrs. Stanley Martin, Miss Maude Griswold, Miss Rita Taylor, Mrs. A. P. Meeks, Mr. E. D. Gilliard.

West Green School

Mr. J. O. Wingard, Mr. Jim Tom Bush, Mrs. Jim Tom Bush, Miss Mildred G. Carmichael, Miss Elvira Jackson, Miss Erma Cross, Mrs. J. O. Wingard, Mrs. L. L. Denton.

Pridgen School

Mr. E. M. Horne, Miss Lucille Lewis, Miss Arloa Pridgen, Miss Blanche England.

Rocky Creek School

Mrs. W. C. Smith.

Rocky Pond School

Mr. E. C. Wideman, Mrs. W. J. Cavenaugh, Miss Rubye Burkett.

New Forest School

Mr. M. B. Allman, Miss Lucille Douglas, Miss Johnnie Byrd.

Sears School

Mr. Ira Moore, Mrs. Myrtle Harrell Gillis.

Stokesville School

Mrs. Estelle Robinette, Miss Vera Gillis, Miss Estelle Gillis.

Ward School

Mrs. W. R. Vickers, Mr. Felder Vickers, Miss Gertrude Kirkland.

Vickers School

Mrs. D. P. McKay, Miss Beatrice Vinson.

Vickers Chapel

Mrs. Dorris Brown, Miss Bonnie Sumner.

St. Illa School

Miss Lillian Tanner, Miss Gladys Griffis.

Salem School

Mrs. Fisher Gaskin, Miss Annie Clough, Miss Myrtice Griffis.

Sunny Side School

Mrs. J. S. Wilkerson, Miss Vida Lou Kight.

McClelland School

Mr. Pittman Vickers, Miss Bessie Butler.

Douglas Public School Teachers

High School

Mr. J. L. Fortney, Supt.; Mr. F. M. Chalker, Prin.; Mr. J. A. Pulley, Coach; Miss Esther Strong, Supervisor; Miss Elizabeth Neal, Supervisor, Public School Music; Miss Miriam Edwards, Teacher of Expression; Miss Vivian Smith, Teacher of Piano; Miss Elizabeth Voigt, Librarian; Miss Agnes Saunders, Dom. Science; Miss Mary Stanford, Latin; Miss Marion Coile, History; Miss Willie Pearl Davis, French; Miss Agnes McNair, Math.

Elementary

Miss Marion DuBose, Miss Myrtle Jackson, Mrs. Esther Clements, Miss Melva Coffee, Mrs. Milton Cole,

Miss Fannie Mae Norman, Miss Blanche Thornton, Mrs. G. L. Spivey, Miss Olive Rogers.

Primary

Mrs. Melvin Tanner, Miss Sybil Shelnutt, Miss Corinne Jackson, Miss Nora Huss, Miss Lola Mae McLean, Miss Lucy Hall, Miss Carolyn Hall, Miss Elizabeth Brown.

South Georgia State College

The South Georgia State College was formerly the Eleventh District Agricultural and Mechanical School. In 1906 the General Assembly passed an act establishing an Agricultural and Mechanical School in each of the eleven congressional districts. Douglas won the school for the eleventh district by offering fifty-two thousand dollars, three hundred acres of land, and water and lights for a term of ten years.

The first year's work began in the fall of 1907. Three splendid buildings were ready for the students and nearly every department had good equipment. The school continued to do general high school work, including Agriculture and Mechanical Arts and Home Economics, until the summer of 1927, at which time the General Assembly passed an Act creating the South Georgia Junior State College, the new college absorbing all of the property including buildings, equipment and grounds, of the Eleventh District A. & M. School. The new charter permitted the South Georgia Junior State College to do two years of college work and continue its high school work so long as the Board of Trustees and Faculty deemed it wise to do so. In 1929 the General Assembly changed the name of the college by dropping the word "Junior." It is now the South Georgia State College.

The South Georgia State College offers freshman and sophomore work in courses leading to the following degrees: Bachelor of Arts, Bachelor of Science, Bachelor of Education, Bachelor of Music.

Charles W. Davis was the first principal, serving from 1907 to 1914. J. W. Powell from 1914 to 1917, C. W. Fraser from 1917 to 1918, L. G. Procter, 1918-19, J. M. Thrash from 1919 to 1927, at which time the charter was changed, creating a college, J. M. Thrash was elected president, serving to date.

The Faculty 1930-31

J. M. Thrash, President, Georgia School of Technology; special work Mercer University.

C. C. Childs, B.S., M.A., Dean, History and Social Sciences, Mercer University.

T. A. Clower, A.B., M.A., Education, University of Georgia, Emory University.

C. E. Lancaster, B.S.C., M.A., English, Mercer University.

C. A. Johnson, B.S., Science, University of Georgia.

R. C. Childs, A.B., M.A., French, Spanish, Louisiana State University, Georgia, Peabody College for Teachers, Nashville, Tenn.

Charles A. Reed A.B., M.S., Physics and Mathematics, University of Oklahoma.

J. H. Breedlove, L.I., History, Science, Georgia, Peabody College for Teachers, Iowa State College of Agriculture.

H. F. Johnson, B.S.C., Athletic Coach, Instructor in Mathematics, University of Georgia.

Miss Mary T. Collins, A.B., Instructor in English, Georgia State College for Women, Milledgeville.

Miss Jimmy Carmack, Home Economics, Girls' Disciplinarian, Georgia State College for Women, Valdosta, Graduate Student University of Georgia; Mercer University, Georgia, Peabody College.

Miss Lucile Wheeler, Secretary and Registrar, Georgia State College for Women.

Miss Ethel Wilkerson, Piano, Voice and Expression, Shorter College, New York School of Music, Bush Conservatory of Chicago.

W. P. Richey, Mechanic Arts, Superintendent of Boys' Dormitory, South Georgia Junior State College, South Georgia A. & M. College.

Mrs. B. J. Moye, Superintendent of Dining Hall, Warthen College.

Georgia Normal Business College

The Georgia Normal College and Business Institute came into being at Abbeville in 1897 with Prof. A. A. Kuhl and Prof. W. A. Little its head.

It was operated there for about ten years, hundreds of students graduating in shorthand, bookkeeping, teachers' courses and business training courses. Douglas at that time was little more than a village, but far-seeing citizens sought Little and Kuhl and persuaded them to come to Douglas. Within five years from the date of their coming to Douglas in 1908, the population trebled. Conservative estimates reveal that 5,500 students have graduated from the college since it came to this city. Further interesting information in connection with the development of both the school and the city, reveals that approximately $1,250,000 has been expended by students attending the school. The thirty-two years of activity have presented to the business world in practically every state of the Union and Cuba, graduates that are now leaders in the business world. Many of the G. N. B. C. have gained places prominent in political and financial circles as well as high places in the religious world.

For the past several years, Prof. and Mrs. A. A. Kuhl have operated the institution since Mr. Little severed his connection to accept the chair of English at the University of Florida.

The new home will be ready for occupancy with the fall term in 1930, and will be more spacious and suited to the needs and purposes of the school. At present equipment is owned that invoices approximately $30,-000. There is not a commercial school in the State that has enjoyed greater success, or done more effective work.

Coffee County, 1930

Size, Altitude—Longitude and Latitude—
Population about 20,000.

Coffee County, Georgia, January 1, 1930, consists of six hundred thirty-two square miles of territory situated about ninety miles west of the Atlantic Ocean, is about three hundred feet above sea level. Its latitude is 31° 30", longitude 82° 83". Population about 20,000

About 1800 when this section of the country was first settled it had the appearance of a beautiful pine park with many streams of water. With beautiful hills and valleys, with hammocks on the east side of nearly all the large streams. There was plenty of game here, birds, turkeys and deer and the streams had plenty of fish. It will be observed that the hammocks and sand ridges are located on the east side of all the large streams. It is said by those who profess to know that when the waters of this country were flowing into the Atlantic Ocean the waters moved east and washed the sands into the streams from the west side over on the east side and that is why great banks of sand, covered with black jack oaks grow on the east side of the streams. You will further observe that the east side of the stream contains many springs. This is especially true of the Seventeen-Mile Creek. The reason for this is said to be when the rain falls on the sand hill on the east side of the stream it sinks down into the clay some ten or twenty feet and then seeps down to the stream and bursts out into a spring which contains the best and purest water in the world. It has been strained through a mile and more of sand. Gaskin Springs on the east side of the Seventeen-Mile Creek, two miles from Douglas, is a good illustration of what is here stated.

About the year 1800 there was not a decent road or bridge in all the territory now occupied by Coffee County. Later on the Blackshear Road and the Columbus Road were "cut out" but were never graded nor bridges built. The only road which tradition has brought to our notice is a single pathway that led from old man Daniel Lott's home, near where John Peterson now lives to the old Ward home where Mr. B. W. Tanner now lives. There was not a public road anywhere to any place in this territory. The first bridge in Coffee County was built many years after the civil war.

In addition to the wildwoods and a few pioneer citizens we had the Creek Indians and as they owned this country and lived here when we came here, we have thought it proper to give a somewhat extended write-up of the Creek Indians. It seems that no real history of the Creek Indians has ever been written—nothing describing their personal appearance, their habits of life, nor their real economic lives as they once lived in Coffee County. As a rule the Indian commissioners in their reports to the Government, consisted of some Medicine Men or green corn dance or some other matter that did not make a history of the Creek Indians.

A short biography of Billy Bow-Legs, the celebrated Seminole Indian Chief of Florida will appear in another place.

The information upon which the story of the Creek Indians is written has been obtained from many sources. From the reports made to the Government by Indian

Commissioners. Drake's History of American Indians and the "Seminoles" of Florida written by Mrs. Wilson of Kissimmee, Florida. I am also indebted to Mr. George W. Powers who lived in Florida in 1846 and many years after that time; he had a personal acquaintance with Billy Bow-Legs. Much has been learned from tradition about the Creek Indians who lived in this section. They were friendly and were good mixers with the Pioneers of this section of the country.

Coffee County has several varieties of native trees. Also many native birds, native fish, and native snakes. Each of these items is more fully discussed in spearate articles in this book. And it may be truly said that Coffee County is well watered. It is bound on the north by the Ocmulgee River. The Satilla River runs all the way through the southern section of the county. The Seventeen-Mile Creek is a large creek with numerous runs and lakes all through it. It rises in the northwestern part of the county and runs southeast entirely through the county.

There are several smaller streams throughout the county. Otter Creek and Tiger Creek are in the central eastern part of the county and flow south into Seventeen-Mile Creek. In addition to these streams there are many other smaller streams such as gullies, branches, spring heads, etc. Many of the smaller streams never go dry. There are ever-running springs and so it can be truly said that Coffee County is well watered. In Pioneer days there were thousands of fish in these creeks and streams, but sad to say, poison, dynamite, seines, traps, etc., have destroyed nearly all the fish in small streams, and in like manner many of the birds have been destroyed by high-powered shot guns and bird dogs. Forest fires have greatly injured the trees and all growing plants in the wild woods; but it is worthy of note, that in two or three years an abundance of fish will raise in the streams, and when fire is kept out of the woods, pine trees come back rapidly and when the hunter gives the birds a chance, it only requires a few years to fill the woods again with quail and other birds. The good Lord seems to be on the giving hand and when we destroy one gift he sends another and so we find ourselves always in "God's Country in Coffee County."

Douglas, the Capital City of Coffee County

COURT HOUSE, DOUGLAS, GEORGIA

The Legislature of Georgia created Coffee County in 1854. Mr. James Pearson gave the county fifty acres of land on which to build the public buildings for the county. This fifty-acre tract of land was surveyed into lots and blocks. The court house was not built until 1858. The lumber for building the court house was sawed at a mill on the Ocmulgee River. The lumber was floated down the river to Barrows Bluff and then hauled out to Douglas with ox teams. The court house was located back of the Overstreet building. The offices for the county officials were located on the second floor of the auditorium where the cases were tried on the first floor. It is said that Coursey Cato nailed the last shingle on the court house when it was covered and that he stood on his head as a signal that the building was finished.

Several jail houses have been built in Douglas. The first jail was a brick building and stood on the corner where the Tanner brick residence now stands. The brick out of which the building was built was a very poor grade and in a year or two the building fell down. The next jail that was built was located about where the Coca-Cola building now stands and was built of hewn logs. The first story had no doors. The prisoner was taken upstairs and the ladder let down from the upper floor and the prisoner went down the ladder to his quarters in the jail below. When the ladder was taken up the prisoner was safely in jail. The prisoner was taken out in the same manner. The last jail is the building that you now see on the court house square. It has stood there more than thirty years and two men have been hanged within its walls.

The next building in Douglas was built for a hotel and boarding house. It was built of logs and was situated on the lot where the Peterson home now stands. The building was constructed by J. K. Hilliard, who came from Holmesville, Georgia. The log hotel was a big success and was the only hotel in Douglas for many, many years.

The first store house built in Douglas was occupied by Ive Kirkland. It was located near where the Chevrolet building now stands. The Spivey home and store stood where the court house now stands. He had a big family of girls and boys. The next store house was a small wooden building with a back room and a side room and stood where the Union Bank building now stands. That building was occupied by Dr. Barber as an office and drug store and post office.

From time to time other buildings were constructed and other little store houses were scattered around. The mail was brought here on horse back from Stockton, Georgia, about twice a week.

There was a race track leading from about where the court house now stands down the road by the side of a fence and ended about where the A. B. & C. depot now stands. We had some wonderful races on that track by some wonderful horses by some wonderful riders. It often happened that the worse looking horse won the race.

All the matters and things written above transpired before the Civil War. When the war came on Douglas went to pieces. There was nothing here to make a town and no town was made.

When the war was over and the soldiers returned home, Douglas was only a wide place in the road. It is said a troop of Yankees rode several days coming to Douglas, Georgia. When they reached here, it is said they walked out in the middle of the streets and looked north and east and south and west, and not a man was in sight, and they said in wonder and astonishment, "Is this Douglas?" "Are you sure this is Douglas?"

The old court house and an acre of land on which it stood was sold to B. Peterson and a new court house was built of wood where the present court house now stands. The old court house was used as a school house, as a church house, for shows, for political meetings, and for everything else that a house was needed for in Douglas. I might add also that the goats had possession of it a long time.

For many years after the war Douglas was only a little country hamlet. There was nothing here except big court twice a year. All the business that Douglas should have had went to Hazlehurst and to Pearson. We had no railroads and nothing to build up the town.

The first train came to Douglas from McDonalds Mill, now Axson, about 1895. The next train that came to Douglas was the Waycross Air Line, a small railroad built by the Southern Pine Company from Nicholls up to Douglas in 1898. In a short time we had railroads to Fitzgerald and to Broxton. These roads have now grown into the great railroad systems of the A. B. & C. R. R. and the Georgia and Florida Railroad.

With the coming of the railroads various enterprises came to Douglas. The Ashley-Price Lumber Company, the Agricultural School, G. & F. R. R. shops, and the Georgia Normal Business College.

The first brick building in Douglas was a school building. It was built in 1896. The railroad was extended from Downing to Douglas primarily for the purpose of hauling the brick to build the middle building on the campus in Douglas. Professor John R. Overman taught the first school in the new building. The next building was a large wooden building with auditorium upstairs and is still standing on the southwest corner of the campus. The money for that was one thousand dollars paid by Lucius Guthrey for permission to sell liquor in Douglas.

Eighteen hundred and ninety-eight the court house was burned, and in 1900 the present brick court house was built.

With the coming of the many enterprises mentioned above, Douglas put on a new life. Water and lights were installed. Later on the streets of the city were paved. Side walks were laid along the principal streets of the city. The Baptist and Methodist churches were built. And from time to time improvements have been made in the business section of the city and also in the residential section.

Douglas has one of the most beautiful cemeteries in South Georgia. The place is well kept and has many beautiful trees and shrubbery of all kinds. There are many very expensive tombstones. Among some of the very nice monuments are those of J. M. Ashley, Frank Sweat, B. Peterson, and others. At this writing, 1930, Douglas is a beautiful city of 5,000 inhabitants, with all the advantages of a real city and the pleasures of a country town. The water for the city is furnished by an artesian well which affords an abundance of pure, fresh water. Douglas is a good city in which to live and no one who lives here has ever been ashamed to say, "My home is in Douglas, Georgia."

Towns in Coffee County

Ambrose

The town of Ambrose, in Coffee County, was started in 1899. Soon after the A. B. & A. Railroad had reached that place, Dennis Vickers and J. J. Phillips gave the land on which to build the town. H. L. Vickers put up a store and Dr. Moorman built a drug store. Soon afterwards H. L. Vickers built a brick building and ran a general merchandise store. Dennis Vickers built a gin, and other enterprises came in from time to time. At the present time Mr. T. J. Holland is manufacturing guano in Ambrose. The Seaboard Farms have their warehouses at Ambrose and make that their shipping point to north and west. Mr. H. B. Macklin, who manages these truck farms, is now trying an experiment by transporting the products of his farm to New York and other large cities with trucks. He has eighteen trucks which go from South Georgia points to northern points in thirty-six hours.

In 1927 the Ambrose School District voted for bonds to build a school building and the building has been completed and is a credit to Ambrose and to Coffee County. In 1915 the Christian Church was built at Ambrose. Mr. T. J. Holland is one of the leaders of that denomination at Ambrose.

October 1st, 1930, the Georgia Power Company began to furnish power for Ambrose and they now have lights. The town has about five hundred people and is in a good farming section and will grow as the country grows.

Ambrose is about twelve miles west of Douglas on the A. B. & C. Railroad.

Broxton

Broxton was named after Broxton Creek near by. The tract of land where Broxton is now situated was owned many years ago by John Passmore.

Mr. Jesse Lott bought the entire tract of land and built a log cabin on what is now the center of the town. He and his wife moved there, later replacing the cabin by a large two-story dwelling.

HIGH SCHOOL, BROXTON, GEORGIA

Broxton was known first as Gully Branch. The mail was carried on horseback from Pearson on Tuesday of each week by a crippled Confederate soldier named Bryant Douglas.

Mr. Jesse Lott was first postmaster. Next Mr Thomas Young. Following him was Mr. B. R. Leggett, who was postmaster twenty years, and is now serving in the capacity of assistant postmaster. Now Miss Mae Gibbs is postmistress.

Mr. Jesse Lott, Mr. Thomas Young and Mr. B. R. Leggett are the outstanding men who figured in the founding of Broxton and making it a town worthy to live in.

Mr. Leggett came here from Jesup and was the third man to build a home here. For two years he was in the mercantile business. In 1902 he was appointed railroad agent of Georgia and Florida, which position he held three years, when he was appointed postmaster.

Dr. Ricketson, deceased, was born and reared here and was once a Representative of Coffee County.

J. L. Palmer, deceased, was first mayor.

The Methodist Church, named "Monroe Chapel" after the sainted Rev. J. M. Wilcox, is the oldest church in the town, built in 1890.

The Baptist Church (as well as can be learned) was organized in 1902.

From a little section of wildwood Broxton has grown to a fine town with its three churches, Methodist Church, Baptist, and Primitive Baptist, its consolidated schools, twenty-four hour service electric lights, water, excellent mail service, good banking system.

Broxton also has the credit of having one of the first newspapers in the county. The organ known as the Broxton Journal was printed in 1905, and also has possibly had some part in telling to outsiders the advantages to be gained by living in Broxton. One year prior to that, Broxton's first public school was erected. Today that institution stands as one of the foremost in the county. It is of the consolidated variety and offers to children of the territory surrounding the city an education on par with that to be secured in larger municipalities.

Outstanding as the oldest active civic body in Broxton is the Womans Club, an organization founded in 1917 by twelve women of the community who had determined that steps should be taken to place the city in its rightful place as one of the leading sections of Coffee County.

Mrs. Ben Poer was named president and Mrs. John Lewis and Mrs. E. L. Bledsoe were named Secretary and Treasurer respectively. Soon after this organization the Womans Club became connected with the State Federation.

Schools of Broxton

Many years ago, after Pioneers had first settled in the city now known as Broxton, children of this section went to a little wooden school house each morning to receive the rudiments of reading, writing, and arithmetic.

No longer do pupils walk many miles to school. Today students of Broxton and the section surrounding the town are carried to a modern building in busses built for that purpose. Their school building is an architectural design followed in larger cities and the courses offered are on par with the curriculums of greater institutions.

The thirteen rooms of the two schools afford ample accommodations for the 480 pupils enrolled, and the fourteen teachers are well qualified to instruct in the most modern subjects. Probably outstanding among the courses offered in addition to the usual ones required in all schools is a home economics class for girls and a pig club for the boys.

A library of 500 volumes, which was installed by the Broxton women, is one of the leading assets of the school and is used by the students.

Nicholls

PUBLIC SCHOOL, NICHOLLS, GEORGIA

The town of Nicholls, Georgia, is situated on the A. B. & C. Railroad, twelve miles east of Douglas. The town was settled by the Southern Pine Company in 1895. The post office was named for Captain John C. Nicholls, who represented this district in Congress for several years. The first post office to bear the name of Nicholls was located at old man Dan Lott's country store, about four miles north of Nicholls. This store was established about 1869, and for many years the post office at Hazlehurst served all that section of Coffee County near the Lott store. When the A. B. & C. Railroad, then the Waycross Air Line Railroad, was built from Waycross to Nicholls, 1895, the post office was established at Nicholls.

The first school in Nicholls was organized in 1895 and was a one-teacher school. Mr. Ingram was the first teacher, and later was a Methodist minister. At one time the school was operated in a large two-story building located near the site of the L. B. Cole residence. In 1909 bonds were voted and the present brick school building was built. The town is yet in need of better school facilities. The next big project will be the erection of a modern school plant. With the building of the schoolhouse came the churches. First the Missionary Baptist Church was organized by Rev. M. A. Grace. The building was located near the railroad, near where the Cason home is now located. The Union Missionary Baptist Church was organized by Rev. Gilford Lastinger about a mile east of Nicholls. About the year 1920, while Rev. H. M. Meeks was pastor of both these churches, they united into one church and built a church house in Nicholls. The Baptist Church has a membership of about three hundred and fifty.

The history of the Methodist Church in Nicholls dates back to about 1870. Rev. Daniel Morrison, of sainted memory, and Rev. W. A. McDonald were Pioneers in Methodism in this section. The church was situated where the Meeks cemetery is now located, about a mile east of Nicholls. Later the church was located in Nicholls, near the Edinfield home, where the Methodists worshiped for many years. The present Methodist Church was built in 1910.

The Primitive Baptist Church was organized by Elder Richard Bennett, a pioneer preacher of his faith. It is situated about two miles northwest of Nicholls. And Elim Church is now one of the strongest Primitive Baptist Churches in Coffee County.

The telephone system was installed about the year 1904. The first brick building built in Nicholls was constructed in the year 1908 and was occupied by W. M. Robinowitz as a general store.

The tobacco business in Coffee County had its origin on a farm two miles south of Nicholls which was occupied and cultivated by S. J. Brown. The farm is now known as the McGee farm. Nicholls also had one of the first tobacco warehouses in Coffee County. It is said that the territory adjacent to Nicholls produces the best grade of tobacco in Coffee County.

While the Southern Pine Company operated a saw mill in Nicholls, all sorts of people from everywhere lived in Nicholls. But when the mill moved, the town was then occupied by the pioneer families of Coffee County. The pioneer families are: Meeks, Halls, Waters, Bagleys, Vinsons, Cannons, Kirklands, Powers, Davis, Testons, Lewis, Tanners, and Taylors.

The population of the town is about a thousand people.

Nicholls is lighted by the Georgia Power Company.

West Green

About the year 1900 The Southern Pine Lumber Company extended its tramroad south from Hazlehurst twenty miles. One branch extending toward Nicholls, the other leading west to Broxton. And the junction was known to the earlier settlers as "The Twenty." "The Twenty" at that time boasted of one residence, a shanty occupied by an old slavery darky known as "Mammy." In a short time the J. P. Courthouse, as it now stands, was erected with B. T. Burkett presiding J. P.

The first enterprise of "The Twenty" was "The Boyd Bird Cross Tie Company," who operated a commissary, which was the first store.

About six or seven years later the railroad changed hands and the name was known as the D. A. and G. "The Twenty" becoming Garrant. J. J. Ward built a house with living quarters on one side and a room on the other side was used as the first depot. In the center room the first general store was operated by J. J. Ward. T. W. Thompson was the first agent and operator at the railroad. About a year later the railroad became the Georgia and Florida. A new depot was built, with section houses.

After this the people became optimistic, and G. W. and W. L. Lott formed a real estate company, building several houses and laying off streets. They also built a modern gin and grist mill which was operated by J. L. Denton, who was one of the pioneer citizens.

The second mercantile business was that of W. B. Courson and son, W. R. Courson.

The next enterprise of importance was a saw mill owned and operated by N. S. Boyd, which later became "The Garrant Lumber Co." T. J. Dickey, Lon Dickey of Fitzgerald, and N. S. Boyd formed the company. About the same time L. D. Long and J. C. Brewer of Douglas operated a saw mill.

The first organization to erect a building here was the K. of P., who built a two-story building. The upper story of which was used for "Castle Hall" by the organization. It was also used for schools and church purposes. The lower floor was used for a drug store, which was operated by R. E. Darnell, who later sold out to Dr. W. L. Hall and was the first physician the village had.

G. W. Lott gave ten acres of land for school purposes and upon this site a two-story building was erected.

A short time later G. W. Lott sold practically his entire real estate possessions to The South Georgia Farm Company, who are the present owners. It was through their influence a number of citizens were brought here from South Carolina, Tennessee, and other states. About this time the town was incorporated, and the name was changed to West Green, honoring a member of the company whose name was Westbrook. Mr. John A. Cromartie of Hazlehurst was employed by the above company to look after their interests. He moved his family here and they meant a great deal to the social, civic and religious life of the town.

In 1915 the Baptist and Methodist churches were erected, with Rev. S. G. Taylor pastor of the Baptist Church. In 1921 the Free Will Baptist Church was built, through the influence of Rev. C. C. Coursey of Baxley, who became its first pastor.

As time passed and the people progressed and became more aggressive they realized their institute of learning was inadequate to the needs of the time, and in 1925, through the efforts of J. H. Green, a sentiment was erected to vote bonds and a modern building was erected with ten class rooms, domestic science department, and an auditorium with seating capacity of 500.

About 1912 B. B. Jackson installed a modern telephone exchange, which was a great means towards the development of a modern town.

The Turpentine Industry

By Mrs. Lon Dickey

The Pine Tree is the most valuable asset that Coffee County ever had. Perhaps the cotton crop comes next. There was not a turpentine still in Coffee County till after 1870. Among the first turpentine stills operated in Coffee County was operated by McNeil and McNeil. The still was located at Rock Falls, near the northern part of Coffee County. Their shipping point was Bare Lake on the Ocmulgee River. Soon after this business began Mr. William C. Vereen from Cheraw, S. C., joined the firm. Mr. Vereen located his still near the town of West Green. He secured leases on thousands and thousands of acres. In 1890 Mr. Vereen moved to Colquitt County and has become a very prominent, wealthy citizen of that county. However he was not forgotten in Coffee County by his friends here. A short time ago in speaking of Coffee County, he says: "I spent four very happy years in Coffee County and formed a number of friendships among the good people of that county, among them were John M. Lott, J. S. Lott, Mr. Samp Smith, Daniel Peterson, and others. I recall Rev. J. M. Wilcox, who lived near our place, as one of the best men I ever knew."

Among other turpentine operators in Coffee County were J. J. Lewis and Marshall Ashley. Another firm was Merritt and Powell, also McLean and Powell and Lott and McLean.

In the southern section of Coffee County, near Pearson, D. F. Bullard had a large turpentine place and became very wealthy. He moved to Savannah but never forgot his Coffee County friends. Mr. J. J. Lewis was married to Miss Lou Ashley, a daughter of Captain Matt Ashley. Mr. Rufus R. Perkins, who was associated with Mr. John McLean in the turpentine business, married Miss Dora Lott, a daughter of Mrs. Jesse Lott of Broxton.

An interesting problem of the turpentine business was securing labor sufficient to operate so many stills. At the close of each year's work the turpentine men would go back to the Carolinas and secure negroes by the train-loads. They would unload at Hazlehurst and haul the negroes and their families out to the stills and deposit them in the cabins prepared for them.

At each of these stills a church was built for the negroes, which they attended with great regularity. They also had baseball clubs and other things for their entertainment. Most all negroes are religious and musical. They have guitars, banjos, fiddles, and they all sing. They all have what you call spirituals; sometimes they sing like fighting fire and sometimes like you are at a funeral. Here is a sample of a turpentine song:

"A ban' of angels done come after me,
　Come for to carry me home,
Come on, bred'ren, jes' come an' see,
　Come for to carry me home.

"Come on, chilluns, and le's go home,
　Le's take us wings an' fly,
Wrap me up in a little white sheet
　For I want to go to Heb'n when I die."

It is thought by those well acquainted with negroes, their habits of thought and plan of living, that their religious inclinations is a very good thing. Negroes have a lot of energy which they work off in religious exercises in preaching, singing, shouting, etc. Of course all this is harmless. Many other nations of people work off their surplus energy in strikes and walk-outs and things of that sort.

Other turpentine firms are Mr. John Peterson, who married Miss Maggie Smith, a daughter of Samp Smith, who operates a business at Huffer, Ga. And Mr. A. G. Coffee is working the Vereen timber near West Green, Ga. Mr. John M. Cook of McRae has recently purchased the large turpentine interests formerly owned by J. L. Sapp and covers the same tracts of land formerly worked by McLean and Howell.

Another extensive turpentine operator in Coffee County was Mr. E. A. Buck. His interest was in the neighborhood of Douglas. One of the best known turpentine operators in Coffee County was Tony Howell. His name was Miles Wilson Howell. He came to Coffee County from Portsmouth, Va. Mr. Howell was born in Gatts County in 1845. He is buried in Fitzgerald, Ga. He was a great church man and gave liberally to all denominations.

Fifty Uses of Turpentine

(By U. S. Department of Agriculture Forest Service Office of Forest Products.)

Volatile thinner for paints, varnishes and wood fillers.

To accelerate oxidation of drying oils (as ozonizer).

Solvent for waxes in shoes and leather polishes, floor polishes, and furniture polishes.

Solvent for gums in lacquers and varnishes.

Ingredients of waterproof cement for leather, rubber, glass, metals, etc.

Solvent for waterproofing compositions.

Cleaner for removing paints and oils from fabrics.

Pharmaceutical purposes, including disinfectants, liniments, medicated soaps, internal remedies, ointments.

Raw material for producing synthetic camphor and indirectly, celluloid, explosives, fireworks, and machines.

Raw material for producing terpineol and eucalyptol.

Raw material for producing terpin-hydrate used in medicines.

Raw material for producing isoprene used in making synthetic rubber.

In the manufacture of sealing wax.

In glazing putty.

Ingredients of some printing inks.

In color printing, processes in lithography.

Lubricant in grinding and drilling glass.

As a moth repeller and in moth exterminators.

Constituent of insecticides.

For cleaning fire-arms (alone or in combination with other materials).

In laundry glosses.

In washing preparations.

In rubber substitutes.

In wood stains.

In stove polishes.

In molding wax and grafting waxes.

In belting greases.

In drawing crayons.

In the manufacture of leather.

As a substitute of pine oil.

In flotation concentration of ores.

Solvent for rubber, caoutchouc and similar substances.

Used to prevent "bleeding" in the manufacture of cotton and print goods.

Laboratory reagent, as substitute for more expensive organic solvent.

Oxygen carrier in refining in petroleum illuminating oils.

Colored turpentine, reagent for wood and cork in Biological technique.

Scab Timber

One source of wealth to the early settlers of Coffee County was "getting out scab timber" and running the same down the river to the markets, Darien and Bruntfort. Much of this timber in Coffee County was floated down the Ocmulgee River, the Satilla River, and other smaller streams such as Pudding Creek and the Seventeen-Mile Creek. The men who got this timber were called "Timber Cutters." They selected large trees and cut them down with club axes and then hewed the tree on four sides till it was square. These trees averaged from twelve inches to twenty-four inches square and were from twenty-five to fifty feet long. When thus prepared for market they were hauled to the water with mules and oxen and rafted on the water. The men then prepared themselves with provisions, got on the raft of logs, and drifted down to market. A raft would drift about twenty miles a day. The large logs would measure fifteen and sixteen hundred feet and would bring about twelve cents per foot. The smaller logs would contain about five and six hundred feet and would sell for nine and ten cents per foot. The farmers would "cut timber" in the fall and winter months when they were not engaged on the farm. Many of our most prosperous farmers, such as old man Elijah Tanner and his sons, the Gillis family, the Griffis, and other citizens along the big creeks and rivers. Many of men and boys got a good start in life by "scab timber." When the saw mills came this kind of business went out of fashion.

Scab timber was rafted and floated down the following streams, to-wit: The Satilla River down to

Burned Fort; down the Seventeen-Mile Creek into the Satilla River; down Pudding Creek; down Seventeen-Mile Creek; down Red Bluff into the Seventeen-Mile Creek. Burned Fort was the market for all "scab timber" floated down the Satilla River.

On the northern part of Coffee County the only stream was the Ocmulgee River. All timbers floated down the Ocmulgee River went to Darien, Ga., to be marketed.

A Study in Human Hands

Last Tuesday morning I looked into the hands of one thousand school children. Each little hand was open to receive a card or button which admitted the child to the Fair Grounds of Coffee County. I saw all sorts of hands. Some fat and some lean. Some long and thin and others short and chubby. But they were all human hands, the most unique piece of mechanism in all the world. Some of the little hands were full of plunder—pictures, cards, fruit, candy, strings and the like—that I could scarcely find room for a button.

When I was a little boy my grandmother took my hand in hers and said, "I wonder what these little hands will find to do?" It made a profound impression on my young mind. Now I find myself asking the same question about these thousands of Coffee County hands. I wonder what they will find to do?

The Bible tells us about clean hands and bloody hands. There are also smart hands and lazy hands—hands that toil and hands that play, hands that steal and hands that bless and help. The world would be better off if some boys and girls had no hands with which to do mischief. God gave us our hands for a good purpose. It is a grand sight to see a thousand children hold up their hands. They are all charged with dynamite to the finger tips for good or evil. The poet has said:

"I wonder where their little feet will stray,
And what their little hands will do,
I wonder what their little lips will say,
When they go from me and you?"

The human hand has played a large part in the history of the world. The most skilled labor is done by hand. What would a generation do who had no hands? Then if hands are so important don't you think we should make the best possible use of them? If we have clear heads, pure hearts and clean hands life will be a glorious success.

So here is a good hand-shake for each child who reads this letter. Take good care of your hands while you live, for at last they will be laid across your breast, their work finished forever.

From Ward's Scrapbook, Coffee County, Georgia. Ward's Scrapbook, 1905.

Education

There is no royal road to learning. In these good old days there was hardly a road of any kind. The state had no public school system. The churches had some colleges and the state a few, but the common people had not a place to learn a lesson till they provided for it. The school masters were, as a rule, men who had made a failure of life, and who were hanging on to the ragged edge and taught for a living. A community would join together and hire a teacher and put him in some little out-house, with poor seats and no heat. Only reading and writing were taught. The teacher would board around with the parents and the school would last about three months in a year and many of the children would walk four and five miles to school. Children took their dinner to school, and the noon hour was spent in games, such as "cat," town ball, marbles, role-a-hole. People generally wanted a teacher to be tight on the children. A teacher who did not whip was regarded as a poor make out for a teacher. "Spare the rod and spoil the child" was good Bible with them.

They paid the teacher about $15 and $20 per month and fed him. Of course, towns had better teachers and better schools.

Some of the old teachers who taught in this section were Prof. Nash, Elisha Graham, Samuel Isaacs, Prof. Holiday, W. B. Byrd, "Doggie" Young, J. M. Wilcox, Eton A. Howell, and others.

You must not get the idea that all the people in this section were ignorant. Many of them came here from Virginia and the Carolinas and had good educations.

But most people lived the pioneer life and paid little attention to education. Many of the best men and women who grew up in the forties and fifties could not read nor write, but in spite of these handicaps they made good citizens.

Inferior Courts and Courts of Ordinary

The Acts of 1854, pages 294-6, approved February 9th of that year, creating Coffee County, provided that an election should be held on the first Monday in January, 1855, at which county officers, including five justices of the Inferior Court, should be elected. Justices of the Inferior Court were elected and given charge of all of the fiscal affairs of the county and charged with the duty of procuring land and locating the county site, and erecting the public buildings. The Justices of the Inferior Court continued to administer all the fiscal affairs of Coffee County up to and through the year 1868, when under the Amendment to the Constitution, approved the second time December 5, 1851, the office and Court of Ordinary was created, and the first Ordinary of Coffee County was elected during the year 1868, and assumed office beginning with the year 1869. The last Justices of the Inferior Court were Daniel Newbern, J. M. Wilcox, John M. Lott, and James S. Pearson, who went out of the office under the Constitutional Amendment at the end of the year 1868, and the first Ordinary who assumed office in January, 1869, was Daniel Lott. The first official act recorded on the Minutes by the Ordinary was to fix the pay of jurors in the Superior Court of Coffee County at the sum of $1.00 per day.

Coffee County Justices of the Inferior Court

Mark Lott, Jr.................Apr. 8, 1854-Jan. 12, 1857
Joel Lott ....Apr. 8, 1854-Jan. 12, 1857
Alexander Mobly ....Apr. 8, 1854-Jan. 12, 1857
Hardy Hall ....Apr. 8, 1854-Jan. 12, 1857

Elijah Pickren ....Apr. 8, 1854-Jan. 12, 1857
Mark Lott, Jr..............Jan. 12, 1857-Jan. 10, 1861
Hiram Sears ....Jan. 12, 1857-Jan. 10, 1861
Hardy Hall ....Jan. 12, 1857-Jan. 10, 1861
Hiram Swain ....Jan. 12, 1857-
Daniel Newbern ....Jan. 12, 1857-Jan. 10, 1861
Calvin A. Ward ....June 15, 1858-Jan. 10, 1861
Mark Willcox ....Jan. 10, 1861-Jan. 25, 1862
John Vickers, Jr...........Jan. 10, 1861-Jan. 23, 1865
Daniel Newbern ....Jan. 10, 1861-Jan. 23, 1865
William H. Walker ....Jan. 10, 1861-Jan. 23, 1865
George C. Dearing ....Jan. 10, 1861-Jan. 25, 1862
C. A. Ward................Jan. 25, 1862-Jan. 23, 1865
Micajah Paulk ....Jan. 25, 1862-
James M. Wilcox ....June 20, 1862-Jan. 23, 1865
James R. Smith ....Jan. 23, 1865-1868
J. M. Wilcox ....Jan. 23, 1865-1868
Daniel Newbern ....Jan. 23, 1865-1868
J. M. Lott ....Jan. 23, 1865-1868
J. S. Pearson ....Jan. 23, 1865-1868

Hon. William M. Gaskin

HON. WILLIAM M. GASKIN

Hon. William M. Gaskin, representative from Coffee County in the legislature, 1880-1, had been impressed with rowdiness and drinking on passenger trains running through the county carrying excursionists to the seashore and he introduced, and had passed by the legislature, a general law giving the conductors on all passenger trains in Georgia the right of police power with authority to eject any passengers guilty of rowdiness, disorderly conduct or playing cards for value, or the right to arrest parties who violated any criminal law of Georgia and turn them over to the proper authorities of the county where the crime was committed, to be prosecuted for such offenses. The conductor was given authority to command the assistance of the train crew and of any other passengers on the train to eject the offending passengers or to arrest them and deliver them to the proper authorities for prosecution.

This act is still in force in Georgia and was first incorporated in Acts 1880-1, page 138.

In honor of Mr. Gaskin and in memory of his great service for the State the conductors of the Brunswick and Albany Railroad presented Mr. Gaskin with a gold medal about the size of a twenty-dollar gold piece with the following inscription, to-wit: "Presented to Honorable W. M. Gaskin by the Conductors of the B. & A. R. R. for introducing bill No. 187, on July 11, 1881, passed September 13, 1881."

The History of Newspapers in Coffee County

One of the most outstanding pioneer newspaper men of this section of the state was James M. Freeman, of Coffee County, known to everybody as "Uncle Jim." He has been dead only a few years, but his memory will live for years to come.

It would be hard to give in detail his locations in the newspaper game but suffice it to say that he spent the last quarter of a century in Douglas with formerly the Douglas Breeze; later the Douglas Enterprise. At the time of his death he was Justice of the Peace for this militia district, a part of his time being given to writing "Uncle Jim's Note Book" for the Douglas Enterprise.

Uncle Jim was a typical country editor, loved the work, and knew every phase of it. He was quoted so often by the daily press, and known throughout the state. He began the work with the old Washington handpress, and long before the linotype was in evidence. Mr. Freeman was associated with William Parker in the publication of the Coffee County Gazette at Pearson, Georgia, and later with W. P. Ward in the publication of the "Waycross Headlight."

At one time during his career his newspaper carried at the mast head the names of "J. M. Freeman and Daughters, Publishers." Perhaps this was the only paper in the state with such an unique head.

Uncle Jim was not an old man at his death. He gave up newspaper work after he was elected J. P., only contributing weekly to his old love, the Douglas Enterprise.

Uncle Jim frequently made talks over the country. He was invited to all the gatherings, especially the singing conventions, where he would play his cornet and always made a speech, filled with anecdotes and stories of various kinds. The children all knew him and loved him.

During his last days Uncle Jim had an office at the court house. His friends from over the country and in the city called often. He always had a word for them and they enjoyed hearing what he had to say. He was "Uncle Jim" to all of them. His friends in the country would bring him various things to eat, often swapping them to him for a subscription to the paper. This was a great part of his life in his last days, and he would sit for hours with his pipe and tell them stories that would please them.

Uncle Jim never accumulated much money. He was not in a money-making game, but he earned more than money or fame, giving to the world an honest and useful life, always doing something to please.

Douglas Enterprise, formerly the Douglas Breeze, started in 1888. J. M. Freeman was editor for over twenty five years. W. R. Frier bought the paper in 1908 and is the present editor.

In 1891, E. V. Newbern published the Coffee County Gazette for only a short time.

The Douglas Leader was operated by Quincey & McDonald for a few years about 1900. Later absorbed by The Douglas Enterprise.

Coffee County Gazette started by W. P. Ward in 1904 and was sold to The Douglas Enterprise.

Coffee County News started in 1906 by S. H. Christopher and was sold to Douglas Enterprise.

Broxton, Georgia

The Broxton Journal was started at Broxton in 1903 by C. O. Beauchamp. Bought and operated for four years by W. R. Frier, in 1904.

Willacoochee, Georgia

The Willacoochee Times is operated at Willacoochee. Garrett, editor. Same plant was operated under several other names for several years, starting about 1910.

Coffee County Progress was started in 1912 by T. A. Wallace and others. Present editor, Fred Ricketson.

Nicholls, Georgia

The Nicholls News was started by a number of Nicholls people in 1912. Suspended in a short time.

Map of Roads in Coffee County, Georgia

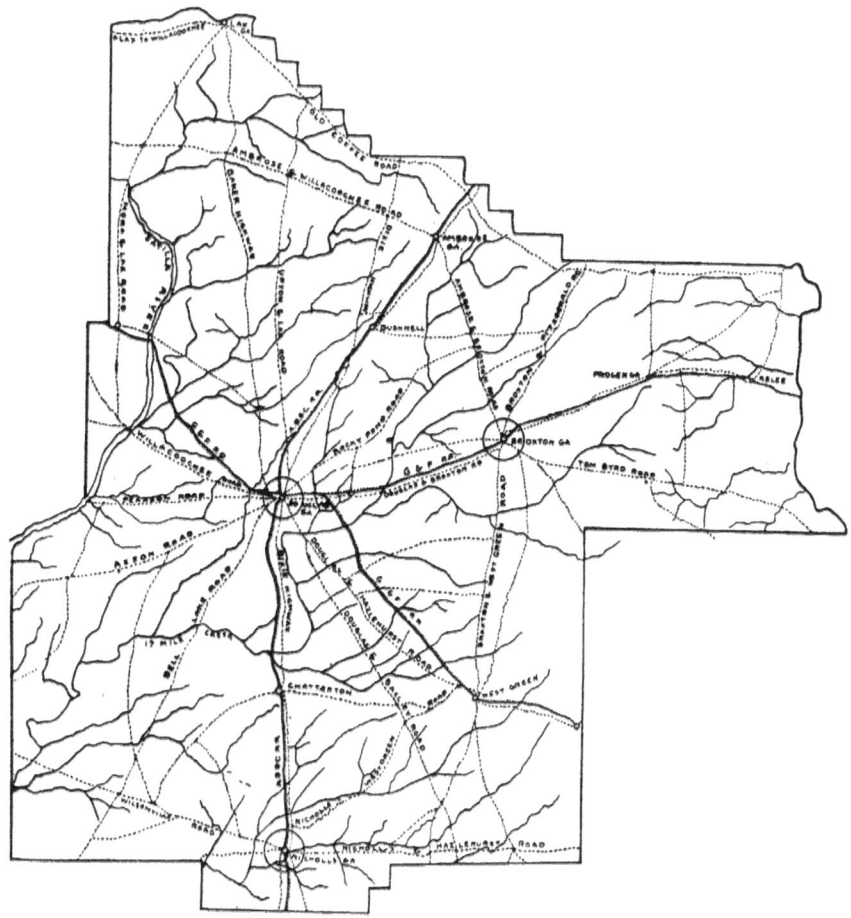

This map was drawn primarily to show the location of the roads. We have two hundred and fifty miles of graded roads surfaced with clay. We have six hundred and ninety-two miles of public roads.

There are twelve bridges on the Seventeen-Mile Creek. All making a total of a mile in length. There are six bridges on the Satilla River, having a total length of forty-two hundred feet. There are many other bridges across the smaller streams of the county, making in all a distance of five miles of bridges. The names of the bridges are as follows: Solomon Bridge, Raccoon Bridge, Belle Lake Bridge, Indian Ford Bridge, New Highway Bridge, Broxton Road Bridge, Tom Young Bridge, Rocky Pond Road Bridge, Ambrose Road Bridge, Leaston Harper Bridge, Marvin Day Bridge, Satilla River Bridge, Old Coffee Ford Bridge, Old Johnnie Vickers Ford Bridge, Bridgetown Bridge, Starling Bridge, Pearson Road Bridge, Reedy Creek Bridge.

Confederate Soldiers Who Went to the War From Coffee County

Anderson, William...4th, Ga.
Anderson, David....26th, Ga.
Anderson, Aaron....47th, Ga.
Adams, P. J.........20th, Ga.
Allen, T. C.........10th, Ga.
Adams, Willanghly..63rd, Ga.
Bennett, W. J.......26th, Ga.
Beverly, John W.....4th, Ga.
Bailey, Thorpe......26th, Ga.
Blount, J. B........2nd, Ga.
Bowen, J. H.........49th, Ga.
Burke, A. D.........25th, Ga.
Beecher, H. H.......25th, Ga.
Beasley, W. M.......1st, Ga.
Bowen, W. C.........49th, Ga.
Cowart, K. C........50th, Ga.
Cook, Henry.........14th, Ga.
Culbreath, L. M.....48th, Ga.
Cross, Richard......10th, Ga.
Courson, W. S.......4th, Ga.
Cato, W. R..........50th, Ga.
Canley, John........26th, Ga.
Corbett, M..........29th, Ga.
Chaney, Harrison...50th, Ga.
Childs, W. H........45th, Ga.
Corbett, M. L.......29th, Ga.
Crosley, Abraham...47th, Ga.
Crosley, Spencer....47th, Ga.
Channell, John......2nd, Ga.
Douglas, B. W.......31st, Ga.
Dobson, W. B........27th, Ga.
Duren, Richard......29th, Ga.
Davis, Stafford.....32nd, Ga.
Douglas, Warren....18th, Ga.
Deen, Jamia.........4th, Ga.
Douglas, Stephen....31st, Ga.
Elmore, Thomas J....5th, Ga.
Ellis, Joshua.......50th, Ga.
Edinfield, Jesse....4th, Ga.
Ellis, H............1st, Ga.
Findley, A. B.......29th, Ga.
Folds, T. J.........13th, Ga.
Grantham, Jackson..50th, Ga.
Gilliard, W. H......63rd, Ga.
Hutto, William......4th, Ga.
Harris, Matthew....26th, Ga.
Hays, B. F..........50th, Ga.
Hall, Joel..........29th, Ga.
Hersey, Joshua T....26th, Ga.
Henderson, J. T.....24th, Ga.
Hesters, S. B.......5th, Ga.
Jowers, J. J........31st, Ga.
Johnson, J. C.......12th, Ga.
Johnson, W. M.......4th, Ga.
Joiner, Hardy S.....50th, Ga.
Joiner, Thomas......6th, Ga.
Johnson, John.......47th, Ga.
Kelley, J. R........14th, Ga.
Kirkland, M.........4th, Ga.
Lott, J. P..........4th, Ga.
Mansell, Hiram......31st, Ga.
Morgan, Jacob.......50th, Ga.
Murrey, William....10th, Ga.
Mack, W. J..........25th, Ga.
Miller, Frank.......18th, Ga.
Merritt, Robert.....4th, Ga.
Merritt, Mark.......61st, Ga.
Myers, J. M.........14th, Ga.
Myers, S. F.........14th, Ga.
Maddox, W. J........35th, Ga.
Mixon, John.........63rd, Ga.
Mansel, H...........31st, Ga.

McLeod, F. M........26th, Ga.
McCormick, G. E......20th, Ga.
McGough, Talley.....3rd, Ga.
Newbern, Thomas...29th, Ga.
Newbern, E. D......50th, Ga.
O'mally, James.....13th, Ga.
Odum, H. W........26th, Ga.
O'Berry, D. E........1st, Ga.
O'Neal, T. P.........4th, Ga.
Peterson, Dan........31st, Ga.
Ricketson, Vincent..21st, Ga.
Royal, Harmon......4th, Ga.
Ricketson, J. P......26th, Ga.
Roberts, Gray......29th, Ga.
Rogar, John D......49th, Ga.
Sauls, T. J..........26th, Ga.
Stephens, J. E.......50th, Ga.
Sweat, F. R.........26th, Ga.
Shea, S..............3rd, Ga.
Snipes, John A......45th, Ga.
Spikes, John........50th, Ga.
Stewart, Joshua.....29th, Ga.
Surrency, John M....26th, Ga.
Stone, J. J..........50th, Ga.
Sapp, Joseph........21st, Ga.
Smith, David.......63rd, Ga.
Sapp, Enoch.........4th, Ga.

Spears, George P.....3rd, Ga.
Sapp, John Dr........4th, Ga.
Sloughter, T. H.....57th, Ga.
Spivey, D. P........26th, Ga.
Spivey, Franklin....20th, Ga.
Stone, William......50th, Ga.
Thompson, W. A.....26th, Ga.
Tompkins, D. J.......9th, Ga.
Taylor, Josiah.......4th, Ga.
Thompson, J. S.......4th, Ga.
Thomas, Edward....47th, Ga.
Taff, J. J...........50th, Ga.
Tarrant, W. B.......20th, Ga.
Thomas, D. F........4th, Ga.
Tucker, John T......4th, Ga.
Thompson, John A....4th, Ga.
Trowell, A. J........4th, Ga.
Taylor, W. P.........4th, Ga.
Varnadoe, J. Q......26th, Ga.
Vickers, Willie .....50th, Ga.
Vining, James......50th, Ga.
Vinson, C. C.........8th, Ga.
Woods, Josiah.......4th, Ga.
Williams, R. G......56th, Ga.
Ward, John E.......50th, Ga.
Yeomans, Ashford...26th, Ga.

World War Veterans—Coffee County

Army

Adams, Bobbie (col.).Broxton
Adams, Marshall.....Broxton
Adams, Will ....Broxton
Allen, Ed. (col.).Willacoochee
Allen, Lee ....Ambrose
Amerson, A. (col.)...Douglas
Anderson, F. (col.)...Broxton
Anderson, G. (col.)..Ambrose
Anderson, J. (col.)..Ambrose
Anderson, Salter.....Nicholls
Anderson, W. (col.)..Ambrose
Andrews, Leon ......Douglas
Arburthnot, Wm. J.....Wray
Arnold, E. (col.).....Douglas
Austin, William B...Broxton
Avriett, Byron A.....Douglas
Bagley, J. J. B.......Nicholls
Bailey, William Z....Douglas
Baity, James (col.)...Douglas
Baity, John G. (col.).Douglas
Baker, C. V..........Douglas
Barnes, D. S. (col.)..Douglas
Barringer, C. A.......Douglas
Bazemore, G. T.....Kirkland
Beasley, O. (col.)....Douglas
Becton, Kato (col.).Kirkland
Belamy, S. (col.).....Douglas
Bell, Oscar M........Douglas
Bennett, C. H........Nicholls
Bennett, J. (col.)....Ambrose
Berry, Charles J......Douglas
Bethea, William C....Nicholls
Beverly, Lawrence D..Douglas
Blount, J. O. (col.)...Douglas
Blunt, Adams ....Douglas

Boatright, Marian E..Douglas
Boone, Usher (col.)..Broxton
Bordeaux, George W..Ambrose
Bouyer, Robert ......Douglas
Bowyer, R. (col.)....Douglas
Boyd, Hollie (col.)...Broxton
Boyd, James H.......Broxton
Boyd, Wiley ....Broxton
Branch, James....West Green
Brazel, Oner (col.)...Douglas
Brazel, Sam (col.)...Douglas
Brice, Mitchell F.....Douglas
Bridges, Erastus H...Douglas
Brigman, John B.....Nicholls
Brigman, Willie F....Nicholls
Bright, Charlie (col.).Douglas
Brinson, G. (col.)....Nicholls
Brogdon, Fort. E.....Douglas
Brown, Ballie (col.)..Broxton
Brown, B. (col.).Willacoochee
Brown, Harry J......Douglas
Brown, Josh (col.)...Ambrose
Brown, James C.....Ambrose
Brown, Leroy (col.)..Broxton
Brown, R. (col.)..West Green
Brown, Samuel ....Wray
Bryant, George G.....Douglas
Bryant, Jule (col.)...Douglas
Bryant, Walter (col.), Nicholls
Bryant, Wesley (col.), Nicholls
Buchanon, James ....Douglas
Bugg, Frank (col.)....Morey
Burgis, Burny (col.)..Douglas
Burkett, James M....Nicholls
Burkett, T. L.....West Green

Burrows, E. (col.)...Nicholls
Busby, Julious O..West Green
Butler, G. (col.)..West Green
Byrd, Lewis A.......Nicholls
Byrd, Zeanus W......Broxton
Campbell, Frank ....Ambrose
Cannon, Goode S.....Douglas
Cargile, Ishmael .....Douglas
Carson, Fado (col.)..Douglas
Carter, George (col.).Douglas
Carter, Geo. B.......Broxton
Carter, Joseph (col.).Douglas
Carver, Jesse ....Ambrose
Cason, Oscar R. .....Nicholls
Cason, Silas D.......Douglas
Cauley, Brantley ...Ambrose
Chancey, W. (col.)...Nicholls
Chappell, John R.....Douglas
Christian, Willie W...Douglas
Claridy, William T...Broxton
Clark, J. H. (col.)..Ambrose
Clark, Lucius (col.)..Ambrose
Clark, M. (col.)..West Green
Clements, Edd ......Douglas
Cobb, H. (col.)..Willacoochee
Coffee, Sam (col.)...Douglas
Coleman, E. (col.).....Axson
Coleman, J. H.,
  Wm. H. (col.).....Nicholls
Collins, Coy (col.)...Ambrose
Combs, John (col.)..Ambrose
Cone, Hiawatha .....Douglas
Cook, A. (col.).......Douglas
Cook, C. (col.).......Broxton
Cook, Eddie (col.)...Douglas
Cook, W. J. (col.).West Green
Cook, Willie (col.)...Douglas
Cooper, Willie (col.).Douglas
Corn, Ira George.....Douglas
Corbitt, Homer ......Broxton

Corbitt, William R....Pearson
Courson, Robert ..West Green
Courson, Archie C....Nicholls
Courson, Oliver M...Douglas
Cowart, Wilburn ....**Douglas**
Cray, Enles (col.)...Broxton
Crawford, Archie L...Pearson
Cribb, James M...West Green
Cribb, Marvin H.....Nicholls
Cribb, Thomas L.....Nicholls
Crosby, Melvin L.....Douglas
Cross, Charlie (col.)..Douglas
Crumbley, H. (col.)..Ambrose
Curry, Essie (col.)...Douglas
Cutno, Matt (col.)...Douglas
Darley, Lee C........Douglas
Davenport, H. J. S.
  (col.) ....Douglas
Davis, Archie ....Douglas
Davis, C. (col.)......Douglas
Davis, Luther ....Nicholls
Davis, Oza E.........Douglas
Dawson, W. (col.)....Douglas
Day, Ashel M........Douglas
Dedge, Edward D.....Douglas
Deen, William H.....Pearson
Dees, John M........Douglas
Dent, Ira ....Douglas
Dickerson, Carl .....Ambrose
Dill, G. (col.)....West Green
Dixon, Henry (col.)..Douglas
Dixon, Zone (col.)...Douglas
Donaldson, L. (col.).Nicholls
Dorminey, Daniel F..Nicholls
Douglas, Avner F...Kirkland
Douglas, Elisha ....Kirkland
Douglas, James L....Nicholls
Drake, David (col.)..Nicholls
Drummer, S. (col.)...Douglas
Dubose, Bennie L....Ambrose

Dudley, Carlos D..West Green
Duncan, J. (col.).....Douglas
Dupree, A. (col.).....Douglas
Duvall, Howard R....Douglas
Edgerton, M. (col.)..Douglas
Edmond, W. (col.)...Broxton
Edmondson, C. (col.).Douglas
Edmondson, G. (col.).Douglas
Edwards, John (col.).Broxton
Edwards, M. (col.)...Broxton
Elliott, A. (col.)....Nicholls
Ellis, James T.......Douglas
Ellison, B. (col.).Willacoochee
England, Fred C.....Broxton
English, John H.....Broxton
Epton, M. (col.).....Douglas
Fairly, Green (col.)..Broxton
Faison, Henry (col.)..Broxton
Fales, Ira ....Douglas
Fason, Joe (col.).....Douglas
Felder, Andrew Lee.Ambrose
Fennell, Sam (col.)...Douglas
Fielding, Henry .....Douglas
Fillmore, N. (col.)...Douglas
Fletcher, H. (col.)...Douglas
Floyd, John H........Douglas
Floyd, Warrar ......Bushnell
Francis, W. (col.)...Ambrose
Friar, Dock (col.)....Douglas
Friar, M. (col.)......Douglas
Fryer, E. (col.)......Douglas
Fryer, Henry (col.)..Douglas
Fuller, Norman (col.).Douglas
Fuller, Orzie (col.)..Bushnell
Fullmore, J. (col.)...Pearson
Funderbunk, S. (col.).Douglas
Fussell, D. W. (col.)...Wray
Fussell, J. M. (col.)..Ambrose
Gainey, James M.....Douglas

Gallon, V. (col.)....Ambrose
Gamble, James L.....Broxton
Gamble, Pless ......Broxton
Garvin, J. W. (col.).Douglas
Gaskin, Daniel M....Douglas
Gaskin, L. (col.).....Broxton
Gaskin, Spurgeon S...Broxton
Gaskin, William J....Douglas
George, Walter L..West Green
Gibson, Clarence E...Nicholls
Giles, Walter H......Nicholls
Giles, William L.....Nicholls
Gillis, Charlton J.....Douglas
Gillis, James M......Douglas
Gillis, Jesse ....Nicholls
Ginsburg, Nathan ...Douglas
Gipson, W. (col.)....Douglas
Girtman, A. (col.)....Douglas
Goddard, Sam (col.)..Douglas
Goodyear, Marian ...Douglas
Goodyear, Paul A.....Douglas
Grady, John (col.)...Douglas
Graham, James (col.).Douglas
Grantham, Charlie ...Douglas
Green, Sam (col.)....Nicholls
Green, Thomas M....Nicholls
Griffin, Monroe ......Douglas
Griner, John W......Douglas
Grisson, George W....Douglas
Guess, Aaron ....Pearson
Gutman, A. (col.)...Ambrose
Hall, Cicero S........Nicholls
Hall, Calvin A.......Nicholls
Hall, Dock (col.).....Douglas
Hall, Thomas L......Nicholls
Hancock, Melvin E...Pearson
Hardy, R. J. (col.)..Leliaton
Harmon, Will (col.)..Douglas
Harper, Berry ....Douglas

Harper, Dennis .....Bushnell
Harper, Elijah ......Douglas
Harper, Henry .....Ambrose
Harper, James ......Douglas
Harrell, James ......Douglas
Harris, Henry (col.).Broxton
Harris, John (col.)..Broxton
Harris, W. (col.)....Broxton
Harrison, A. (col.)...Douglas
Haskins, William M..Broxton
Hatcher, C. (col.)...Ambrose
Hayes, Christ (col.)..Douglas
Haynes, Joe (col.)...Douglas
Head, Anthony .....Leliaton
Henriet, George ..West Green
Henriot, Warren A...Nicholls
Henson, Taylor N....Douglas
Herris, Hezzie R.....Nicholls
Herrin, Lewis ......Nicholls
Hersey, Eddie ......Nicholls
Higgs, Thomas R.....Douglas
Hill, A. (col.).....Sapps Still
Hodge, C. (col.).......Douglas
Hollenworth, E. (col.).Douglas
Holton, Weaver ....Douglas
Hooten, W., Jr. (col.).Douglas
Howard, Edward C...Douglas
Howard, Shepherd ..Bushnell
Howard, T. (col.)....Douglas
Huggins, G. (col.)....Douglas
Huggins, R. (col.)....Douglas
Hughes, Jim (col.)...Douglas
Hunter, Louis (col.)..Douglas
Hursey, Arthur .....Douglas
Hursey, Emmett S....Broxton
Hutchinson, H. D....Douglas
Hutto, Richard, Jr......Wray
Ingram, Henry (col.).Douglas
Jackson, Eli (col.)...Douglas

Jackson, Henry N..Bear Creek
Jackson, W. (col.)...Broxton
Jardine, A. R........Douglas
Jardine, James B.....Douglas
Jeffcoat, Joel G., Jr...Douglas
Jeffrey, A. (col.)....Ambrose
Jefferson, C. (col.)...Douglas
Johnson, Ed (col.)...Douglas
Johnson, Eddie (col.).Broxton
Johnson, Grover C....Nicholls
Johnson, H. (col.)...Douglas
Johnson, Isaac F.....Douglas
Johnson, Joe (col.)..Ambrose
Johnson, N., Jr. (col.).Douglas
Johnson, R. (col.)...Broxton
Johnson, S. (col.)....Douglas
Johnson, Truman H...Douglas
Johnson, William S...Nicholls
Joyce, Benjamin J...Ambrose
Joyce, William ......Douglas
Joiner, Hardy ....Douglas
Joiner, Mose ....Douglas
Jones, A. (col.)......Douglas
Jones, E. (col.)......Broxton
Jones, Jake (col.)....Douglas
Jones, Lim B....(No address)
Jones, Royce L....West Green
Jordan, Joe (col.)....Douglas
Jowers, Earnest E...Ambrose
Jowers, J., Jr. (col.).Douglas
Jowers, Pink ....Bushnell
Kelley, J. (col.).....Broxton
Kendrick, J. (col.).West Green
Kight, Rufus........Broxton
Kight, Thomas W....Broxton
King, E. G. (col.).West Green
Kirkland, Dixie .....Nicholls
Kirkland, Edward L..Douglas
Kirkland, Emmitt ...Nicholls

Kirkland, J. B......Douglas
Kirkland, L. F...West Green
Kirkland, Patrick ...Nicholls
Kirkland, Stafford ..Nicholls
Kirkland, Thomas P..Douglas
Kirkland, Zean W....Nicholls
Knight, James M......Broxton
Knowles, Kile W.....Douglas
Knowles, P. (col.)....Douglas
Laidler, J. H. (col.)..Douglas
Laird, John B........Douglas
Lairsey, George W....Douglas
Lamar, H. (col.).....Douglas
Lane, C. (col.)....West Green
Lane, L. W. (col.)...Nicholls
Lasseter, William ...Nicholls
Lee, J. M. (col.)..West Green
Lee, Joe ....Douglas
Lemons, Arthur .....Douglas
Lewis, Earnest ......Nicholls
Lewis, J. S. (col.)....Douglas
Lewis, Joe ....Douglas
Lewis, R. (col.)......Douglas
Little, T. (col.)......Douglas
Long, John F........Douglas
Lott, Clinton ....Douglas
Lott, James M.......Douglas
Lott, John D........Broxton
Lott, Lester ....Douglas
Lott, Warren ....Douglas
Lott, Lonnie J.......Douglas
Lowery, Clarence E...Douglas
Lowery, John T.....Ambrose
Luke, David F.......Douglas
Lyons, George (col.).Douglas
McCall, A. (col.).....Douglas
McCallum, Henry N..Broxton
McCarthy, Daniel ...Nicholls
McClain, T. (col.)....Douglas

McClendon, E. (col.).Ambrose
McClendon, R. (col.).Ambrose
McCranie, B. G......Douglas
McDonald, C. L.(col.).Broxton
McDonald, Eugene J..Nicholls
McDonald, John C....Douglas
McFadden, L. (col.)..Douglas
McGee, John W......Douglas
McLean, C. (col.)....Douglas
McLean, James F....Douglas
McLean, J. (col.)....Douglas
McLean, Roy G.......Douglas
McLean, William A.....Wray
McMillian, N. (col.)..Douglas
McNair, B. (col.)....Douglas
McPhail, A. (col.)...Ambrose
McQuaig, James W...Nicholls
McRae, Jack (col.)..Douglas
McWhite, Tom (col.).Douglas
Mainor, Jesse M.....Douglas
Malpass, Clyde .....Douglas
Mancil ....Kirkland
Manley, J. (col.).....Douglas
Marshall, Lee ....West Green
Martin, Joseph .....Douglas
Martin, Seba .....West Green
Mayo, John ....Ambrose
Meeks, Charlie H.....Douglas
Meeks, Dan M.......Nicholls
Meeks, Demery ......Douglas
Meeks, Emery C.....Nicholls
Meeks, Ira J.........Nicholls
Meeks, Malcom .....Nicholls
Meeks, Spencer .....Nicholls
Meeks, Spurgeon ....Nicholls
Meeks, William G....Nicholls
Merritt, Elijah .....Ambrose
Merritt, John ......Ambrose
Merritt, John ....Broxton

Merritt, William S...Ambrose
Miller, Archibald P..Broxton
Miller, W. E. (col.)..Douglas
Minchew, James M....Douglas
Minchew, Willoe ....Nicholls
Minchew, Julian M...Douglas
Minix, Albert ....Douglas
Mixon, John H.......Douglas
Mixon, Thomas M......Axson
Mobley, G. M. (col.).Broxton
Mobley, Lim (col.)..Broxton
Mobley, Marvin M...Broxton
Mobley, M. C. (col.).Douglas
Mobley, Otis (col.)...Douglas
Moore, Charles W....Nicholls
Moore, Clifton F.....Nicholls
Moore, Carl (col.)...Ambrose
Moore, Henry C......Douglas
Moore, Robert ......Nicholls
Morgan, John (col.).Douglas
Morris, James B....Nicholls
Morris, Jim (col.)...Douglas
Mosely, Lawson R...Broxton
Mote, Cecil E........Douglas
Music, James ......Nicholls
Nance, Emery L......Douglas
Nance, Mayo (col.)..Douglas
Nettles, Henry ......Nicholls
Newbern, Daniel F...Broxton
Newcurte, L. (col.).Chatterton
Newkirk, M. (col.)..Bushnell
Nicholson, A. (col.)..Douglas
Nickson, A. (col.)....Broxton
Nipper, Willie ....Douglas
Nixon, A. (col.)......Broxton
Norris, George W....Nicholls
Odom, Rowan E......Broxton
Oldsmith, J. (col.)...Douglas
Oneal, Pearl (col.)...Douglas

Oneal, S. (col.)......Douglas
Oneal, Luther ....Douglas
Osteen, Dunk ....West Green
Osteen, Herbert Q....Douglas
Owens, Sam (col.)....Leliaton
Paramore, L. (col.)....Ozark
Parks, Rufus (col.)..Douglas
Parker, James L.....Nicholls
Parker, John W......Nicholls
Parker, John A......Douglas
Parrish, Rufus ......Douglas
Patton, Frank ......Ambrose
Paulk, Clifton C....Douglas
Paulk, Homer ......Ambrose
Paulk, Willie ......Ambrose
Payne, Joseph P...Enterprise
*Peace, Leonard H...Douglas
Pearson, J. (col.)....Douglas
Perry, A. L. (col.).West Green
Peterson, M. W......Broxton
Peterson, Rexford ...Douglas
Phillips, B. R.......Ambrose
Philips, Samuel J.....Douglas
Pitts, Isome (col.).Hilder Sta.
Pittman, Martin E....Douglas
Pouncie, R. (col.)....Nicholls
Powell, D. G. (col.)..Douglas
Powell, John (col.)..Douglas
Powell, P. (col.).....Douglas
Price, C. (col.)...West Green
Prickett, James Roy.Douglas
Pridgen, Arthur .....Broxton
Pridgen, E. (col.)....Douglas
Pridgen, George W...Broxton
Pridgen, Jesse ......Broxton
Purvis, Reason ......Douglas
Quincey, Hately J....Douglas
Rawls, H. (col.)......**Fairfax**
Relihan, James E.....Douglas

WARD'S HISTORY OF COFFEE COUNTY 339

Relihan, Maurice P...Douglas
Rentz, P. (col.).....Ambrose
Redden, Julius (col.).Douglas
Reed, George (col.)..Douglas
Reed, Perry (col.)...Broxton
Reed, Sam (col.).....Broxton
Reeves, George.......Bushnell
Reeves, S. J. (col.)....Upton
Rewis, Earnest ......Nicholls
Rhem, James (col.)...Douglas
Rickardson, James J..Douglas
Ricketson, Fred .....Douglas
Ricketson, Oscar ....Broxton
Riggnes, Lewis (col.).Douglas
Roan, Bruce J........Douglas
Rollie, E. W. (col.)..Nicholls
Roberts, Danile .....Ambrose
Roberts, Henry C....Douglas
Roberts, James A....Douglas
Roberts, J. A. (col.).Nicholls
Roberts, Rufus O.....Pearson
Roberts, Ralph H....Nicholls
Rollins, Lester C....Douglas
Rowell, Clifton .....Nicholls
Rowland, Ike M......Douglas
Rowland, Matthew ..Douglas
Rozier, J. E. (col.)..Ambrose
Rudolph, Milton O...Douglas
Ruff, Major (col.)....Douglas
Rushing, B. T........Douglas
Salter, Burke ....Douglas
Samuel, G. (col.).....Douglas
Sanders, J. (col.).West Green
Sanders, Zeb B.......Douglas
Sapp, David C........Douglas
Sapp, Mitchell ......Douglas
Schumpert, J. E., Jr..Douglas
Scott, Hardie E......Broxton
Scruggs, G. (col.)....Douglas

Sears, Cary J........Nicholls
Sears, Charlie ......Nicholls
Sears, Elias ....Douglas
Sears, Elijah ....Douglas
Sears, Wesley ......Nicholls
Shady, George ......Douglas
Shappell, Clinton E...Douglas
Shappell, Rauss .....Douglas
Shaw, Fred H. (col.)..Douglas
Shaw, Tom (col.).....Douglas
Shepherd, A. (col.)...Douglas
Shrouder, Selma M...Broxton
Slaughter, Forest T...Douglas
Small, John (col.)...Douglas
Smith, Ashely ......Broxton
Smith, Don (col.).West Green
Smith, F. (col.)......Broxton
Smith, J. L. (col.)...Douglas
Smith, James W.....Ambrose
Smith, James D......Broxton
Smith, Jesse W......Douglas
Smith, Rufus J......Nicholls
Smith, Stacey Lee...Douglas
Smith, Willie C......Broxton
Snipes, Jesse ....Broxton
Southerland, A. F....Nicholls
Southerland, W. C...Douglas
Solomon, David L....Ambrose
Solomon, E. (col.)...Broxton
Solomon, Shaver ....Broxton
Springer, Billie (col.)..Mova
Spears, Marvin G.....Douglas
Speight, H. M. (col.).Douglas
Spencer, Eugene ....Douglas
Spikes, Henry (col.).Nicholls
Spivey, James E......Douglas
Spivey, Wiley L.....Douglas
Stalnaker, Ralph T...Broxton
Stalvey, Mose ......Douglas

Stalsvey, C. M.......Douglas
Stanton, Howard W..Douglas
Starling, Edward O...Douglas
Stephens, G. (col.)...Ambrose
Stevens, Fred ....Douglas
Stewart, Andrew J...Douglas
Stewart, E. (col.)...Ambrose
Stewart, Malcom ...Ambrose
Stone, Jack ....Douglas
Story, Andrew S.....Douglas
Strickland, B. S......Douglas
Stubbs, Francis S....Douglas
Summerlin, Allen ...Kirkland
Sutton, C. (col.).....Douglas
Strozier, E. (col.)...Douglas
Stubbs, Clyde Mc.....Douglas
Swails, James ....Douglas
Swanson, Ernest C....Douglas
Sweat, Estell.........Nicholls
Tanner, Allen ....Nicholls
Tanner, Elijah H.....Douglas
Tanner, Mitchell ....Nicholls
Tanner, Samuel ......Axson
Taplye, Sephus......Ambrose
Taylor, Aud A....West Green
Taylor, Bennie (col.).Broxton
Taylor, C. (col.).....Nicholls
Taylor, Charlie.......Nicholls
Taylor, Henry ......Nicholls
Teston, Millie ....Nicholls
Teston, Thad ....Nicholls
Teston, Willie ......Nicholls
Teston, Jesse ....Nicholls
Terrell, Ruel ....Douglas
Therrell, James R....Broxton
Thorne, Grover (col.).Douglas
Thorne, James (col.).Douglas
Thigpen, William M..Nicholls
Thomas, Elmo ......Nicholls
Thomas, Henry (col.).Douglas

Thomas, Isiah (col.).Douglas
Thomas, J., Jr. (col.).Douglas
Thomas, Snow H.....Nicholls
Thompson, W. F......Douglas
Tillman, Claude A....Pearson
Tillmon, O. (col.)....Douglas
Toole, J. W. (col.)...Douglas
Toombs, E. (col.)....Douglas
Touchton, George D.:Douglas
Townsel, H. (col.)...Broxton
Toombs, Emery ....Axson
Todd, John T........Douglas
Trapnell, Barney L...Douglas
Traynham, James G..Broxton
Trowell, Leonard ...Ambrose
Trowell, Oliver .....Ambrose
Turner, Leonard W..Nicholls
Vickers, Cornelius ...Douglas
Vickers, Homer .....Douglas
Vickers, John R.....Nicholls
Vickers, Michael......Douglas
Vinson, Roy G. .....Nicholls
Waddell, H. (col.)...Broxton
Walker, Fachion..West Green
Walker, Frank (col.).Douglas
Walker, M. T. (col.).Douglas
Walker, T. J. (col.)..Douglas
Wall, John A.........Axson
Wallace, Edd (col.)..Douglas
Walton, Joe (col.)...Broxton
Ward, Warren P., Jr..Douglas
Ware, A. (col.)......Douglas
Washington, J. H.
   (col.) ....Nicholls
Weitman, Glenn C....Douglas
Weathers, T. A......Ambrose
Wells, Bennie J......Broxton
Wesley, Frank G.....Douglas
Whelchel, Garnett W..Douglas
Whelchel, Hugh C....Douglas

White, John L.......Nicholls
Whitehead, Eli (col.).Broxton
Whitley, Charles ....Nicholls
Wilds, Edward M...Douglas
Wilds, John F.........Axson
Wilkerson, R. (col.)..Broxton
Wilcox, App (col.)...Douglas
Wilcox, D. (col.)....Ambrose
Williams, C. (col.)....Broxton
Williams, Ed (col.)...Douglas
Williams, Elias .....Nicholls
Williams, G. (col.)...Douglas
Williams, J. (col.)...Douglas
Williams, John (col.).Broxton
Williams, Lewis F...Douglas
Williams, L. (col.)....Upton
Williams, Oliver ......Axson
William, P. (col.)...Douglas
Wilson, Allen ....Douglas
Wilson, Ellie (col.)..Broxton
Wilson, Henry (col.).Douglas
Wilson, James F.....Douglas
Wilson, Jeff (col.)...Douglas
Wilson, Moses (col.).Nicholls
Wilson, Ottis Otto...Douglas
Wilson, Preston ....Ambrose
Wilson, R. (col.).....Douglas
Worth, Daniel D.....Douglas
Wood, Daniel S......Douglas
Worthy, King D..West Green
Wright, R. (col.).....Douglas
Wright, W. (col.).West Green
Yancy, J. (col.)......Douglas
Yarberry, Theodore..Ambrose
Yoemans, Kyler ....Ambrose
Young, John ....Broxton
Young, Willie J......Broxton
Young, William S....Nicholls
Young, Wykie........Broxton
Youngblood, Acey ...Douglas
Youngblood, J. L....Nicholls
Youngblood, Willie ..Nicholls

Among the first to volunteer from Coffee County were: Howard W. Stanton, W. P. Ward, Jr., J. E. Relihan, J. E. Schumpert, R. W. Terrell and J. H. McColskey. They enlisted with the 7th Engineers, which was later changed to the 17th Engineers, the only regiment of Engineers in militant division equipped with rifles. Howard W. Stanton and W. P. Ward, Jr., served in France eighteen months.

Deceased

Baisden, Bryant ....Ambrose
Chancey, Oler ......Ambrose
Cowart, Riley J...McDonald
Edwards, J. (col.)...Broxton
Crutchfield, W. C....Nicholls
Gaskins, Joe F.......Douglas
Johnson, F., Jr. (col.).Douglas
Pearsall, T. (col.)...Nicholls
Shepherd, J. A...West Green
Taylor, Rand ....Douglas
Turner, A. W........Nicholls
Vaughn, Jesse J.....Broxton

Officers

Brown, Adolphus H...Douglas
Burns, Gordon........Douglas
Clark, Thomas H.....Douglas
Coleman, A. S. M...Douglas
Hall, Warren Lee....Nicholls
McLean, James E.....Douglas
Naab, Henry ....Douglas
Newber, Jefferson L..Broxton

Pafford, Jefferson L..Nicholls
Sibbett, William A...Douglas
Smith, John Roy.....Douglas
Stubbs, S. J., Jr......Douglas
Siddeth, Jewel J.....Broxton
Tanner, Elijah H.....Douglas
Touchton, George L...Douglas
Ward, John F........Douglas
Whelchel, Emmett V..Douglas
Yeomans, Ralph N...Douglas

Navy

Bailey, Louie M......Douglas
Barnes, Ashley P.....Douglas
Brown, Carl Hardy...Douglas
Canady, John F......Nicholls
Canon, Jake ....Broxton
Carter, Addison W...Nicholls
Carter, Ira ....Nicholls
Cato, Scott ....Douglas
Cole, Gordon ....Nicholls
Conner, Genevie .....Douglas
Currie, Fletcher T...Douglas
Daley, Herman W....Bushnell
Day, John Josh......Douglas
Day, Robert Valpo...Douglas
Davis, Roderick S...Douglas
Dent, Marion Lester..Douglas
Dubose, John Lester..Douglas
Edenfield, David ....Nicholls
Edenfield, Homer ....Nicholls
Gillis, Homer D........Axson
Green, John ....Nicholls
Green, Willie ......Nicholls
Griffin, Burney E.....Douglas
Griffin, Ralph W......Douglas
Hancock, Edd M.....Douglas
Harrell, Randall H...Douglas
Hays, Ealey ....Nicholls
Hayes, Gaines E....Douglas
Higgs, Frank G......Douglas
Howard, George P...Douglas
Hubert, Wiley C.....Douglas
Hughes, Lewis W....Douglas
Hunt, Joseph J.......Douglas
Johnson, Doctor T...Douglas
Johnson, Homer A...Douglas
Kirkland, Daniel ....Douglas
Kirkland, Fisher L...Nicholls
Kirkland, Richard C..Nicholls
Lott, Daniel D.......Douglas
McKinnon, Virgil ...Pearson
McLane, John M.....Douglas
Moore, Jesse C......Douglas
Nixon, Jesse ....Broxton
Pearsall, Robert M...Douglas
Shaw, Thomas W....Douglas
Sims, James H.......Douglas
Sims, Raymond T...Douglas
Slappey, Hammond ..Broxton
Stalnaker, Sebron C..Broxton
Suddath, Carl Zack...Broxton
Suddath, Foy N......Broxton
Tanner, Amos G......Nicholls
Terrell, William B...Douglas
Teston, John D.......Nicholls
Tomlinson, Frank M..Douglas
Upton, Thomas H...Douglas
Vickers, Cleon ......Douglas
Vickers, Harry B....Ambrose
Vickers, Johnny J...Douglas
Vickers, Micajah J...Douglas
Wilson, Franklin F...Douglas
Zachary, John Key..Nicholls

Deceased

Carter, Carl ....Nicholls
Lewis, Claude A......Douglas

List of Coffee County Officers Dating From 1854

Date Elected	Name	Office
1854	B. H. Tanner	Sheriff
	Whittington Moore	Clerk Superior Court
	Whittington Moore	Clerk Inferior Court
	Thomas Mobley	Ordinary
	John W. Machet	Tax Receiver
	James R. Smith	Tax Collector
	——— Carver	Surveyor
	Sim Parker	Coroner
1855	James R. Smith	Tax Collector
	Timothy Fussell	Tax Receiver
1856	James McKinnon	Sheriff
	Edward Ashley	Clerk Superior Court
	Edward Ashley	Clerk Inferior Court
	Timothy Fussell	Tax Receiver
	James R. Smith	Tax Collector
	Benjamin H. Sturges	Surveyor
	Archibald McLean	Ordinary
1857	Timothy Fussell	Tax Receiver
	James R. Smith	Tax Collector
1858	Mark Wilcox	Sheriff
	James K. Hilliard	Clerk Superior Court
	James K. Hilliard	Clerk Inferior Court
	Green Gill	Coroner
	Timothy Fussell	Tax Receiver
	David Kirkland	Tax Collector
	Daniel Morrison	Surveyor
1859	Timothy Fussell	Tax Receiver
	James W. Overstreet	Tax Collector
	Benajah Pearson	Treasurer
1861	A. McLean	Ordinary
	James K. Hilliard	Clerk Superior Court
	James K. Hilliard	Clerk Inferior Court
	James Pearson	Sheriff
	John I. Pickren	Tax Receiver

Date Elected	Name	Office
	Alfred A. Smith	Tax Collector
	Daniel Morrison	Surveyor
	John T. Minix	Coroner
1862	James K. Hilliard	Clerk Superior Court
	James K. Hilliard	Clerk Inferior Court
	J. A. Spivey	Sheriff
	B. H. Sturges	Surveyor
	Benajah Pearson	Treasurer
	A. A. Smith	Tax Receiver and Collector
	Joel Wilcox	Tax Receiver and Collector
	Timothy Fussell	Clerk Superior Court
	Timothy Fussell	Clerk Inferior Court
1864	D. Lott	Ordinary
	M. Daniel	Sheriff
	Timothy Fussell	Clerk Superior Court
	J. M. Ashlang	Clerk Inferior Court
	A. Lott	Tax Receiver
	E. Pickren	Tax Collector
	D. Anderson	Coroner
	J. Ellis	Surveyor
	G. W. Smith	Treasurer
	W. Byrd	Coroner
1866	John Hill	Sheriff
	John J. Smith	Clerk Superior Court
	John J. Smith	Clerk Inferior Court
	L. B. Daniels	Surveyor
	George W. Smith	Treasurer
	John J. Pickren	Tax Receiver
	Alfred A. Smith	Tax Collector
1868	L. P. Gaskin	Clerk Superior Court
	J. Denton	Sheriff
	J. C. Wilson	Tax Receiver
	B. H. Sturgis	Surveyor
	J. Anderson	Coroner
	W. B. Overstreet	Tax Collector
1870	Louis C. Wilcox	Ordinary
1871	James M. Denton	Sheriff
	Simon P. Gaskin	Clerk Superior Court

Date Elected	Name	Office
	Daniel Gaskin	Tax Receiver
	Henry L. Paulk	Tax Collector
	Benajah Pearson	Treasurer
	Tharpe Bailey	Surveyor
	Benjamin Minchew	Coroner
1873	Timothy Fussell	Ordinary
	Simon P. Gaskin	Clerk Superior Court
	Riley Wright	Sheriff
	Jesse Lott	Tax Receiver
	Henry L. Paulk	Tax Collector
	Vincent Ricketson	Treasurer
	Tharpe Bailey	Surveyor
	Benjamin Minchew	Coroner
1875	Riley Wright	Clerk Superior Court
	Thomas N. Cady	Sheriff
	John J. Pickren	Tax Receiver
	Daniel Gaskin	Tax Collector
	Vincent Ricketson	Treasurer
	Tharpe Bailey	Surveyor
	Henry Love	Coroner
1877	Thomas Young	Ordinary
	Riley Wright	Clerk Superior Court
	Jonathan Jowers	Sheriff
	Daniel Newbern	Tax Receiver
	Daniel Lott	Tax Collector
	Vincent Ricketson	Treasurer
	Hiram Ellis	Surveyor
	Joseph Ward	Coroner
	W. H. Love	Clerk Superior Court
1879	C. A. Ward	Clerk Superior Court
	James Stevens	Sheriff
	John Tucker	Tax Receiver
	Allen Carver	Tax Collector
	Vincent Ricketson	Treasurer
	Hiram Ellis	Surveyor
	Joseph Ward	Coroner
	A. H. Ennis	Sheriff
1881	Elijah Paulk	Ordinary

Date Elected	Name	Office
	Calvin A. Ward	Clerk Superior Court
	A. H. Ennis	Sheriff
	John Tucker	Tax Receiver
	B. W. Douglas	Tax Collector
	Vincent Ricketson	Treasurer
	David Summerlin	Surveyor
	Byril Merritt	Coroner
1882	Manning Peterson	Sheriff
1883	C. A. Ward	Clerk Superior Court
	Manning Peterson	Sheriff
	John Fussell	Tax Receiver
	B. W. Douglas	Tax Collector
	Elias Roberts	Treasurer
	James Gillis	Surveyor
	Henry Love	Coroner
1885	Elijah Paulk	Ordinary
	C. A. Gaskin	Clerk Superior Court
	John H. Hall	Sheriff
	B. W. Douglas	Tax Collector
	David Summerlin	Tax Receiver
	Elias Roberts	Treasurer
	J. S. Heriot	Surveyor
	Matthew Royal	Coroner
1887	J. J. Lott	Clerk Superior Court
	J. H. Hall	Sheriff
	T. P. O'Neal	Tax Receiver
	J. J. Carver	Tax Collector
	Elias Roberts	Treasurer
	Mark Lott	Surveyor
	Elias Batten	Coroner
1889	H. L. Paulk	Ordinary
	Giles J. Lott	Clerk Superior Court
	William Tanner	Sheriff
	David Summerlin	Tax Receiver
	B. W. Douglas	Tax Collector
	Richard Kirkland	Treasurer
	James C. Gillis	Surveyor
	Burwell Merritt	Coroner

Date Elected	Name	Office
1891	J. J. Lott	Clerk Superior Court
	W. M. Tanner	Sheriff
	J. W. Roberts	Tax Receiver
	J. J. Meeks	Tax Collector
	Vincent Ricketson	Treasurer
	J. W. Solomon	Surveyor
	George Chaney	Coroner
1893	John Vickers	Ordinary
	Giles J. Lott	Clerk Superior Court
	W. A. J. Smith	Sheriff
	Thomas Daniel	Tax Receiver
	B. W. Douglas	Tax Collector
	Vincent Ricketson	Treasurer
	Tharpe Bailey	Surveyor
	William Hutto	Coroner
1895	D. W. Gaskin	Clerk Superior Court
	W. M. Tanner	Sheriff
	M. E. Vickers	Tax Receiver
	B. W. Douglas	Tax Collector
	R. G. Kirkland	Treasurer
	Tharpe Bailey	Surveyor
	W. F. Liedfelt	Coroner
1897	Thomas J. Young	Ordinary
	D. W. Gaskin	Clerk Superior Court
	William Tanner	Sheriff
	Dennis Vickers	Tax Receiver
	T. L. Paulk	Tax Collector
	R. G. Kirkland	Treasurer
	Tharpe Bailey	Surveyor
	H. M. Teston	Coroner
1899	D. W. Gaskin	Clerk Superior Court
	William Tanner	Sheriff
	W. B. Courson	Tax Receiver
	T. L. Paulk	Tax Collector
	William Vickers	Treasurer
	D. J. Pearson	Surveyor
	G. M. Ricketson	Coroner
1901	Thomas Young	Ordinary

Date Elected	Name	Office
	D. W. Gaskin	Clerk Superior Court
	W. W. Southerland	Sheriff
	M. Paulk	Tax Receiver
	Thomas Daniel	Tax Collector
	H. Sears	Treasurer
	J. C. Gillis	Surveyor
	Dr. William Carter	Coroner
1902	D. W. Gaskin	Clerk Superior Court
	W. W. Southerland	Sheriff
	D. S. Wall	Tax Receiver
	T. T. Tanner	Tax Collector
	Hamilton Sears, Sr.	Treasurer
	G. L. Miller	Surveyor
	William Vickers	Coroner
1904	W. P. Ward	Ordinary
	D. W. Gaskin	Clerk Superior Court
	W. W. Southerland	Sheriff
	C. W. Corbett	Tax Receiver
	§W. L. Kirkland	Tax Collector
	W. M. Vickers	Treasurer
	W. B. Mills	Surveyor
	Eugene Merrier	Coroner
1906	Sessions Fales	Clerk Superior Court
	J. R. Overman	Clerk Superior Court
	David Ricketson	Sheriff
	Daniel Vickers	Tax Receiver
	Ben Morris	Tax Collector
	J. T. Relihan	Treasurer
	G. L. Miller	Surveyor
	Eugene Merrier	Coroner
1908	W. P. Ward	Ordinary
	J. R. Overman	Clerk Superior Court
	David Ricketson	Sheriff
	C. D. Kirkland	Tax Receiver
	Solomon Sears	Tax Collector
	Richard Vickers	Treasurer
	D. M. Douglas	Surveyor

§E. M. Paulk, first elected—died.

Date Elected	Name	Office
	W. B. Adams	Coroner
1910	J. R. Overman	Clerk Superior Court
	David Ricketson	Sheriff
	B. W. Tanner	Tax Receiver
	Daniel Vickers	Tax Collector
	J. T. Relihan	Treasurer
	B. M. Douglas	Surveyor
	E. Smith	Coroner
1912	W. P. Ward	Ordinary
	J. R. Overman	Clerk Superior Court
	J. C. Gillis	Sheriff
	D. S. Wall	Tax Receiver
	Daniel Moore	Tax Collector
	W. L. Kirkland	Treasurer
	C. B. Porter	Surveyor
	G. L. Sims	Coroner
1913	George W. Kight	Surveyor
1914	A. W. Haddock	Clerk Superior Court
	Dan Wall	Clerk Superior Court
	David Ricketson	Sheriff
	Lige S. Sapp	Tax Receiver
	Dan Vickers	Tax Collector
	Tim Tanner	Treasurer
	George W. Kight	Surveyor
	G. L. Sims	Coroner
1916	W. P. Ward	Ordinary
	A. W. Haddock	Clerk Superior Court
	W. M. Tanner	Sheriff
	E. S. Sapp	Tax Receiver
	Ben Morris	Tax Collector
	J. A. Crosby	Surveyor
	G. L. Sims	Coroner
1920	W. P. Ward	Ordinary
	Sessions Fales	Clerk Superior Court
	W. M. Tanner	Sheriff
	John R. Vickers	Tax Receiver
	Willis Newbern	Tax Collector
	D. H. Peterson	Surveyor

Date Elected	Name	Office
	G. L. Sims	Coroner
	George W. Kight	Surveyor
1924	Ivy W. Bryant	Surveyor
	W. P. Ward	Ordinary
	Sessions Fales	Clerk Superior Court
	William Tanner	Sheriff
	J. M. Lott	Tax Receiver
	G. L. Sims	Tax Collector
	S. H. Christopher	Surveyor
	W. W. Southerland	Coroner
1926	Cleon Fales	Clerk Superior Court
1928	H. F. Brown	Tax Collector
	W. P. Ward	Ordinary
	Cleon Fales	Clerk Superior Court
	R. C. Relihan	Sheriff
	J. M. Lott	Tax Receiver
	Noah Burkett	Tax Collector
	D. H. Peterson	Surveyor
	W. W. Southerland	Coroner

COFFEE COUNTY (Created February 9, 1854)

Placed in Southern Circuit, February 9, 1854. Acts 1853-54, p. 294.

Placed in Brunswick Circuit, February 8, 1856. Acts 1855-56, p. 215.

Placed in Alapaha Circuit, October 17, 1870. Acts 1870, p. 37.

Changed from Alapaha to Brunswick Circuit, December 4, 1871. Acts 1871-72, p. 31.

Changed from Brunswick to Waycross Circuit, January 1, 1910. Acts 1910, p. 94.

SOLICITORS GENERAL

Southern Circuit

John S. Winn, February 1st, 1854-November 10th, 1855.

Edward T. Sheftall, November 10th, 1855 - October, 1859, resigned.

Brunswick Circuit

William H. Dasher, February 9th, 1856; October 5th, 1857; October 7th, 1861; October 1st, 1865.

Joseph S. Wiggins, October 1st, 1865; July 21st, 1868. (Vacant by change in government.)

Peter Bedford, October 3rd, 1868. (Term from July 21st, 1868.)

Isaac W. Christian, September 1st, 1869-January 19th, 1870.

Alapaha Circuit (Abolished December 4th, 1871).

Andrew J. Liles, November 29th, 1870-December 4th, 1871.

Brunswick Circuit

Simon W. Hitch, January 19th, 1872-January 1st, 1873; January 1st, 1877-January 1st, 1881.

George B. Mabry, January 1st, 1881-January 1st, 1885.

J. L. Carter, January 1st, 1885-1889.

William Gordon Brantley, January 1st, 1889-January 1st, 1893-September 1st, 1896, resigned.

William M. Toomer, September 1st, 1896-January 1st, 1897.

John William Bennett, January 1st, 1897; January 1st, 1901; January 1st, 1905; January 1st, 1909.

E. Lawton Walker, January 1st, 1909; died 1909.

Joseph Henry Thomas, February 6th, 1909; January 1st, 1911; January 1st, 1913; January 1st, 1917.

Waycross Circuit

Marcus David Dickerson, October 5th, 1910 (App. term from January 1st, 1910; qual. December 17th, 1910); January 1st, 1915; January 1st, 1919.

Allen B. Spence, January 1st, 1919; January 1st, 1923; January 1st, 1927 to date.

JUDGES

Peter Early Love, Judge of the Superior Courts in the Southern Circuit, November, 1852, to October, 1859.

Judges of the Brunswick Circuit

Arthur Erwin Cochren, from February, 1856, to January, 1860.

William Moultrie Sessions, from January, 1860, to 1864.

Arthur Erwin Cochren, from January 10th, 1864, to 1865.

William Moultrie Sessions, from September, 1865, to January, 1873.
John W. O'Neal, from November, 1870, to 1871.
John L. Harris, from January, 1873, to January, 1879.
Martin T. Mershon, from May, 1879, to October, 1886.
Courtland Symns, from November, 1886, to January, 1887.
Spensor Rome Atkinson, from January 1st, 1887, to April, 1892.
Joel L. Sweat, from April, 1892, to January, 1899.
Joseph William Bennett, from January, 1889, to July, 1902.
Francis Willis Dart, from January 1st, 1902, to January 1st, 1903.
Thomas Augustus Parker, from January, 1903, to January, 1910.

The Waycross Circuit

Thomas Augustus Parker, from January, 1910, to January, 1914.
J. W. Quincey, from January, 1914, to January, 1915.
J. I. Summerall, from January, 1915, to January, 1924.
Harry Day Reid, from December, 1924, to February, 1928.
J. Dorcey Blalock, from February, 1928, to January, 1929.
Marcus David Dickerson, from January, 1929, to date.

SENATORS

Coffee County

1855-56	Mark Lott	1857-58	Matt Ashley
	1859-60	Mark Lott	

Note: Coffee County was placed in the Fifth Senatorial District by an ordinance of the Constitutional Convention of 1861. (Confederate Records of Georgia, vol. 1, p. 727.)

Fifth Senatorial District

1861-63	Thomas Hilliard	1877	George W. Newbern
1863-65	Rowan Pafford	1878-79	William Bardin Folks
1865-66	B. B. Pedford	1880-81	C. A. Smith
1868-70	Newsom Corbitt	1882-83	Wm. A. McDonald
1871-72	M. Kirkland		(Rev.)
1873-74	M. Kirkland	1884-85	J. M. Wilcox (Rev.)
1875-76	George W. Newbern	1886-87	Franklin B. Sirmans

WARD'S HISTORY OF COFFEE COUNTY

1888-89	Frank V. Folks	1905-06	Franklin B. Sirmans
1890-91	J. W. Boyd	1907-08	George W. Deen
1892-93	Franklin B. Sirmans	1909-10	Calvin A. Ward, II.
1894-95	Leon A. Wilson	1911-12	Walter T. Dickerson
1896-97	Jeff. Wilcox, M.D.	1913-14	Joel L. Sweat
1898-99	Robert G. Dickerson	1915-16	Calvin Augustus Ward
1900-01	Lemuel Johnson		
1902-04	Frank L. Sweat	1917-18	Robert G. Dickerson

Note: By a constitutional amendment approved in 1918 seven additional senatorial districts were created. Coffee was placed in the Fourth District (Acts 1918, p. 84).

Forty-Sixth District

1919-20	John K. Larkins	1925-26	Samuel F. Memory
1921-22	George W. Taylor	1927	Walter Bennett
1923-24	E. L. Grantham	1929	J. C. Brewer

Under an act approved December 23rd, 1843 (Acts 1843, pp. 17-19) the state was divided into forty-seven senatorial districts. Up to this time each county was entitled to one senator. See Georgia's Official Register, 1927, p. 446.

On January 19th, 1852, a constitutional amendment was adopted providing a return to the former basis of representation, viz., one senator from each county, chosen biennially by the electors thereof. (Acts 1851-52, p. 48.) See Georgia's Official Register, 1927, p. 470.

In 1859, the State Senate contained 132 members. . . . Governor Brown, in his annual message to the Legislature dated November 3rd, 1859, recommended a reduction of membership. . . . Governor Brown recommended only 33 Senatorial Districts. However, it was deemed best to create 44. . . . A constitutional amendment, approved in 1918, added seven new districts, bringing the total to 51, which is the number at present. See Georgia's Official Register, 1927, p. 480.

COFFEE COUNTY REPRESENTATIVES

1855-56	Rowan Pafford	1863-65	Elisha Lott
1857-58	John P. Wall	1865-66	John P. Wall
1859-60	James R. Smith	1868-70	James R. Smith
1861-63	Elisha Lott	1871-72	John M. Spence

1873-74	John Lott	1900-01	Arthur Lott
1875-76	J. M. Wilcox	1902-04	T. L. Paulk
1877	James Pearson	1905-06	C. A. Ward
1878-79	S. D. Phillips	1907-08	C. A. Ward
1880-81	William Gaskin	1909-10	J. I. Hatifield
1882-83	Dennis Paulk	1911-12	Elias Lott, Sr.
1884-85	Arthur Lott	1913-14	C. E. Stewart
1886-87	William Vickers	1915-16	C. E. Stewart
1888-89	Elijah Tanner	1917-18	C. E. Stewart
1890-91	Thomas P. O'Neal	1919-20	J. W. Quincey
1892-93	Jeff Wilcox	1921-22	J. W. Quincey
1894-95	John Fussell	1923-24	Daniel H. Meeks
1896-97	Daniel Lott	1925-26	George M. Ricketson
1898	————	1927-28	J. M. Thrash
1899	Elijah Tanner	1929-30	J. M. Thrash

Index to: Ward's History of Coffee County, Georgia

ADAMS, ...65
    Annie Belle 89
    Harold.......................240
    John 22
    Joseph J. 105
    Susan 80
    Susan Harrell..............78
    William.......................78
    Willoby.......................23
ALDERMAN, Dr. 50
    Eunice........................50
ALEXANDER, W.H. 151
ALLMAN, M.B. 285
ANDERSON, Aaron................109
    E. 80
    Elizabeth.....................82
    Jake.............................78
    L. 78
    Miriam.......................284
    Nellie..........................83
ANTHONY, J.D. 109, 113, 115
APPLEBY, F.M. 235
ARNOLD, Mary.........................80
ASBELL, Joseph.......................21
ASHLEY, ...261
    Bill..............................261
    Burrows Maxey........261
    Caroline....................110
    Cornelius..........260, 261
    Ed..............................261
    Elizabeth...........260, 262
    Ellen..........................261
    J.M. 233, 264, 301
    John Marshall...........277
    Jonathan..260-262, 264
    Lou.............................312
    Marshall...........261, 311
    Mary..........................261
    Matt........110, 127, 261, 270, 312
    Maxey.......................261
    Nat. 261
    Nathaniel...21, 110, 221, 260
    Susan Caroline.........262
    William.....234, 264, 270
AUSTIN, M.C. 113, 202
BAGLEY, ...308
    B.T. 78
    Ben............................111
    Dick...........................183
    Janie.....................40, 41
    John Davis..................41
    L.C. 78
    Lisa..............................41
    Lottie..........................41
    Mary............................41
    Nina............................41
    Penny..........................41
    Rachell........................41
    Rila..............................63
    Sarah..........................41
    William..........40, 41, 111
BAGWELL, Archie...................240
BAILEY, ...64
    Belle............................43
    Bessie.........................50
    Joe..............................78
    Levicey........................81
    Mary............................78
    M..ary A. 78
    Tharp..........................78
    Thomas.......................50
BARKER, ...63

Index to: Ward's History of Coffee County, Georgia

    Eula............................68
    June............................68
    Lou..............................68
    Maggie.........................68
    S.S. 68
BARBER, Dr. 298
BARNES, Herman....................245
    Ruth.............................50
    S.H.D. 235
BARR, Ruth................................71
BARWICK, Zella........................284
BAZEMORE, A.H. 109
BEAUREGARD, General.220, 267
BELLINGER, W.P. 235
BENFIELD, Mathew....................22
BENNETT, A.D. 245
    Adline...........................82
    Cassey..........................63
    Jeff................................62
    Jesse..............................22
    Liza................................41
    Richard.............112, 307
    Tennessee....................62
Beverly.......................................74
BLACKSHEAR, David.................85
BLALOCK, A.C. 63
    David..........................109
    Dora..............................63
    Rev. 115
BLEDSOE, E.L. 305
    K.K. 66
    Minnie...........................66
BLITCH, Rev. 153
BLOUNT, Emma........................284
BLUNT, Betty..............................54
    Major.............................54
BOGGAN, Mary...........................45

BOOKER, John W. 78
    Nancy E. 78
BOOTH, R.M. 109
    Sallie............................71
BOWEN, Ellen............................80
    L. 78
    Seaborn......................21
BOWERS, Alma.........................49
BOYCE, William.......................239
BOYD, Asbury............................62
    Augustine Moore....262, 263
    Ella Jane...................263
    Ellen............................62
    Eva............................262
    Georgia.......................55
    J.W. 6, 115
    James........................262
    Julius Warren..262-265, 274
    Leila..........................266
    Marcella............264, 265
    Mary Ann...................262
    N.S. 309
    Rhoda..........................80
    Wilie.............................55
BRAGG,..................................220
BRANTLEY, Aaron.....................84
    W.G. 86
BRATCHER, Nancy....................80
BRECKINRIDGE, John C. 219
BREEDLOVE, J.H. 290
BREWER, Fred.........................240
    J.C. 236, 250, 309
    Turner........................235
BRICE, Mother.........................278
BRIGGS, George R. 279

Index to: Ward's History of Coffee County, Georgia

BRISBANE, ...148
BROOKER, ...114
    Annie..............................83
    Clem..............................109
    D.E. 83
    Eland..............................63
    Joel W. 78
    Mattie..............................63
    R.M. 78
    Rebecca..........................82
BROOKS, Johns......................21
BROWN, Dorris......................285
    Elizabeth..........................287
    Rubye..............................284
    S.J. 308
BRYAN, W.C. 240
BUCK, E.A. 313
BUIE, Cornelius......................111
BULLARD, D.F. 311
BUNN, Duddley.......................63
    Idell..............................63
BURCH, John W. 78
    Mary..............................78
    Sarah..............................79
BURKETT, ...68-70
    Angel..............................69, 70
    Angeline..........................41
    Ann..............................68, 78
    Annie..............................70
    B.T. 308
    Bartillery..........21, 68, 69
    Betty..............................48, 68
    Betty Dean.......................68
    Billie..............................68
    Boss..............................69
    Carleen..........................68
    Carrie..............................69
    Coolege..........................68
    Dock..............................68
    E.H. Mozell....................68
    Elisha..............................70
    Eliza..............................69
    Ellen..............................69
    Emily..............................69
    Emmie..............................69
    Enos..............................68
    Gray..............................70
    Ida..............................69, 70
    Jack..............................70
    John........67, 69, 70, 115
    Johnie..............................69
    Laura..............................60, 69
    Leonard..........................60, 69
    Lige..............................69
    Linnie..............................69
    Lucinda..........................69
    Lucynida..........................67, 69
    Lura..............................68
    Maggie..........................70
    Marine..............................68
    Martha..............................69
    Mary..............................70
    Mary J. 69
    Mary Jane.......................69
    Mintie..............................69
    Missouri..........................68, 82
    Nancy..............................69
    Naomi..............................70
    Nealey..............................70
    Noah..............................69
    Preston..........................70
    Quincey..........................68
    Robert..............................68
    Ruby..............................70

Index to: Ward's History of Coffee County, Georgia

- Rubye..........285
- Sarah..........68
- Sophronia..........69
- Texas..........68, 78
- Tom R. 69
- Vine..........115
- Viney..........69
- William..........68
- Wilma..........68

BURROWS, Anna..........78
- Charles C. 78

BUSH, Jim Tom..........284

BUTLER, Bessie..........286
- J.C. 256

BUTTS, James R. 257

BYRD, E. 81
- Eliza..........54
- Elizabeth..........48, 78, 80
- Fannie..........51
- Johnnie..........285
- Lizzie..........68
- Nathan..........21
- S.S. 78
- Thomas..........51
- W.B. 320
- Wiley..........78, 114, 270
- Wiley, Jr. 65
- Willie..........54

CADY, Christian..........62
- Lilah..........62
- Mark..........62
- Mary A. 60
- Minnie..........62
- T.N. 60
- Tom..........62
- Zona..........62

CAIN, M.P. 240

CALLIS, Charles A. 106

CANNON, ...308
- David..........78
- S. 78

CANOVA, Annie..........73

CARMACK, Jimmy..........290

CARMICHAEL, Mildred G. 284

CARTER, ...69
- Betty..........66
- Jesse..........66
- Jim..........41
- John..........41
- Joshua..........40, 78
- Martha..........40, 78
- Mina..........41
- Rhoda..........41

CARTON, Clement..........284

CARVER, ...70
- Allen..........70
- Bede..........70
- Bill..........70, 153
- Boyce..........70
- Braz..........70
- Eliza..........48, 51, 70
- Gabe..........70
- Hariot..........78
- Hulda..........70
- Jabriel..........78
- James, Jr. 23, 78
- Jesse..........70, 78
- Jim..........70
- Joe..........70
- John..........70, 109
- Josh..........70
- Lige..........70
- Mary..........71, 78, 82
- Minnie..........70

Index to: Ward's History of Coffee County, Georgia

Nancy...........................78
Patsy............................70
Peggy............................63
Pink..............................70
Polly.............................42
Rhoda...........................78
Sammie...................70, 71
Samp.............................70
Samson........................73
Sarah......................70, 81
Silas........................70, 78
Sol................................70
Solomon......................21
Vincent.......................70
W.M. 114
William.................22, 114
CASHWELL, Ruby.....................70
CASON, Frances.......................284
CATO, Bede................................70
    Betty.....................39, 49
    Coursey.......................297
    Delila.............................71
    Gemima........................71
    Henry............................48
    Joe..................................70
    Sallie.............................48
CAVENAUGH, W.J. 285
CHALKER, F.M.....................287
CHANCEY, Alexander............ 21
CHANEY, George.....................78
    Lucendia......................78
    Mary..............................78
    William..........................78
CHASTAIN, R.V. 245
CHILDS, C.C............................289
R.C. 289
CHRISTOPHER, S.H. 156, 328
    156, 326, 327
CLARK, T. H. 236, 245
CLEMENS, Isabel McRae.......277
CLEMENTS, Esther................287
    John Wooten...........277
    Winnie...........................54
CLOWER, T.A. 240, 289
CLOUGH, Annie.....................286
COFFEE, A.G. 313
    John.................................20
    Melva...........................287
COILE, Marion.......................287
COLE, Addie..............................68
    L.B. 306
    Mae.................................60
    Milton.........................287
    Minnie...........................62
    Screven.........................60
    William........................112
COLEMAN, A.S.M. 245
COLLINS, David.......................31
    Mary T. 290
COMER, A.J. 261
    Burrows 261
COOK, Int 54
    John M. 313
    Marjorie......................54
CORBETT, ...52
    Elisha............................52
CORBITT, Belle......................39
    M.L. 36
    Mary Ann 113
CORNELIUS, R.J. 278
COTHERN, E. 78
    John...............................22
    Melvinia........................78
COTTINGHAM, Eula........42, 174,

Index to: Ward's History of Coffee County, Georgia

268
W.T. 4, 42, 231
COURSEY, C.C. 310
COURSON, Bettie....................41
    Janie...........................41
    Lem..............................41
    Mattie..........................78
    Monroe 41
    Rachell..........................41
    W.B. 78, 309
    W.R. 309
    William........................41
COWART, L. 78
    Nancy..........................78
CRABB, J.E. 240
CREECH,................................ 117
    S.S. 78
    William.......................114
    William W. 21
CRENSHAW, David.................109
CRIBB, ...55
    B. H. 55
CROMARTIE, John A. 310
CROSBY, Martha......................82
CROSS, E.R. 50, 108, 231
    Erma...........................284
    Fannie..........................50
CROW, Brother Jim 227
CROWDER, George W. 152
Culver: Burrows....................261
    Ellen...........................261
CURREY, ...55
CURRY, ...270
    Abner W. 78
    Mattie..................54, 78
    Neal..............................54
DANIELS, Elizabeth................44

Rebecca....................44
DARNELL, R.E. 309
DART, Francis Willis 16
DASHER, Colonel 119
DAUGHTREY, J.A....................235
DAVIS,.................40-42, 70, 308
    America....................40
    Ann............................68, 78
    Arthur........................40
    Bettie.........................40
    Betty..........................40
    Betty..........................67
    Charles W. 289
    D. 79
    Dan.............................40
    Delilah....................40, 41
    Delilah........................42
    E. 79
    Eliza...........................78
    Elizabeth..............38, 82
    Ella.............................40
    Emma........................40
    Georgia Ann..............62
    Henry.........................61
    High............................40
    Hiriam........................70
    Hoke........................235
    Janie..........................40
    Jefferson..................219
    Jim.............................38
    Joe........................40, 64
    John..........................40
    L. 79
    L.C. 78
    Lewis........................245
    Margaret.............40, 66
    Mark...........................40

Index to: Ward's History of Coffee County, Georgia

Martha.....40, 59, 63, 78
Mary.....................40, 41
Mary A. 82
Mary Ann.....................67
Mary J. 79
Mary Jane....................40
Mattie.......................61
Mose.....................40, 79
Nine.........................67
Patsy........................40
Pennie...................40, 49
Penny........................40
Penolope.....................82
Rhoda...............40, 41, 49
Richard......................79
Roxie....................40, 64
S. 79
Sallie...............40, 41, 64
Simon........................40
Stafford...21, 40, 41, 49,
  59, 62, 93, 94
Thomas...................51, 79
Tom.........................122
Travis.......................41
Willie Pearl................287
DAY,........................126
  Charles...................257
  Fannie..................38, 79
  Harry G. 271
  Ida Barrett...............271
  J.B. 79
  James.......................79
  Joe.....................38, 122
  John L. 271
  Mary........................79
  Tommy.....................271
DEARING, George C. 323

DEDGE, C.W. 60, 62
  Eliza Ann..............60, 62
  Ellen........................62
  James........................62
  Joe..........................62
  Lula.........................62
  Lydia....................54, 62
  Martha.......................62
  Mary Ann.....................62
  Squire......................112
DEEN, George W. 6
  Mary E. 279
  Nettie.......................50
  Thomas Shelton.............279
DENT, ...110
  Elda.........................61
  Eliza A.E.J. 79
  Henry......................106
  Ira..........................61
  James........................53
  Joshua A. 61
  Lula.........................61
  Mary Ann.....................61
  Neila 61
  Olive........................53
  R.H. 79
  Sarah........................61
  Thomas.....................106
  Thomas R. 125
  Tommie.....................196
  Ursula.......................68
  Walter.......................61
  William.21, 75, 125, 153
DENTON, Barbara...........62, 81
  Bartillery...................69
  Bill.........................65
  Cora........................270

Index to: Ward's History of Coffee County, Georgia

  Fannie..........................54
  J. L. 309
  J.M. 51, 140, 145
  Jim...............................65
  John........................54, 65
  Johnie...........................69
  L.L. 284
  Mary..............................67
  Mary..............................73
  Mary E. 80
  Priscilla.........................63
  Priscilla....................65, 72
  Sam..........................65, 72
  Shug.............................55
  Tom..............................69
  Vinney..........................69
  W.M. 73, 125
  William..........55, 74, 270
DICKERSON, David.................169
  Ethel..........................169
  M.D. 3, 235, 245
  Marcus D. 168, 169
  R. G. 16
  Sula..............................53
  W.T. 22
  Will...................169, 245
DICKEY..266
  Lon....208, 255, 260, 309
  T.J. 309
DORMINEY: Rebecca.............267
  Willis..........................267
DOUGHTERY, Betsie................49
  Matt..............................49
DOUGLAS, ...104
  Bryant........................303
  Dorcas..................63, 80
  Dunk.......60, 90-92, 121,

       153, 196, 246
  Eliza.............................42
  Elizabeth.....................81
  John.............................21
  Jug...............................69
  Lizzie............................42
  Lucille........................285
  Lucinda..................69, 79
  Lucy.......................50, 51
  Mary.......................48, 51
  Penny...........................40
  Q. 79
  Rebecca................60, 80
  Robert.........................42
  Simo......................... 51
  Stephen A. 20
  Tempie..........48, 50, 231
  Thad.............................40
  Virgil.............................50
DUBOSE, Gladys.....................284
  Josh..............................66
  Marion..........................28
  Mattie..........................66
DUPREE, Rev. 110
DUREN, Linnie..........................61
DURHAM, John........................23
  Seth....................21, 113
DURHAN, ...41
DYAL, ...68, 110
  David..........................21
DYER, W.H. 152
EDENFIELD, Fannie..................55
  Jim................................55
EDINFIELD................................307
  Jesse............................78
  Rena............................78
EDWARDS, Miriam................287

Index to: Ward's History of Coffee County, Georgia

ELLIS, ...69, 187
    Bettie..................41
    Dewey..................70
    Elmira..................54
    Emma..................68
    Gaines..................41
    H.C. 41
    Hiram..................21
    Hiram, Jr. 22
    Ida..................69
    Jack..................69
    Joe..................54, 70
    Penny..................41
    Sophronia..................69
    Zelphia..................67
ENGLAND, Blanche..................285
ETHERIDGE, H.C. 113
EVERETT, Demps..................23
EVERITT, William..................23
FALES, Cleon..................124
    Margaret..................64
    Session..................124
FENDER, ...64
FENTRASS, H.C. 109
FIELDING, C.N. 235
FINELY, A.B. 41
    Susan..................41
FINLEY: A.B. 155
    Ben..................113
FITZGERALD, Eva..................262
FLANDERS, J.W. 79
    Sarah..................79
    W.J. 109
FLETCHER, Polly..................284
FOREMAN, Jake..................61
    Viola..................61
FORTNEY, J.L. 287

FORTUNE, Catherine..................55
    Clifford..................70
    Willie..................55
FOSTER, D. 284
FRASER, C.W. 289
FREEMAN, Dollie..................235
    J.M. 156, 326-327
    James M. 157-158, 326-327
FRIER, ...54, 110
    Aaron..................265
    America..................40
    Dr. 40
    Josh..................111
    Joshua..................114
    Joshua H. 264, 265
    Narcissa..................264, 265, 270, 275
    W.R. 107, 327, 328
FRINK, Ethel..................169
FRYER, Aaron G. 21
FUSSELL, ...42, 115, 268
    Ann..................79
    Elizabeth..................79
    Fannie..................79
    John..................79, 281
    Mary..................268
    William T. 79
GABBITT, Cecil..................151
GARDNER: Elizabeth..................60
    J. R. 60
GARRETT..................329
    Joe..................114
GASKIN, Betty..................52
    Betty..................44
    Boyce..................70, 278
    Carrie..................61

Index to: Ward's History of Coffee County, Georgia

Charlotte..............48, 52
Cyrus.......................124
Dan W. 124
Daniel......................230
David..........................52
Delilah........................52
E. 79
Elizabeth....................55
Fannie......48, 50, 51, 52
Fisher......................286
James..........................21
Jimmie.........................52
Joe F. 277
Joel...........................201
John............................52
Martha........................52
Martha..................38, 49
Nancy..........................78
Patsy...........................52
Penny..........................64
Sarah.....................52, 67
Simon P. 124
Symeria.......................82
W.M. 278
William.................46, 70
William M. 324-325
GASKINS: Aleph.....................230
Bell..........................230
Dan.................153, 229
Daniel.......106, 125, 230
Estell..........................66
Fannie......................108
Fisher......................230
Joe.............................66
John...........................39
Mary.................39, 231
S.P. 107
GEIGER, L.D. 109
GIBBS, ...74
Abram.................56, 72
Mae.........................303
Priscilla...........55-59, 74
GIBSON, John........................245
GILL, Mary.............................. 67
William......................67
GILLIARD, E.D. 284
Penny..........................41
William.......................41
GILLIS, ...316
Angus........................22
Annie..........................70
Arthur......................114
Cicero......................114
Dave............................63
Douglas...................114
Estelle......................285
Mamie.........................63
Myrtle Harrell...........285
Vera.........................285
GIRTMAN, ...117
Aliff............................54
Ive..............................54
Jack............................54
Maggie........................54
Tiny............................54
Vicey..........................67
GLENN, V.E. 284
GODBOLD, Renna Thompson.67
GOODYEAR, Duncan S. 279
Maggie F. 279
GOOGE, Annie.......................265
Fannie.........................51
James Allison............265
Jefferson Lee............265

Index to: Ward's History of Coffee County, Georgia

Walter..........................265
William Robert.........265
GRACE, M.A. 307
GRADY, Henry W. 223
GRAHAM, ...110
    Elijah..........................21
    Elisha..................220, 320
    Elizabeth..................65, 72
    James........................65, 72
    Ophelia.....................269
GRANTHAM, ...31
    Betty.........................45, 68
    C.H. 45
    D.L. 45
    Dewey........................45
    E.L. 6, 45
    Elisha........................245
    Ethel..........................45
    G1ennis......................45
    John............................4
    Johnie.....................45, 50
    Lucile.........................45
    Mary...........................45
    Mary Jane............45, 50
    Minnie........................45
    Nancy.........................45
    Rebecca.....................45
GRAVES, Sarah Jane................44
GREEN, J.H. 310
GREER, Mamie.......................80
GREGORY, Thomas................284
GRIFFIN, Moses.....................53
    Narcissus..................53
GRIFFIS, ...316
    Gladys......................286
    Myrtice.....................286
GRISWOLD, Maude...............284

GUTHREY, Lucius...................300
HADDOCK, A.W. 124, 235
HALE, Naomi............................70
    Robert.......................70
HALL, ...41, 54, 245, 308
    Bettie..........................41
    Carolyn....................287
    Dan.............................41
    Delilah..................40, 41
    Delphia Ann...............41
    Emminie.........,,,.........67
    Emmie..........,,..........69
    Hardy............20, 40, 41, 322, 323
    John...........................41
    Lee..............................41
    Leon............................42
    Lucy.........................287
    M.M. 51, 79
    Mark......................41, 69
    Mattie...................41, 61
    Nettie........................41
    Pollie..........................41
    Rachell........................4
    Rebecca B. 79
    Seaborn............219, 220
    W.L. 309
    Winnie....................41, 42
HAMMOND, ...270, 274
    A.P. 79
    J.Q. 79
HAND, Jasper........................187
    Maria..........................68
    Susan.........................79
    William S. 79
HARDEN, Beulah....................284
HARDMAN, L.G. 2

Index to: Ward's History of Coffee County, Georgia

HARGRAVES, ...74
    Abe/Abram..........21, 56, 73, 75-77, 137, 138, 139, 140, 146, 197-200
    Abram, Jr. .74, 137, 138, 139, 140
    Bartow.........................74
    Christopher............73, 74
    Ellen............................74
    Feraby.........................73
    Jack.....................56, 74
    John....56, 73, 74, 75, 79
    Laura...........................74
    Leon.............................74
    Linnie...........................73
    Lucinda........................73
    Mary......73, 74, 144, 145
    Nancy..........................79
    Parthenia....................74
    Priscilla...........55-59, 74
    Rhoda...................73, 75
    Susan..........................73
    Sydney.73, 74, 144, 145
    Teresa..................73, 137
    Tom......................56, 74
HARGRAVES negroes..............221
HARGROVES, Hiley.................109
HARPER......................................245
    Archie..........................53
    C.O...............................79
    Charlotte....................52
    Eliza.........................,..55
    H.S. 79
    Henry..........................79
    John............................52
    Julia..........................284

Lewis...................21
Lila......................53
Lucinda..............79
Mary...................79
Mary Jane.........53
Osie....................53
Sarah.................79
HARRELL, Delphia Ann............41
    John.................258
    Love...................41
    Lovett...........23, 79
    Mary................78, 79
    S.M. 70
    Susan...............78
HARRIS, ...119
    Ambrose (slave).......221
    Hade (slave)............221
HART, T.S. ....,.........................235
HARVEY, ...113
HATFIELD, J.I. 278
    Z.I. 49
HATTON negroes..................274
HAYS, Joe.................................69
    Lyman................69
    Mary Jane..........69
    Minnie................69
HEAD, Mary Ella....................268
HEALD, ...55
HEATH, L.E. 235, 236, 245
HEN (slave)....197, 198, 199, 200
HENDERSON, G.G. 43
    Martha...............43
    Nancy.........,........52
HENSON, J.P. 79
    Lilah....................62
    Mary Ann............54
    Nancy.................79

Index to: Ward's History of Coffee County, Georgia

Nephi 105
HERRIN, William 23
HERRINGTON, Bertie 39
HERSEY, Emma 40
    Enoch 41
    John 40
    Mary 41
HIGGS, Isaac 258
HILL, Dot 31
    Elizabeth 82
    Jacob J. 21
    L.A. 235
HILLIARD, Cuyler W. 73, 137, 138, 140
    J.K. 127, 298
    James K. 136
    Sarah 65
    Susan 64, 65
    Teresa 73
HINSON, ... 110, 117, 261, 270
    Aleph 230
    Elias 49, 51
    Eliza 42
    Frank 49, 51
    James 88
    Jim 110
    Marian 88
    Mary J. 49, 51
    Nancy 81
    Nancy 49, 51
    William 21, 261
HIXON, W. F. 109
HOGAN, Pet 270
    William 270
HOLIDAY, ... 63, 320
HOLLAND, T.J. 302
HOLTEN, ... 54
Maniza 54
HOLTON: R. 51
    Seab 112
HOLDZENDORFF, B.F. 152
HORNE, E.M. 285
HOWARD, Mary 71
HOWELL, ... 44
    A.T. 53
    Eton A. 320
    Leila 266
    Mary Ellen 53
    Melissa 44
    Miles Wilson ... 266, 272, 313
HUGHES, Archibald 263
    Ella Jane 263
HUGHS, Dr. 245
HULETT, Nancy 79
HURSEY, E. 79
HUSS, Nora 287
HUTCHINSON, David 21
HUTSON, H.L. 79
    Mollie 79
HUTTO, Ellen 80
    Emiline 81
    Henry 23
    Mary A. 83
    Sarah A. 82
    William 23
INFINGER, C.W. 279
    Tobitha T. 279
INGRAM, ... 306
ISAACS, Samuel 320
ISABELLA 148
JACKSON, ... 42
    B.B. 310
    Corinne 287

Index to: Ward's History of Coffee County, Georgia

Elvira...................284	Sarah......................80
Myrtle..................287	Squire...................114
JAMES, Capt. 151	Thaney...................79
JARDINE, Alexander........278	William..................79
Allie......................50	KELLEY, Lawson........245
James...................231	KEENE, Lucille..........284
Jim........................50	KETRON, Cora............53
JOHNS, Enoch..................15	KIGHT, M. 196
JOHNSON, ...68, 231	Vida Lou................286
C.A. 289	KILPATRICK, Gladys....284
Daniel...................23	KING, M. 61
Elizabeth................54	Minnie....................53
H.F. 290	Neila......................61
Harris....................21	Riley......................15
Lem........................22	KIRKLAND, ...63, 64, 65, 308
JOINER, Allen................80	Abbie J. 80
Bessie....................44	Alice......................64
Mary......................78	Ann J. 79
Nancy.....................78	Annie....................278
Susan.....................80	Ben....................64, 65
JONES, Hanna Neal,........284	Benajah..................65
Mother.....55-59, 72, 73, 74, 75, 144	Bettie.....................61
	Bettie...................50, 65
Sister Sealey..........225	Betty......................52
JORDEN, Rachell.............41	C.D. 51
JORDON, David..............79	Creasy....................64
Henry....................68	David..................64, 117
Mary......................79	David H. 278
Nancy....................68	Doll........................65
JOWERS, Delilah.............79	Delilah....................67
Dicey M. 79	Doryann..................65
E. 79	Eliza....................,..51
Eli.......................114	Eliza....................,..64
Elijah....................80	Elizabeth.............64, 78
J.J. 126	Eliza J. 80
Joe........................79	Ella........................66
John.....................188	Elmer.....................65

Index to: Ward's History of Coffee County, Georgia

Emma Jane..................69
Estell..........................65
Gertrude..................285
Harris.........................23
Harrison.......52, 65, 277
Ivey...21, 65, 76, 77, 298
J.C. 64
Janie...........................65
Janie....................49, 51
Jeff................65, 80, 281
Jim.......................50, 65
Joe................50, 64, 65
Joseph.....................185
Josh............64, 117, 125
Josh, Jr. 64
Joshua..................64, 72
Jud..............................65
Kyler............................65
Laura...........................65
Leila............................66
Lila..............................61
Lizzie..........................65
Lock............................65
Lucy............................65
Lydia...........................66
M. J. 22
Mack............22, 64, 65, 113, 126
Mamie........................80
Manning.....................64
Margaret....................42
Margaret....................64
Marjorie.....................80
Mattie.........................65
Minta..........................73
Moses/Mose.......61, 63, 64, 66, 67, 70, 72, 117, 125, 145
Mose J. 80
Hose, Jr. 64
Pate............................65
Peggy...................63, 70
Penny.........................64
R.G. 39, 52, 279
Rebecca.....................64
Roxie Ann............40, 64
Sarah..........................65
Susan.........................64
T.J. 65
Tim......................64, 69
Timothy.........63, 64, 65, 72, 113
V.W. 278
William.........64, 65, 126
Z.W. 117
Zene.........................125
Zenus.........................64
Zylphia..................64,72
KUHL, A.A. 291, 292
LAFAYETTE, ...116
LAINE, Marion..........284
LANCASTER, C.E. 289
LANIGAN, M.T. 152
LANKFORD, Ellen.......80
  Jim..........................145
  Mary.........................79
  Mattie...............50, 170
  Parrish......................22
  R.E............................80
  W.C. 50, 168-70
LAPRADE, Clara.......235
LASSITER, ...69

Index to: Ward's History of Coffee County, Georgia

Delphia..................62
John........................62
LASTINGER, Gilford......106, 107, 109, 114, 307
LATIMER, Anne....................266
LEE, ...41
    Eliza A. 80
    Eliza Ann....................62
    Eliza Ann....................62
    Mattie.................60, 62
    Newton........................41
    Pollie..........................41
    Sam.............................62
    Thomas M. 80
    Tom..............................62
LEGGETT, B.R. 303, 304
    Dora Ann....................65
    Russell B. 65
LEVINS, Eliza....................71
    Jack............................71
LEWIS....................261, 308
    Angel...........................70
    Elda.............................61
    J.J. 261, 311, 312
    Jeff.............................68
    John...........................305
    Lou............................312
    Lucile........................285
    Mary Jane..................68
    Mattie........................62
    Mich...........................62
LITTLE, Mary Jane................40
    W.A. 291
LOFTIN, R.L. 152
LONG, L. D. 309
LOTT, ...38, 44, 49, 54
    Aliff............................45

Allie..............................50
Alma.............................49
Amanda........................80
Arminta...........49, 65, 72
Arthur......38, 43, 47, 48, 51, 70, 259
Arthur, Jr. 51
Avie/Avy.................50, 8
Beedy............................43
Bessie...........................50
Betsie....................48, 49
Betsie...........................48
Bettie...........................52
Betty..............38, 44, 50
Cecil...........................170
Charlotte.....................48
Chester......................170
Clinton.........................50
D.W. 49, 50
Daisy............................45
D.P. 43, 45
Dan....38, 43, 45, 49, 50, 51, 52, 54, 108, 115, 186, 196, 231, 250, 306
Dan P. 105
Daniel........7, 21, 48, 49, 51, 58, 145, 278, 294
Daniel, Sr. 21
David..................48, 80
Delilah................47, 48
Dora..................51, 312
Elias, 47, 48, 50, 51, 230, 231
Elisha........38, 43, 48, 50, 51, 80

Index to: Ward's History of Coffee County, Georgia

Eliza..............................51
Eliza................48, 51, 70
Eliza J. 80
Elizabeth Peterson....39, 51
Elizabeth...............48, 80
Ely...............................45
Eunice..........................50
Fannie.....48, 50-55, 278
G.W. 309, 310
Henry............................45
Hester................48, 49
Hortense.....................50
J.B. 43
J.D. 51
J.J. 51, 24
J. M. 28, 323
J.P. 50
J.S. 48, 50, 80, 151, 170, 235, 311
James................50, 231
Janie......................49, 51
Jesse.......43, 48, 51, 145, 303, 312
Joe........................38, 50
Joel....20, 21, 43, 48, 49, 322
John.....38, 48, 49, 50, 51, 54, 115, 121, 188, 228
John M. .. 23, 46, 51, 80, 278, 311, 322
Johnnie........................43
Laura..........................170
Laura............................50
Lewis..........................146
Lila...............................39
Lillian Fillingim............51
Lucinda...............79, 278
Lucinda.......................79
Lucy......38, 43-45, 48-51
Maggie........................51
Mark, 20, 38, 47, 48, 49, 52, 65, 72, 80, 144, 145, 195
Mark, Jr. 322, 323
Martha...............43, 48
Martha.........................52
Mary.........46, 48, 50, 51, 74, 144, 145
Mary Ann.....................51
Mary J. 49, 51
Mary Jane..........45, 278
Mary Jane....................51
Mary Jane.....48, 51, 54
Matilda..........43, 45, 49
Mattie.................50, 170
Mattie...................45, 50
Minnie.........................45
Mitchell........................51
Nancy..............49, 51, 79
Nancy........48, 49, 51, 54
Narcissus.......43, 48, 50, 51, 59
Nettie...........................50
Penny..............40, 48, 49
Pink.......................48, 50
Polly..........41, 48, 50, 49
R. 80
Reason........................45
Rebecca...43, 45, 51, 53
Rebecca......................51
Rebecca......................54
Rebecca B. 79

Index to: Ward's History of Coffee County, Georgia

Rhoda...................49	MCDONALD, ...53, 149, 156, 327
Richard..................52	Mary...................53, 74
Robert...................50	W.A. 307
Ruth......................50	W.W. 151, 236
Sallie...................48, 49	William A. 6, 74
Sallie.....................50	Willis.......................278
Sarah............39, 52, 65	MCDONALDS, ...175
Sarah.....................50	MCDUFFIE, Rebecca...............267
Stanford..................51	MCEACHIN, Emma..................44
Tempie...48, 50, 51, 231	MCGOVERN, ...38, 115, 149
W.L. 309	Eli........................38, 49
Walter....................163	Fannie.........................38
Wash......................51	John....................38, 116
Wiley.................43, 51	Lizzie..........................47
William................43, 51	Matthew................38, 49
Willie.....................50	Thomas......................38
LOTT negroes.........145, 146, 221	Tom Boy...................38
LOVE, Abbie J. 80	MACHET, John H. 21
Artie..............80	MCKAY, D.P. 285
Henry.............80	MCKINNON, ...104
W.H. 80, 281	Abbiegal..................80
LOWE, ...110	Jim.............................113
LUKE, Sallie.................50	H. S. 80
LUTES, L.A. 155	MACKLIN, H. B. 302
MCADOO, William G. 56, 74	MCLEAN, Albert....................269
MCARTHUR Negroes.............274	Anderson..........266, 269
MCCALL, Millie.....................71	Anne 266
MCCALLIE, Dr. 271	Archibald...........21, 182,
MCCALLUM, J.W. 284	265, 268, 269
MCCLATCHEY, D.F. 2	Duncan............215, 266,
McClelland: E. 80	268, 269
E.H. 80	Edna.......................269
Ida.........................67	Flora Ella....................269
Mattie.....................67	Frank.......................269
MCCRANIE, George..................53	Jewel.......................269
Ida.........................53	John.........151, 266, 269,
MCDANIEL (family)...............116	272, 279, 312

Index to: Ward's History of Coffee County, Georgia

Lola..........................269	MATHIS, J.E. 152
Lola Mae..................287	MAULDEN, ...115
Mae..........................269	J.D. 109
Margaret Ann...........269	Nettie........................41
Mary..................268, 269	MEDLOCK, Mary....................261
Ophelia.....................269	MEEKS, ...40, 61, 63, 308
Oscar........................269	A.P. 284
Roy............................269	Abbie........................60
Walter.......................269	Albert...................60, 61
MCLENDON, B.E. 81	Aleph....................61, 63
E. 82	Alex..........................49
Josephine..................81	Amos.........................63
Vernon E. **119**	Andrew J. 61
MCMILLAN, ...53	Angel.........................62
MCMILLEN, Fronney................44	Annie.........................61
Kattie.........................44	Archie...................61, 67
Melissa......................44	Beatrice....................284
Thomas.....................44	Bessie.......................61
MCNAIR, Agnes.....................287	Bettie.......................61
McNeill, Major 271	Billie..........38, 48, 50, 59
MCRAE, Duncan...................269	Billy..........................59
Maddock H. 21	Bryant...................59, 63
Murdock...................115	Burrell......................62
MADDOX, ...31	Burton.......................61
MAIN: Dede..............................50	C.F............................80
Elmo............................50	Carrie........................61
MAINE, Elmore........................43	Cassey........................63
MAMMY (slave)......................308	Charles................60, 112
MANCIL, Hiram, Jr. 80	Charles C. 59
Hiriam......................113	Charles F. 63
Mary..........................80	Charles W. 60, 62
Manning...........270, 274	Charlie..................59, 60
William R...................21	Clarence.....................63
MARTIN: C) Burkett.................69	Cora..........................61
Sarah..........................69	D.H. 58, 60, 245
Stanley.....................284	Dan......................61, 63
Will.............................69	Daniel..................59, 61

Index to: Ward's History of Coffee County, Georgia

Delphia Ann..............62
Dorcas..............63, 80
Dorcus.....................61
Dorsey 63
E. A. 70
E.S. 22
Early.........................61
Effie.........................61
Elias.........................63
Elijah.......................59
Elisha..............60, 61, 63
Elisha A. 63
Eliza..................62, 66
Eliza.........................62
Eliza A. 80
Eliza Ann..............60, 62
Eliza Ann..................62
Elizabeth...60, 66, 80, 83
Eliza Jane..................62
Elmira......................61
Emily..................62, 67
Emma Jane..........42, 62
Emmett....................63
Ethel........................61
Fannie......................61
Fat Charley...............49
Fleeta......................61
Frances....................61
Frank..................59, 61
George.................60, 63
Gilbert..................... 61
Gray.....................59, 60
R. 63
H.M. 41, 61, 307
Hymrick..........40, 59, 61,
62, 63, 117, 153
Irsa..........................61

Jeff...........................63
Jesse....................59, 60
Joe...........................61
John....................59, 60
John J. 80
Julian.......................61
Kenneth....................63
Laura............59, 60, 69
Legrand....................63
Leon........................61
Lila..........................61
Linnie......................61
Lizzie.......................62
Lois..........................63
Lonnie.....................60
Loyd........................61
Lucy..........49, 60. 61, 62
Lula..........................61
Lydia...................60, 62
Lydia....................59, 60
Mack........................62
Mae..........................60
Maggie.....................60
Maggie................61, 70
Malcolm...59, 60, 61, 66,
80, 117, 281
Martha.................59, 63
Martha Jane..............62
Martha Jane..............68
Marvin......................61
Mary........................60
Mary Ann........59, 60-62
Mary J. 79
Mary Jane.........61, 69
Mattie............41, 60-63
Melvin.....................60
Merritt.........59, 61, 62

Index to: Ward's History of Coffee County, Georgia

    Merritt 59, 61
    Minnie........................61
    Mintie........................61
    Nancy........................62
    Narcissus..38, 48, 50, 59
    Oliver........................61
    Patsy.........................40
    Pearl..........................61
    Penny............61, 63, 67
    Polly..........................49
    Priscilla.....................63
    Rebecca...............60, 80
    Redding....... 62, 66, 112
    Riley..........................63
    Roan..........................63
    Ruby..........................61
    Sarah....................59, 67
    Sarah Ann.................59
    Shafter......................61
    Simpson...............59, 60
    Spurgeon...................61
    Stafford................59, 61
    Tempie.................59, 61
    Tennessee..................62
    Truit..........................63
    Viola..........................61
    Warren G. 42, 62
    Wesley.......................61
    Will............................62
    Willie.........................60
    Willoughby............59, 62
MELTON, W..M. 284
MEMORY, S. F 6
MERIER, Eugene.....................80
    B.A. 80
MERRITT, Alfred.....................21
    Fred..........................31

    Mollie........................79
    P. 22
METTS, ...31, 70
    Elias..........................80
    Ellen..........................80
    John..........................80
    M.. 80
    Nancy........................80
    Redding....................31
    Rhoda.......................80
MIDDLETON, John...................21
MILHOLLIN, J.M. 51
    Rebecca....................51
MILLER, ...258
    Archibald..................21
    Archie...........64, 72, 114
    J.W. 151
    Mills.......................... 80
    E. 80
    Jackson.....................21
MIMS, Emily..........................66
MINCHEW, A.S. 80
    Abraham................270
    Ben..........................114
    Bill............................62
    John..........................80
    Martha Jane...............62
    Mary E. 80
    Rhoda.......................80
MINGLEDOFF, George H. 245
MINIX, Betty..........................39
    Cyrus........................39
    Henry........................39
    Hulda........................70
    Joe............................39
    Lucy..........................39
    Lydia.........................39

Index to: Ward's History of Coffee County, Georgia

Monroe...........39
Thomas...........23, 70
MISS Dollie...........157
MITCHELL, T.A. 4
MIXON, Gussie...........284
    Hariot...........78
    Maxie...........284
    MOBLEY, Alex...........20
    Lula...........62
    Mark...........22
    Thomas...........21
MOBLY, Alexander...........322
MONROE, Mary Ann...........262
MOODY, George...........73
    Linnie...........73
MOON, Mary...........78
MOORE, ...111
    Aaron...........49
    Arthur...........49
    Babe...........117
    Charlie...........70
    Dannie...........49
    E.B. 2, 51
    Elias....21, 38, 48, 49, 60, 113
    Elizabeth...........51
    Hester...........49
    Hester...........38, 48, 49
    Ira...........285
    John...........51, 113
    Johnie/Johnnie, 51, 228
    Lucille...........45
    Lucy...........49, 60, 62
    Maggie...........51
    Mary...........70
    Mary Ann...........51
    Minnie Lee...........51

Polly/Pollie...........48, 50
Rufus...........245
Sandy...........161
Whitington S. 20, 21
MOORMAN, ...302
    LW. 245
MORGAN, Jonathan L. 73
    Parthenia...........74
    Susan...........73
MORRIS, ...104
    W.E. 114
MORRISON, Dan...........115
    Daniel...........21, 59, 110, 113, 307
    Mary Ann...........59
MOYE, B. J. 290
MULLIS, ...41
MUNDY, Bill...........160
MURRAY, Mary...........79
NASH, ...54, 320
NEAL, Elizabeth...........287
NEILL, W. Cecil...........2
NELMS, George W. 81
    Nancy...........81
NELSON, Washington...........22
NETTLES, Bettie...........40
    Susie...........67
NEUGENT, ...38, 116, 149
NEWBERN, ...42, 69, 125
    Abbie...........60
    Bill/Billie.......42, 49, 268
    Dan....42, 228, 229, 230, 268
    Dan, Jr. 42
    Daniel.......21, 41, 42, 49, 54, 231, 268, 322, 323

Index to: Ward's History of Coffee County, Georgia

Daniel, Jr. 231
Delilah.......................42
E.J. 284
E.V. 327
Eliza..........................42
Elizabeth....................81
Emma.......................268
Emma Jane () Meeks, 42
Eula....................42, 268
G. W. 106
George.............114, 153
George W. ...22, 42, 109, 114
J. 81
Jack................41, 42, 49
Jackson................41, 49
Jesse...........42, 231, 268
Joe.......................42, 49
L. 81
Lawrence....................42
Lizzie..........................42
Malissa.......................53
Margaret.....................42
Mark....................42, 49
Mary A. 81
Missouri......................41
Phillip.........................60
Polly...........................42
Polly....................41, 49
William.....................231
Willis...................42, 108
Winnie....41, 42, 54, 268
NEWBORN, Dread..........100, 101
NICHOLS, John C. 306
NOLAN, ...116
   A. 81
   Elizabeth................................81

NORMAN, Fannie Mae..........287
NOWLAND (family)................149
O'BERRY, B.G. 245
O'BRIEN (family).....................149
ODUM, J.M. 81
   Nancy.....................................81
OGLETHORPE, James.....I, 24, 26, 27, 30, 164
O'MALLY, Ida............................81
   James....................................81
O'NEAL, Julia............................82
   Thomas P. 106, 107, 153
OSBORN, Chase S 213
O'STEEN, ...104-105
   Levi.................................57, 231
OVERMAN, J.R. 124, 300
OVERSTREET, Elizabeth..........81
   Frances.........................49, 278
   Jim...49
OWENS, Abe............................67
   Liza...67
PACE (family)................111, 270
PAFFORD, Hester.....................49
   Jesse......................................49
   Joe..50
   Marcus A. 122
   Mary.......................................50
   Newt.......................................49
   Roan.......................................21
PALLICER, Paul........................81
   R. 81
PALMER, J.L. 304
PARKER, ...36
   Alice......................................284
   Annie Belle.................89
   C.G.W. 100
   C.S. 81

Index to: Ward's History of Coffee County, Georgia

Calvin Gordon Berry Washington..............100
Elizabeth....................81
Eugenia....................44
Jacob........................258
Matilda....................49
Sim..........................21
William......89, 100, 155, 156, 326
PARRISH, ...105
   Nancy........................78
PASSMORE, Jane....................81
   John.............21, 31, 303
   L. 81, 122
PAULK, ...52, 53
   Aleph.......................53
   Alonzo.....................51
   Bell...........................53
   Bessie.......39, 44, 53, 66
   Betsie...................38, 48
   Betsie......................49
   Brooks............38, 39, 52
   Cora..........................53
   Dan............................53
   Daniel........................53
   Delilah......................79
   Dennis..................39, 113
   Elijah.....................53, 182
   Elisha...................39, 52
   Elizabeth..............43, 81
   Fannie........................53
   Fannie.............38, 39, 52
   Henry....................49, 53
   Hiram........................53
   Ida.............................53
   Jessie.........................53
   Jim.............................50
   Joel............................53
   John...........38, 39, 49, 52
   John R. 81
   L. 81
   Laura...........................50
   Lila..............................53
   Lilar.............................43
   Lott..............................44
   Lucinda.......................49
   Lucius....................43, 81
   Lucy............................51
   Malissa........................53
   Mary............................53
   Mary Ellen...................53
   Mary Jane....................53
   Micajah.................53, 323
   Minnie.........................53
   Minnie.........................44
   Nancy..........................52
   Narcissus.....................53
   Ola...............................58
   Olive............................53
   Ollie.............................44
   Rachael.......................44
   Rebecca......................43
   Rooks Jodie................49
   Roy........................39, 52
   Sarah...........................50
   Speed..........................50
   Symanthia...................53
   Thomas....21, 49, 51, 52, 188
   Thomas J. 53
   Thomas L. 52, 53, 58
   Tish..............................52
   W. R. 53
PAULK, negroes....................221

Index to: Ward's History of Coffee County, Georgia

PEARSON, Benajah...38, 48, 113, 141
    Bettie..............50, 64, 65
    Delilah.......................52
    E. 80
    J.B. 323
    James............20, 52, 297
    James S. 322
    Mary...........................78
    Pink..............38, 48, 50
PERKINS, Dora...............51, 312
    Hortense....................50
    R.R. 51
    Rufus R. 312
    Tempie.......................51
PETERSON, ...38-40, 298
    Alfred.....38, 39, 49, 228
    Avie/Avy...............50, 80
    B. 151, 299, 301
    Belle............................39
    Benajah....................275
    Bertie..........................39
    Betsie.........................49
    Betty......................39, 49
    Betty...............35, 48, 49
    D.H. 17
    Dan...........38, 39, 51, 52
    Daniel.......................311
    Dave............38, 40, 52
    David.........................81
    Delilah........................49
    E. 81
    Eliza.....................38, 49
    Elizabeth....................40
    Elizabeth....................38
    Elizabeth...............39, 51
    Emmitt........................39
    Essex..........................40
    Fannie...................38, 39
    George.....................100
    Gladys........................39
    Hal....38, 40, 49, 52, 140, 278
    Henry............38, 39, 52, 278, 279
    Iris...............................39
    J.B. 3
    J.H., Jr. 39
    Joe..............................39
    John...31, 38, 39, 40, 48, 49, 108, 231, 294, 313
    L.S., Jr. 39
    Lem.............................39
    Lila..............................39
    Lizzie..........................39
    Lucy......................38, 51
    Maggie.................39, 313
    Manning.....................40
    Martha......................278
    Martha........................49
    Mary............................39
    Mary Jane..................39
    Nicholls......................40
    Patsy..........................52
    Percy..........................69
    Polly...........................40
    Rexford.......................39
    Richard.......................39
    Robinetta....................39
    Rosa Mary..................39
    Ruby...........................39
    Sallie.........................279
    Sallie 48

Index to: Ward's History of Coffee County, Georgia

Simon.................................39
Stella..................................39
Tom....................................39
William........................39, 40
PHILLIPS, ...126
   Charley.........................272
   J.J. 302
   S.D. 81, 114
   Samanthia 81
PICKERN, ...117
   A.P. 79
   Easter..............................82
   Emma............................116
   John...............................270
   Katherine.....................270
   Nancy.............................82
   T.L. 270
PICKREN, Elijah............20, 323
   Emma () Wilcox, 55, 264
   John J. 21
POER, Mrs. Ben..............305
POULAN, ...213
POWELL, J.W. 289
   P.W. 106
   Sadie..............................235
POWERS, ...308
   George W. 295
   Sarah () Burkett..........68
   PRICE, John W. 279
   Lula Drew....................279
   Thomas S. 278
PRIDGEN, ...111
   Arloa.............................285
   Elizabeth........................81
   George............................69
   John................................81
   Mintie.............................69

PROCTOR, L.G. 289
PULLEY, J.A. 287
PURVIS, Eliga....................70
   Elisha..............................81
   H.W. 152
   L. 81
   Needham........................21
   Sarah........................70, 81
QUILLIAN, B.D. 245
QUINCEY, ...156
   Hately............................245
   J.W. 16, 46, 151, 235
   S.D. 245
QUINN, Calvin..................21
REED, Charles A. 289
   Roxie.............................267
REGISTER, Emiline..........81
   Sam................................81
RELIHAM, Minnie............66
RELIHAN, R.C., ...214
   R.T. 235
REMIS, Lydia....................82
RICH, Ben E. 105
RICHEY, W.P. 290
RICKETSON, ...304
   Benjamin........................23
   Dicey M. 79-80
   E. 83
   Fred...........155, 156, 328
   H.E. 82
   John................................22
   John P. 22
   Martha...........................82
   Mary 81
   Mary A. 78
   Mary Ann.......................62
   Rhoda.............................80

Index to: Ward's History of Coffee County, Georgia

    S. 81
    Wesley 62
RICKS, Joel 21
RIDGON, ... 69
ROBERT, Dora A. 81
    John W. 81
ROBERTS, Barbara 62, 81
    Dan 113
    Delilah 49
    Eliza Ann 62
    Elizabeth 79, 81
    Ellen 74
    Georgia Ann 62
    Gray 60, 62, 81
    H.C. 281
    J.A. 245
    J. Wesley 113
    Jack 113
    Jesse 62, 113
    Jimmie 113
    John 62, 81
    Joseph 23
    Mary 60
    Mary Ann 60, 113
    Rob 113
    Robert 21
    S.M. 235
    Sallie 49
    Sarah Ann 62
    Sarah J. 81
    Sherrod 21
    Wash 49
    William 114
    William F. 109, 113
ROBINETTE, Estelle 285
ROBINOWITZ, W.M. 307
RODENBERRY, ... 55

ROE, Bell 53
    Sarah Ann 81
    William 81
ROGERS, Julia Ellen 217
    Olive 287
ROYALS, Dora A. 81
    Elizabeth 81
    James S. 81
    John 81
    Levicey 81
    S. Ann 81
RUDOLPH, Oscar 278
RUIS, Thaney 79
RUSSELL, Richard B., Jr. 2
RYALS, ... 68
    Dock 183
    Lydia () Meeks 59
SALTER, Capt. 256
SANDERS, Mary 51
SAPP, Bettie 71
    Christian 71
    Dan 71
    Dave 71, 245
    Delila 71
    E. S. 71
    Elias 71
    Enoch 71
    Fannie 71
    G.M. 71
    Gemima 71
    H.W. 7
    Henry 71
    J.L. 313
    Jim 71
    Joe 71
    John 71
    Joseph 71

Index to: Ward's History of Coffee County, Georgia

    Levi 71
    Levy 82
    M.C. 71
    Martha 71
    Mary 71
    Missouri 71
    Nancy 71
    Richard 71
    Ruth 71
    Sallie 71
    Sarah 71
    Sarah 80
    Sarah 71, 82
    Tempie 71
    Tilden 71
    Tom 71
    William 71
SAUNDERS, Agnes 287
SEARS, ... 65
    Amanda 82
    Beedy 45
    Elizabeth 1, 82
    Ellen 44
    George 82
    Hamilton 43
    Hamp 45
    Hampton 44
    Harriet 45
    Hiriam .. 21, 45, 113, 121, 323
    Josephine 81
    Julia 82
    Mary 43, 44, 79
    Matilda 45
    Ollie 45
    Rose 67
    Rosa Ann 45

    Sarah Ann 81
    Sol 45
    Symanthia 53
    Wiley 44
SELLERS, Minnie V. 278
SENTELL, Ben L. 109
    John E. 109
SERMONS, James 21
SHELNUTT, Sybil 287
SHELTON, Charles 260
    Elizabeth 260
    J.M. 261
SHEPHERD, Rebecca 49
SHERMAN, ... 141
SHORT-ARM Bill 100
SHUMAN, Mary 41
SIBBETT, ... 65
    W.F. 65, 244
    Will A. 245
    Will F. 245
SIMMIE, ... 157
SIMMONS, ... 55
    Elizabeth 54
    Susan 79
SINGING Tom 122
SISLAR, N.B. 22
SLATER, John R. 245, 277
SMITH, ... 117
    Annie 265
    B.W. 240
    Betty 40
    Creasy 64
    Doc. 64
    Ellen 54
    George 110
    J.R. 58, 11
    James 116

Index to: Ward's History of Coffee County, Georgia

James R. 21, 323
Jane............................81
Jimmie Belle..............67
John...42, 183, 231, 245
John R. 21
Josh.........................111
Joshua......................110
Maggie.............39, 313
Marcella...........264, 265
Martha......................71
Mary............42, 81, 231
Monroe.............108, 231
Nancy..........................81
Nannie......................267
Narcissa....................265
Neil...................266, 267
Pat...........................155
R.S. 82, 109, 230, 231
Ruby.........................284
Sampie....108, 231, 311, 313
Symeria......................82
Tom...........................110
Vivian........................287
W.C. 284
Warren........................40
William C. 21
SOLOMEN, Godden.................52
SOLOMON, Anna..................78
  Delilah......................81
  Henry........................82
  John........................122
  Sarah...................71, 82
  Sarah A. 82
SOLOMONS, ...65
  John..........................81
  S. Ann........................81

SOUTHERLAND, W.W. 214
SPELL, Jim....................41
  Sarah........................41
SPENCE, Allen M. 86
  Feraby.......................73
  John M. 73, 127, 259
  Rena.........................78
SPIKES, Sarah Ann............64
SPIVEY, ...116, 149, 298
  Adline.......................82
  E. 82
  Erwin........................87
  G.L. 287
  J.T. 82
  John..................82, 118
  Lydia........................82
  Mathey.......................82
STALLINGS, ...105
STANFORD, Mary..............287
STARLING, Joe...............60
  Maggie......................60
  Viola....................... 45
STEVENS, H.E. 82
  R. R. 82
  Stella.......................39
STEWART, C.E. 58
  William....................121
STOCKTON, ...298
STRONG, Esther..............287
SUGGS, S. 78
SUMMERALL, J.L. 16
SUMMERLIN, Peterson.........39
  Allen........................21
  Amanda.......................82
  Ben..........................65
  Burl.........................46
  Delilah......................81

Index to: Ward's History of Coffee County, Georgia

Elisha...........................81
Elizabeth.....................81
Elizabeth.....................82
M. 82
Mattie...........................65
Rebecca.......................46
William........................82
SUMNER, ...46
Bonnie..........................85
SURMANS, Ella......................66
John..............................66
SUTTON, Annie......................45
SWAIN, Hiram...............260, 323
SWEAT, ...41
F.L. 151
Frank L. 278, 301
J.P. 126
Lila................................41
Lucinda........................73
Minnie Lee..................51
Thomas........................73
TAFF, Abbiegal......................80
TALLEY, Mattie....................284
TANNER, ...41, 67, 68, 297, 308
A.F. 68
Addie............................68
B.H. ..20, 66, 67, 125, 278
B.W. 68, 81, 82, 294
Barney..........................67
Berry.....................52, 67
Berry H. 82
Bessie....................53, 67
Betty.............................66
Betty.............................67
Bunk................63, 66, 67
Carl................................67
Chappel........................68

Clifton..........................66
Cylia Mose...................67
D.W. 68
Dacy..............................68
Dan................................67
Dave.....................52, 67
Delilah..........................67
Dora..............................63
E.L. 67, 235
Elie................................67
Elijah, 21, 52, 64, 66, 67, 316
Elijah, Jr. 66
Eliza....52, 62, 64, 66 , 79
Eliza A. 82
Elizabeth......55, 60, 64, 66, 80
Elmini...........................67
Elmore..........................66
Emily.....................66, 67
Emma...........................68
Eula...............................68
Fred.....................40, 66
G. W. 82
George..........................67
George W. 63
Green....................66, 67
Hampton..65, 66, 67, 72
Hester.......65, 66, 72, 82
Hiram...........................67
Ida.................................67
Idell...............................63
J.H. 67
J.M. 68
J. W. 82
Jim...............................125
Jimmie Belle...............67

Index to: Ward's History of Coffee County, Georgia

Jinsey............................68
Joe.....................52, 67
John........52, 66, 67, 277
John................................66
Julian..............................67
Leon................................66
Leonard..........................53
Lillian...........................286
Liza.................................67
Lou..................................68
Lucinda...................67, 69
Lucy................................68
Lydia...............................66
Lydia Ann.......................66
Maggie............................68
Mamie.............................63
Manning..........................67
Margaret................40, 60
Maria...............................68
Marshall...................63, 67
Martha............................67
Martha Jane...................68
Mary......................52, 67
Mary A. 82
Mary Ann........................67
Mary Jane......................68
Mattie..............................66
Mattie......................63, 67
Mattie..............................67
Melian.............................68
Melvin66, 280, 281, 287
Minnie.............................66
Monro.............................66
Nancy.............................68
Nine................................67
Penny......................63, 67
Penolope........................82

Renna Thompson........67
Rhuban............................67
Rilze.................................67
Rosa Ann......................278
Rose................................67
Russell............................68
Sarah......................52, 67
Sarah......................52, 67
Staten.....................52, 67
Susie...............................67
Syndia.............................67
Thad................................67
Tom.................................67
Ursula.............................68
Vicey...............................68
Vicey...............................67
W.M. 68, 214
W. M., Jr. 68
Walter.....................63, 67
Warren............................66
William............................63
Zelphia............................67
TARRENT, W.B. 281
TAYLOR, ...68, 111, 258, 270, 308
  Bill................................69
  Eliza......................62, 66
  Eliza A. 82
  Elizabeth.....................66
  Eliza Jane...................62
  Emily............................69
  Green.........67, 115, 201
  Ida................................81
  Jesse...........................68
  Jim...............................66
  John A. 82
  John G. 31, 32
  Johnie.................106, 107

Index to: Ward's History of Coffee County, Georgia

    Johnie G. 114, 153
    Lizzie....................62
    Lydia Ann..................66
    Martha................67, 82
    Mary.......................82
    Nancy..................62, 69
    Rita......................284
    Rube.......................62
    S.G. 310
    Sarah Ann..................62
    Sebe.......................69
    Tal........................62
    Vicey......................68
    Viney......................69
    W.P. 115
    Warren.....................66
TERRELL, Alice Clemens........278
TESTON, ...308
    Angel......................62
    B. W. 40
    Ben....................41, 62
    Lottie.....................41
    Lydia......................62
    Rhoda 40
    Zeck.......................62
THIGPEN, ...41
    Bartow.....................41
    Joe........................41
    Lila 41
    Manning....................41
    Mary...................40, 41
    Susan......................41
    Travis.................40, 41
THOMAS, ...68, 69
    A.F. 62, 116
    Amanda..........64, 65, 72
    Andrew.....................62

    Bartow.....................69
    Ben........................62
    Benjamin...................21
    D.G. 82
    Dave.......................69
    Ella.......................62
    Ellen......................69
    Harley.....................62
    Henry M....................62
    John.......................69
    Lydia..................60, 62
    Martha.....................82
    Mary.......................69
    Mary.......................82
    Melian.....................68
    Nellie.....................62
    Rebecca....................64
    Sallie.................64, 72
    Sam....................64, 72
    Tom........................69
    W.N. 113
    W.J. 62
    Wesley.....................69
    Zeke...................65, 72
THOMPSON, E.M. 284
    T.W. 309
THORNTON, Blanche.............287
THORPE, ...110, 111, 117
    G.W. 114
THRASH, J.M. 46, 289
THRASHER, Sarah................61
TIFT, Nelson..................149
TILLIS, ... 117
TINSLEY, ... 152
TOMBERLIN, ...10
TOMMIECHICHI, Chief.......26, 30
TOOK, Artie...................80

Index to: Ward's History of Coffee County, Georgia

TOWNS, Eliza..................69
    Matthew..................69
TROWEL, Emily..................66
    Joe..................66
TROWELL, Betty..................52
    Eliza A.E.J. 79
    John..................52
    Penny..................40
    Tom..................40
TUCKER, Easter..................82
    Jacob..................82
    John T. 82
    Nancy..................82
    Rhoda..................78
    Richard..................82
    Roxie..................82
TURNER, Arthur..................21
    J.M. 151
    Martha..................49
TURRENTINE, M.H. 245
    M.H., Jr. 245
TYSON, John L. 82
    Martha..................82
    Uncle Ben..................225
    Uncle Ike...225, 226, 227
    Uncle Jim..........157-158
    Uncle Tarrant..........265
VARNEDORE Elizabeth..............82
    J.J. 82
VEREEN, ...313
    William C. 311
VICKERS, ...46, 104
    Amanda..................44
    Annie..................45
    Avie..................43
    Avie Jane..................50
    B.L. 44

Bartley..................45
Bede..................43, 48
Beedie Carver..................38
Belle..................43
Bennie..................45
Bessie..................44
Betty..................44
Betty..................44, 50
Blannie..................45
Bronz..................46
C.E. 44
Calvin..................44
Cora Bell..................55
Dan..................45, 50
Daniel..................43, 278
Dede..................50
Dennis..................82, 302
Dorsey..................45
E.L. 46
Eli..................50
Elias..................44
Elie..................44
Elijah..................43, 45
Elisha..................45, 50
Elizabeth..................43, 81
Elizabeth..................44
Ellen..................44
Ellen..................44
Ely..................43, 44, 45, 47
Emma..................44
Emory..................46
Eugenia..................44
Eunnie..................43
Eva..................44
Fannie..................38, 45
Felder..................285
Flem..................45

Index to: Ward's History of Coffee County, Georgia

Fronney..........................44
George............................44
Gordon...........................44
H.E. 45
H.L. 50, 302
Harriet............................45
Hattie.......................44, 45
Henry....................43, 44, 45
Henry V. 44
Herbert...........................50
Hiram.............................44
Howard...........................46
Hump Back Wiley........38
J.J. 43, 45, 46, 50
Jack..........38, 48, 50, 228
Jacob..............................44
Jesse.......................43, 47
John............43, 44, 47, 50, 55, 102, 103, 182
John, Jr. 323
Johnie..........................188
Johnnie..........................45
Joseph..........................44
Kattie............................44
Leander........................45
Leon..............................44
Leonard........................45
Lewis.............................44
Lila Paulk....................38
Lilar..............................43
Liller.............................45
Lister............................44
Little George Paulk.....38
Lucy...........43, 44, 45, 50
Lydia...........................284
Martha..........................43

Martha........38, 43, 48, 50
Mary..43, 44, 46, 79, 82
Mary Jane..............44, 50
Matilda...........43, 44, 45
Mattie......................44, 45
Mattie............................50
Melissa..........................44
Micajah....42, 43, 44, 45, 50, 231
Michael..........................44
Minnie............................45
Minnie............................44
O.J. 44
Olden.............................46
Onnie.............................45
Pittman........................286
R. 80
Rachael..........................45
Rachael..........................44
Rebecca............43, 44, 45
Rebecca 46
Rebecca..........................44
Rebecca...................43, 47
Richard..........................44
Sarah.............................79
Sarah Jane....................44
Tish................................52
Tishie Burthnot............38
Viola..............................45
W. R. 44, 254
W.R. 50, 285
Warren..........................45
Wiley.........43, 44, 45, 50
William......43, 44, 45, 52
Willie....................58, 109
Willis.............................50
Winnie..................42, 268

Index to: Ward's History of Coffee County, Georgia

- Youngie..............38, 49
- VICKERS negroes...................221
- VINING, Banny..........................82
  - Christian.....................62
  - James........................107
  - Martha........................82
  - Melvinia....................78
- VINSON, ...308
  - Beatrice.....................285
  - S.E. 245
- VOIGHT, Elizabeth................287
- WADLEY, ...151
- WALDEN, Elias.......................109
- WALKER, ...39
  - Dollie V. 83
  - James L. 83
  - William R. 323
- WALL, ... 67
  - Annie...................... 83
  - D. E. 83
  - D.S. 83
  - J.R. 83
  - J.P. 114
  - Old Bill....................141
  - R. M. 78
- WALLACE, T.A. 156, 328
- WALLS, D.S 82
  - Rebecca......................82
- WARD, ... 69, 72, 294
  - Abram.......56, 65, 72, 73
  - Amanda........................80
  - Amanda..........64, 65, 72
  - Angeline....................41
  - Annie...........................73
  - Annie..............73, 279
  - Arminta....49, 64, 65, 72
  - Bettie............................41
- Big John...............41, 195
- Billy...72, 94, 95-97, 109, 191
- C.A., 36, 64, 155, 235, 32
- Calvin A. .16, 21, 46, 69, 72, 279, 323
- Daddy.................27, 125
- Desdemonia...64, 65, 72
- Elizabeth...............64, 72
- Emma J. 279
- Emma Jane.................69
- Frank..................73, 246
- Franklin.....................106
- Gay................................69
- George.......................73
- Hester........64, 66, 72, 82
- J.J. 309
- Jack....................69, 171
- Jackson....21, 40, 41, 64, 72, 184
- James..........................56
- James Franklin.......65, 73
- James Preston.....56, 64, 65, 72, 73, 125
- Janie............................41
- Joab....................56, 72
- Joe.................41, 69, 94
- John.....................65, 191
- John F. 65, 130, 132, 279
- John Franklin..............73
- John C. 73
- Josh.............................73
- Lizzie..........................39
- Lucendia...................78
- Mammy.....................125
- Martha.........................69
- Mary...........................41

Index to: Ward's History of Coffee County, Georgia

Mattie.........................78
Maud..........................73
Minta..........................73
Missouri.....................41
Nancy..................64, 72
Neele.........................73
Penny.........................69
Penny.........................41
Percy..........................69
Preston......................73
Priscilla................64, 72
Priscilla......55-59, 72, 74
Sallie..........40, 41, 64, 72
Sarah.......................153
Sarah.........................69
Sarah...................65, 73
Sarah A. 132, 279
Sarah Ann..................64
Staff...........................41
Tempie...................... 66
Tom......................41, 69
Vinney.......................69
W.P. 155, 156, 235,
                245, 326, 327
Walton, W. 64, 72
Ward..........................73
Warren p. 3, 182
Warren Preston...65, 73
Zylphia.......................64
Zylphia.................64, 72
WARD, negroes..................221
WATERS, ...61, 308
   Elizabeth....................83
   Elmire.......................61
   John A. 83
WATSON, Alma..................284
   Dollie V. 83

WEATHERINGTON, ...105
WELLS, Martha........................62
WESTBROOK, ...310
WESTON, Jesse....................173
WESTONIA, ...173
WHEELER, Lucile.................290
WHEELESS, Clyde.................245
WHELCHEL, Henry C. 279
WHIDDON, Avie.....................43
   Dempsey.....................43
   Eunnie.......................43
   Ola...........................53
WHITE, Elizabeth....................82
   Peter........................111
WHITTEN, Avie Jane...............50
WIDEMAN, E.C. 285
WILCOX, ...54-55, 111
   A.M. 26
   Annie.........................55
   Annie Belle 89
   Augustus...................270
   Betty..........................54
   Betty..........................66
   Buddie........................55
   Cabb..........................53
   Catherine....................55
   Cora..........................270
   Cora Bell....................55
   Dan....................54, 55
   DeKalb.................55, 66
   E.K. 55, 66
   Eli...........................271
   Eliza..........................54
   Eliza..........................55
   Elizabeth...........110, 270
   Elizabeth.............53, 54
   Elizabeth....................55

Index to: Ward's History of Coffee County, Georgia

Ellen..................54
Elmira..................54
Emma..............55, 264
Fannie.............54, 55
Frank..............53, 55
George..........21, 53, 54
Georgia..................55
Henry..................55
Ira E. 88
J.M. 6,54,55,109, 110,116,121,30 4,311, 320,322, 323
J. Mark..................88
J. Monroe..................280
Jack..................53, 55
James H. 21
James M. 323
Jasper..................53
Jeff..............54, 85
Jefferson..........29, 88-89
Jim..................53
Joe..............54, 55, 116
John..............53, 54, 55
John, Jr. 54
Johnie..................54
Johnnie..................55
Jule..................69
Kate..................55
Katherine..................270
Lewis..................55
Lewis C. 54, 145
Linnie..................69
Lucy..................68
Lydia..............54, 62
Maggie..................54
Maniza..................54
Margaret..................53
Marian..................88
Marjorie..............54, 80
Mark......53, 54, 88, 121, 323
Marvin..................270
Mary..................55, 270
Mary Ann..................54
Mary Jane......48, 51, 54
Mattie..............54, 78
Maud..............55, 73
Minnie..................66
Monroe....55, 96, 98-99, 122, 264, 270
Nancy..................54
Nancy........48, 49, 51, 54
Pate..............55, 66
Pet..................270
Piety..................54
Rebecca..................54
Robert..................55
Roxie..................267
Samanthia..................81
Sarah J. 81
Shug..................55
Tempie..................66
Tiny..................55
Thomas....49, 51, 84, 85
Tom....53, 54, 55, 62, 68, 267
Virginia..................55
William..................55
Winnie..............42, 54
WILDEN, E.B. 65
Pate..................65
WILDS, Reuben..................101
WILKERSON, Ethel..................290

Index to: Ward's History of Coffee County, Georgia

J.S. 286	WRIGHT, Mary A. 83
WILKINSON, S.A. 80	Missouri.................68, 82
WILLIAMS, ...63	Riley....................12, 120
A.M. 109	W.J. 82
C.M. 239	WYNN, Decocrat......................66
Calvin W. 105	Leila..............................66
J.H. 245, 281	YARBOUGH, Elizabeth..........270
John L. 109	M.E. 270
John Skelton.....150, 151	YATES, Nancy....................64, 72
Joseph......................258	YEOMANS, Ashford...............109
Rebecca......................45	YONN, Piety............................54
WILLIAMSON, Laura................74	Lewis............................54
WILLIS, Irma..........................284	YOUNG, Bud...........................69
WILSON, ...110	Doggie....................320
F.C. 240	Gay................................69
Leon A. 22	Mattie........................67
WINDFIELD, J.W. 83	Nas................................67
Mary A. 83	Thomas............182, 303
WINGARD, J.O. 284	YOUNGBLOOD, Elijah...........195
WOLFF, Nancy....................45	John............................67
WOOD, Bryant........................82	Mary............................67
E. 83	R. 81
Elizabeth....................82	
G.W. 83	
M. 83	
Mary A. 83	
Nellie..........................83	
Rowan........................83	
WOODS, Carrie........................69	
Mary A. 81	
WOOTEN, ...39, 40	
Bryant........................21	
Elizabeth......................81	
L. 79	
Mary...................55, 270	
Roxie..........................82	
Simon L. 22	

www.ingramcontent.com/pod-product-compliance
Lightning Source LLC
Chambersburg PA
CBHW020636300426
44112CB00007B/137